This book shows for the first time how the global advertising industry works as a business. It will help practitioners and scholars alike who want to know more about advertising beyond their own borders. With more than 80 percent of the world's major markets included, this is an invaluable resource.

Colin Jevons, *Associate Professor, Monash Business School, Australia*

Robert Crawford, Linda Brennan, and Lukas Parker's book provides a refreshing and unique overview of advertising practice in the world. The bird's eye view of the industry and the regional perspectives well highlight the globalization and regionalization realities, opportunities, and challenges facing the advertising industry. The special attention paid to cultural differences and information technology development makes the book even more relevant and more valuable to today's advertising practice. The book is indeed a pleasant and must read for anyone – student, practitioner, and scholar alike – who desires a good understanding of advertising in this "borderless world."

Hong Cheng, *Ph.D., Professor and Director, Richard T. Robertson School of Media and Culture, Virginia Commonwealth University, USA*

Global Advertising Practice in a Borderless World

Cultural and regional differences in creating and managing advertising require unique responses to a dynamic, rapidly globalising business environment. To be global in advertising is no longer to be homogenised or standardised, it is to be at the leading edge of social and cultural trends that are changing the world as we know it.

Global Advertising Practice in a Borderless World covers a wide range of adaptive advertising practices, from major and emerging markets, in mainstream and digital advertising. It focuses on understanding how the globalisation of advertising works in practice, explored in three sections:

- globalising advertising in a media and communications context;
- advertising in a global world; and
- global advertising in a digital world.

Covering past, present and potential futures, through an impressive ensemble of global advertising practitioners and academics, the book combines academic rigour with practical insights to provide a comprehensive analysis of the changing dynamics between advertising and globalisation. It will be of great interest to researchers, educators and advanced students in advertising, global branding, international marketing, international business media, communication and cultural studies.

Robert Crawford is a Professor in the School of Media and Communication at RMIT University, Australia.

Linda Brennan is a Professor in the School of Media and Communication at RMIT University, Australia.

Lukas Parker is a lecturer and researcher in the School of Media and Communication at RMIT University, Australia.

Routledge Studies in International Business and the World Economy

Global Advertising Practice in a Borderless World

**Edited by Robert Crawford,
Linda Brennan and Lukas Parker**

Routledge
Taylor & Francis Group

LONDON AND NEW YORK

First published 2017 by Routledge

2 Park Square, Milton Park, Abingdon, Oxfordshire OX14 4RN

52 Vanderbilt Avenue, New York, NY 10017

Routledge is an imprint of the Taylor & Francis Group, an informa business

First issued in paperback 2019

British Library Cataloguing in Publication Data
A catalogue record for this book is available from the British Library

Library of Congress Cataloging in Publication Data
Names: Crawford, Robert, 1975- editor. | Brennan, Linda L., editor. | Parker, Lukas, 1977– editor.
Title: Global advertising practice in a borderless world / [edited by] Robert Crawford, Linda Brennan, Lukas Parker.
Description: 1 Edition. | New York : Routledge, 2017. | Includes bibliographical references and index.
Identifiers: LCCN 2016055577 (print) | LCCN 2017015108 (ebook) | ISBN 9781315688626 (eBook) | ISBN 9781138918306 (hardback : alk. paper) | ISBN 9781138918306 (paperback : alk. paper)
Subjects: LCSH: Advertising. | Internet advertising. | Globalization–Social aspects. | Culture and globalization.
Classification: LCC HF5823 (ebook) | LCC HF5823 .G5625 2017 (print) | DDC 659.1–dc23
LC record available at https://lccn.loc.gov/2016055577

ISBN: 978-1-138-91830-6 (hbk)
ISBN: 978-0-367-87315-8 (pbk)

Typeset in Times New Roman
by Wearset Ltd, Boldon, Tyne and Wear

To all strategic planners, wherever you are. We hope you find this book useful in designing global brand strategy.

Contents

Figures

Tables

Contributors

Editors

Linda Brennan is a professor in the School of Media and Communication at RMIT University in Melbourne, Australia. In the lead up to becoming a full-time academic, she had an active consulting practice in marketing and strategic insights research. Her research interests are social and government marketing and especially the influence of marketing communication and advertising on behaviour.

Robert Crawford is a professor in the School of Media and Communication at RMIT University in Melbourne, Australia. He is the author of *But Wait, There's More ...: A History of Australian Advertising* (MUP 2008) and (with Jackie Dickenson) *Behind Glass Doors: The World of Australian Advertising Agencies 1959–1989* (UWAP 2016).

Lukas Parker is a lecturer and researcher in the School of Media and Communications at RMIT University in Melbourne, Australia. He has taught in advertising to postgraduate and undergraduate students, and supervises postgraduate research students in Australia and Vietnam. His research interests are in social marketing, digital advertising and marketing communications.

Contributors

Isidoro Arroyo-Almaraz is full Professor of Audio-visual Communication and Advertising at the Rey Juan Carlos University (Madrid, Spain), PhD in Communication and a Master in Communication Techniques in Social Services from the Complutense University. He has been a visiting professor in many European and Argentinian universities including Bournemouth (UK), Catholic University of Portugal, Cordoba National University (Argentina). He is also the main researcher of many projects in social communication.

Julie Bilby is a senior lecturer in advertising in the School of Media and Communication at RMIT University in Melbourne, Australia. Prior to her academic career, she worked as an art director in advertising agencies including

Y&R (Melbourne). Her research interests include advertising and consumer creativity, Chinese advertising and the influence of culture on effective communication.

Jackie Dickenson worked in the advertising industry in Britain and Australia before she completed her PhD in History at the University of Melbourne. Her publications include *Australian Women in Advertising in the Twentieth Century* (2016) and, with Robert Crawford, *Behind Glass Doors: The World of Australian Advertising Agencies 1959–1989* (2016).

Tomasz Domański is a professor at the University of Lodz in Poland, Chair of the Department of International Marketing and Retailing. His scientific interests include strategies of international retail chains, university marketing, marketing of culture, and city marketing. He is the author of more than 150 publications in the area of marketing.

Jean M. Grow is a professor at Marquette University. Her work appears in the *International Journal of Advertising* and *Advertising & Society Review*, among others, and she is the co-author of Advertising Creative. Prior to joining the academy Grow worked in industry with clients such as Coca-Cola and Kellogg's and at agencies such as DDB and Leo Burnett. Her consulting clients include Flamingo International and Nike.

Matthew Hook is Chief Strategy Officer of Dentsu Aegis, with responsibility for leading the strategic direction and product for a 4,000-person group made up of brands in media, creative, data and digital. His career has encompassed global and domestic strategy and general management roles in New York and London.

Peter Ling is author of *Be the Innovators: How to Accelerate Team Creativity* and lead author of *Consumer Behaviour in Action*. He worked in various cities in team creativity, advertising agency, marketing communication, public relations, journalism and academia. He is Deputy Dean International, School of Media and Communication, RMIT University.

Lilia Ivana Mamic holds a PhD in Communication from the Rey Juan Carlos University in Madrid and a Master in Social Communication from the University of Valladolid, Spain. Throughout her career she has collaborated with several NGOs and private organizations in relation to topics including strategic communication, sustainability, and social media.

Dang Nguyen is an associate lecturer and emerging scholar in the Centre of Communication and Design at RMIT University Vietnam. She conducts research into digital communication, communication policy and technology, political communication, international communication and communication for social change.

Rotimi Williams Olatunji (BA First Class Honours, MA, PhD) is Professor of Public Relations and Advertising and Dean at the School of Communication,

Lagos State University, Nigeria. He studied in the University of Ibadan (Advertising as Communication), Obafemi Awolowo University, Ile-Ife, Nigeria (Archaeology). He is the Editor of *Media and Communication Review* and Associate Editor of *Journal of Global Marketing*.

Reza Semnani Jazani is an experienced Senior Account Manager having worked for 12 years in the Middle East, five years for fully integrated advertising agency Publicis Middle East. He has worked primarily in client servicing, assisting both international and local brands navigate the unique landscape of advertising in the Middle East. Reza holds a Masters Degree in Advertising from RMIT University and a Masters of International Business from Wollongong University.

John Sinclair is an Honorary Professorial Fellow in the School of Historical and Philosophical Studies at the University of Melbourne. His internationally published work concerns the globalisation of consumer culture and the media and communication industries, with special emphasis on advertising and television, and a regional focus on Asia and Latin America.

Kunal Sinha has over 25 years of experience unearthing and commenting on consumer and cultural trends, and helping companies profit from them. Based in Shanghai for nearly a decade, he is the author of two books about creativity in business, *China's Creative Imperative*, and *Raw: Pervasive Creativity in Asia*, and has taught at some of the world's leading business schools.

Hari Sreekumar is Associate Professor of Marketing at the Indian Institute of Management Tiruchirappalli. He has carried out interpretive consumer research among migrants and consumers with resource constraints, and also in the field of Indian advertising. Hari has also contributed to the literature on Indian marketing history, with publications in the *Journal of Historical Research in Marketing* and *The Routledge Companion to Marketing History*.

Marta Mensa Torras was born in Barcelona (Spain), but has worked and lived for more than ten years in Peru. She was awarded a PhD by the Universitat Autònoma, Barcelona (Spain). She has worked as a creative in a digital advertising agency in Lima. She undertook postdoctoral research about advertising at University National Autonoma in Mexico (UNAM) with thanks to the Santander Banc Scholarship.

Rohit Varman is Professor of Marketing at Deakin University, Australia. His research interests are in the fields of critical marketing and consumer culture theory. He uses interpretive methodologies in his research and has primarily focused on subaltern consumers, corporate violence, postcoloniality and history of marketing in India. He has published his research in leading journals that include *Journal of Consumer Research, Human Relations, Journal of Retailing, Organization Science, Marketing Theory, Journal of Public Policy* and *Marketing*, and *Consumption, Markets & Culture*.

Acknowledgements

The completion of any book is a task that requires input and talent from many people. We would like to thank the following people without whom this work would not have made it to the publisher:

The Australian Research Council provided funding for Robert Crawford and Linda Brennan who were both investigators on the project 'Globalising the Magic System: a history of advertising industry practices in Australia 1959–1989' ARC DP 120100777.

Thank you to the authors who contributed to this book and who persevered though a sometimes arduous review and revision process. Their ability to collaborate across the virtual and physical boundaries that makes an international book has been a model of cooperation and a clear indicator that advertising is indeed a borderless world!

Additionally, there are the many anonymous reviewers who understood the importance of providing formative advice to sometimes new and non-academic authors. In the extensive review process they managed to see their way through some academic challenges to make the country and regional chapters come to life as theoretically relevant practice. In the process, they helped to create some much needed and practically relevant theory.

We would like to thank our institutions for their support. At RMIT University, we thank the School of Media and Communication and the Centre for Communication, Politics and Culture. At the University of Technology Sydney, we thank the School of Communication in the Faculty of Arts and Social Sciences along with the Australian Centre for Public History.

Also, there are the people at Routledge who from the very first stage of putting this together understood the need for a regionally relevant but globally useful book. Their supportive encouragement throughout the project has made it what it is.

Finally, there are the many supporters who have helped with various stages of production. The foremost of these is Ms Dang Nguyen who has worked with the team and without whom this one would not have come together. We would also like to thank Ms Phan Nhat Tram for her cheerful assistance in the editing process and RMIT University Vietnam for providing the training for these exceptional professional communicators. Thanks also to James Worner for his keen eye for detail and helpful suggestions. And, finally, we would like to thank Julia Mugavin, Grace Carter and Judy Gregory for supporting the review and editing processes and Brian Rodrigo Llagas for his design expertise.

The editorial team
Robert Crawford
Linda Brennan
Lukas Parker

Introduction

Dove's 'Campaign for Real Beauty' was voted by *Ad Age* 2015 in as the best campaign of the twenty-first century. Judges found the campaign's positive message to be an uplifting one for all women. One described it as 'Bold. Brave. Smart. So right for the brand. A message the world needed.... They made their customers' values into their purpose and set out to change the world' (Neff 2015, para. 35), whilst another declared that it 'is one of the most amazingly creative ways to express a true global human truth – an incredible and simple insight beautifully executed' (Neff, 2015, para. 34). A different judge observed that ' "Real Beauty" is a brilliant brand platform for Dove (Ad Age, 2016). "Evolution" and "Sketches" stand out as masterpieces – and notice both are not TV ads' (Neff, 2015, para. 40). This was a campaign that was born digital and reached out to a global audience (Ad Age, 2016). At the time of writing, uploads of 'Evolution' on YouTube had collectively amassed 25 million views. The campaign's success lay in the universality and the accessibility of its central message. Noting that 'As social campaigners, brands can have far-reaching reaching impacts by helping to spread the positive benefits of globalisation' (Clifton, 2009, p. 54), Rita Clifton reveals the ways in which advertising and branding have been drivers of globalisation. Of course, the Dove campaign also demonstrates that advertising and the advertising industry have been the beneficiaries of a globalised world (Clifton, 2009).

In 2016, Ian Verrender, business editor for *The Drum*, wrote a column asking whether globalisation was dead (Verrender, 2016). Citing the debates in the lead up to the US presidential elections and the UK Brexit vote, Verrender notes the ways in which anxieties about globalisation have been expressed by both sides of politics through issues such as economic disparity and immigration. After decades of increasingly open flows of international trade, commercial firms have certainly profited handsomely from globalisation. However, current geo-political anxieties, and the growing sense that these benefits have largely remained the preserve of the elites running these organisations, is changing the nature of the rhetoric surrounding the benefits of globalisation. Such polemical accounts all too easily situate globalisation within a rather narrow frame. Defining globalisation as a 'transplanetary process or set of processes involving increasing liquidity and the growing multidirectional flows of people, objects, places and information as well as the structures they encounter and create that are barriers to, or expedite, those flows' (Ritzer, 2015, p. 2), George Ritzer offers a more holistic account. Venturing beyond the economic, Ritzer reveals that globalisation is intrinsically connected to broader social, political, cultural and technological developments (Ritzer, 2015). The multidirectional flows outlined by Ritzer not only underscore globalisation's inherent fluidity, they also provide an opportunity to revisit and, indeed, reinterpret globalisation as well as its relationship with the advertising industry.

Over the twentieth and twenty-first centuries, globalisation has progressively evolved in line with the companies seeking to extend their operations across the world. Beginning with simple exports, these firms moved on to setting up international operations which functioned in parallel to their headquarters. The next phase was to standardise operations internationally. This then gave way to the 'glocal' model, where the firm's need for global consistency is balanced against the need to cater for the local markets and their distinctive tastes. More recently, it has been suggested that globalisation's latest phase is characterised by collaborative 'co-creation', where ideas and concepts are devised by audiences across the globe and are then integrated into multinational firms' strategic operations. Within advertising circles, the issue of standardisation has long been a point of discussion and debate (Walker Smith, 2012).

Various companies that commenced international trade in the early twentieth century readily dispatched advertising materials to overseas offices. Already, in the 1920s, General Motors was attempting to develop a standardised approach to its advertising by distributing advertising materials and guides to its operations across the globe. When J. Walter Thompson took on the General Motors export account in 1927, it adopted the same process for its own network of offices. From the 1960s, the issue of standardisation began to attract a growing body of literature (Crawford, 2016). Such interest reflected the upward surge in global trade (John *et al.*, 2012). Rising living standards and the expansion of technology encouraged practitioners and scholars alike to view standardisation as an inevitable part of global trade. Writing in the *Journal of Marketing* in 1963, Ilmar Roostal predicted that 'insufficient marketing planning, diversity of languages and media, and government regulations' (Roostal, 1963, p. 20) across western Europe would not prevent the growth of 'standardization of advertising in the internationally developing Western European markets' (Roostal, 1963, p. 20). Twenty years later, Theodore Levitt expressed similar sentiments in the *Harvard Business Review* when he argued that global firms 'will seek constantly to standardize [their] offering everywhere' (Levitt, 1983, p. 6). Levitt conceded that they might 'digress from this standardization only after exhausting all possibilities to retain it' before explaining that these firms would 'push for reinstatement of standardization whenever digression and divergence have occurred' (Levitt, 1983, p. 6).

As standardisation won the plaudits of global marketers, it also elicited a small but growing number of critical responses. In 1969 Warren Keegan observed that standardised products and promotional materials worked for products such as Pepsi, but warned that the firm's 'approach does not work for all products' (Keegan, 1969, p. 58). Keegan suggested that standardisation was only one option, and urged marketers to adopt a more holistic approach to global marketing that took into consideration the product, the market and the costs of adaptation (Keegan, 1969). By the 1980s and 1990s, advertising research was paying greater attention to the challenges posed by culture – from subtle differences in humour or taste to more overt differences in attitudes to gender and sex (Ford *et al.*, 2011). Such scholarship increasingly echoed Keegan's concerns and urged practitioners to adopt a more nuanced approach to standardisation that could find a balance between local and global interests.

Standardisation of advertising assumed that consumers across the globe shared uniform characteristics, hopes and desires. In their 1998 study of consumption and lifestyle of Asian youths, Mariko Yasue and Gu Xiang Wen found that 'Asian youth are moving in the same direction and share similar lifestyle values and traits regardless of the country' (Yasue and Wen, 1998). While Yasue and Wen also cautioned that 'the degree of similarities are still different between countries' (Yasue and Wen, 1998), their findings nevertheless asserted that consumers across the world shared inalienable similarities. Aiming at the 'lowest common denominator' offered advertisers and their agencies a straightforward and, indeed, efficient way of reaching a global audience. Critics' concerns about the perceived homogenisation or 'coca-colonisation' were often premised on similar grounds. There was a sense that advertising threatened to produce a single, indistinguishable consumer market, and, further, that consumers lacked the capacity to maintain their distinctiveness in the face of standardised approaches and appeals.

Concerns about standardisation have long been expressed. The agencies' creative teams had been the first to question its appropriateness. Many were frustrated by the task of localising a global idea, as it often resulted in bland and uninspiring advertisements (Crawford and Dickenson, 2016). On the flip side, mistranslations or a simple lack of attention to local conditions could result in embarrassing and expensive failures. The cultural turn in advertising research posed other questions about the standardisation model. Over the 1990s, the idea that there was that were 'global teens' or 'global businessmen' was progressively being questioned, as research demonstrated the profound impact of local culture on consumption practices (Churkina and Sandler, 2011). Robert Malcolm, senior marketing advertiser to the beverage firm Diageo, underscored this point in 2009 when he bluntly stated that 'There are no specific "global consumers", only local ones who may have some important value similarities across different markets' (Malcolm, 2009, p. 25). The influence of culture was also being recognised in other ways. Concerned that 'the consequences of globalization may not differ significantly from those of the colonialism of the past' (Frith, 2003, p. 50), South East Asian nations looked to regulating advertising content to safeguard their local culture. Such concerns can also flow the other way. Western culture's concerns about quality or environment credentials pose a significant marketing obstacle for aspiring global brands from emerging markets such as Russia or India (Kumar and Steenkamp, 2013). Of course, the impact of culture similarly attracted attention. Describing researchers' propensity to attribute any adverse or unexpected findings to 'cultural differences', Ford *et al.* warn against using culture as 'a nebulous catchall' (Ford *et al.*, 2011).

The concept of a global consumer has been further undermined by emerging digital media platforms. While digital media have enhanced advertisers' capacity to reach global audiences and to develop personal interaction with them, such platforms have also empowered consumers (Okazakin and Taylor, 2013; John *et al.*, 2012). This capacity to engage directly with brands has meant that consumers inevitably insert their own culture/s into these interactions. Significantly, such engagement places an even stronger emphasis on advertisers to pay greater attention to consumers and the context in which they are interacting with the brand (Raynor, 2016). Media platform proliferation has similarly played a key role in disrupting the notion of a single global consumer as audiences fragment into smaller and more distinctive clusters of consumers with their own particular cultural mores.

Since the 1990s, advertising practitioners and researchers have increasingly embraced the concept of 'think global, act local' as an ideal strategy for multinational firms looking to reach global audiences. As Ashish Banerjee notes, such 'glocalisation' functions as something of a middle ground 'between global vision and the consequent needs for standardization … and the validity of the realities of local needs and operating conditions' (Banerjee, 1994, p. 104). John Sinclair similarly notes in this collection, glocalisation is essentially about 'maximising the organisational and economic advantages of standardisation' (Sinclair, 2007).

At a glance, being 'glocal' offers a simple solution: it delivered consistency across global networks on the one hand and facilitated local input on the other. However, a closer inspection reveals complications. Observing that 'Someone who thinks globally is still part of his or her own culture' (de Mooij, 2014, p. 2), Marieke de Mooij suggests that the mantra is inherently paradoxical. De Mooij also expands on this paradox, noting that 'Marketing knowledge has spread across the world, but its use has supported localization of products and services rather than standardization' (de Mooij, 2014, p. 4). Others have taken aim at 'think global, act local' for being too simplistic. C. Frederic John *et al.* thus contend the 'division of labor between global headquarters and country managers is often far more complex, and prone to tension'. In addition, they note that 'there are frequently other levels between the two extremes [local and global], such as regions or sub-regions' (John *et al.*, 2012).

Examining globalisation through a regional lens offers a different perspective to globalisation and the ways that advertising practice is understood. Alan Rugman has been a notable critic of globalisation and its proponents. Claiming that globalisation is little more than a 'myth', Rugman dismisses the literature advocating globalisation as 'far too simplistic' (Rugman, 2003). Although he readily recognises that 'there are some economic drivers of globalisation', Rugman questions their primacy (Rugman, 2003). He argues instead that 'Regions have cultural attributes and political borders that are stronger than the economic forces of globalisation' and that cultural and political barriers have effectively prevented 'the development of a single world market' (Rugman,

2003). Echoing this point, John Sinclair points out that 'globalisation is mediated by regional realities, and that actual nation states are more resistant to global influences that the usual globalisation rhetoric' (Sinclair, 2007, p. 283). Julien Cayla and Giana Eckhardt similarly assert 'Despite media hype about global brands and global business, the world economy is fundamentally regional' (Cayla and Eckhardt, 2007, p. 444).

Rugman's (2003) observation that 'the vast majority of multinational manufacturing and service activity is (and has always been) organised regionally' reveals his thesis to be highly relevant to the advertising and marketing industries. While Fernando Fatoso and Jeryl Whitelock observe that 'the regional level of intentional advertising standardization has rarely been specifically discussed in the literature' (Fastoso and Whitelock, 2010, p. 33), the handful of studies exploring such issues from a regional viewpoint demonstrate the importance of adopting or incorporating such a perspective (Fastoso and Whitelock, 2010). Susan Tai's 1997 pioneering study of advertising in Asia predicted an intensification of regional thinking on account of 'the regionalization of advertising media and the increasing recognition of the applicability of cross-market learning and the advantages and of regional synergy' (Tai, 1997, p. 59). A decade later, John Sinclair and Rowan Wilken confirmed Tai's prediction, noting that regionalisation 'is of continuing interest to global marketers who ... see it as a viable marketing strategy' (Wilken and Sinclair, 2007, p. 9). Expanding on this, Sinclair and Wilken also observed that advertisers were engaging in 'strategic regionalisation ... where organisational structure, ad creation and marketing strategies have ... been realigned to varying degrees and in different ways around the concept of the global region' (Sinclair and Wilken, 2009, p. 155).

Regionalisation shows little sign of abating. Prior to 2012, PepsiCo's Lays potato chip brand had used a highly decentralised approach to its marketing, with local operations autonomously determining the appropriate approach for their respective markets. The 'Do Us a Flavour' of 2012 challenged this order. Devised in the UK in 2008, the campaign invited consumers in each market to suggest possible flavours and then vote to create the most popular one. Despite being directed to implement 'Do Us a Flavour' locally, local operations embraced the campaign as 'it still afforded a great deal of freedom to local brand teams and consumers alike' (White, 2014). The different flavours selected in each market reflected both local palates as well as the unique executions of the campaign. Guinness' 'Made of More' campaign in 2011 was premised on the idea that Guinness was a brand 'that champions those who have the confidence to carve their own path' (Marketing Society, 2015, p. 21). Images of confident trailblazers varied from market to market. Glocalisation was celebrated as the centrepiece of brewer's strategy:

For the first time ever, Guinness has created work that can be shared in many markets crossing borders around the globe, which has led to increased efficiencies and had an overall impact on the quality of the work we do.

(Marketing Society, 2015, p. 48)

In their study of Kimberly-Clark's (KC) global brand management strategy, Tandadzo Matanda and Michael Ewing explore the firm's broader marketing operations. Their interviews with key brand managers found 'that balancing standardization and global best practices with regional empowerment and capacity-buying is paramount to KC's global brand management strategy' (Matanda and Ewing, 2012, p. 9). Interviewees revealed how Kimberly-Clark:

> uses various processes and templates to determine what a brand stands for, and allows the markets to 'adapt what's relevant for them', thereby giving the regions 'almost total autonomy' and creating 'powerful regional organization[s]' that have the ability to 'pick and choose'.
>
> (Matanda and Ewing, 2012, p. 7)

Of course, the shift to glocal strategies and the emphasis on regional issues has not gone unchallenged. Speaking at the Advertising Research Foundation's 2011 'Re:Think' conference, Sir Martin Sorrell, chief executive of WPP, predicted that the rise of 'developing economies' would have a major impact on WPP's global operations. Sorrell predicted that this shift would see 'more power for local agencies and a diminishing of authority for the regional managers who have provided an intermediate management step between the parent company and its site-specific offices' (Precourt, 2011). Observing the ways that technology was enhancing the connections between headquarters and local offices, Sorrell also mused that current trends may 'eliminate the managerial necessity of regional offices' (Precourt, 2011). In academic circles, the arguments proffered by Rugman and other supporters for a regional perspective have similarly been questioned in terms of the classification of global firms and what constitutes 'global' (Osegowitsch and Sammartino, 2008). While Michael Stevens and Allan Bird are not persuaded that the presence of regionalism intrinsically denotes an absence of globalisation, they nevertheless concede that they are 'more than willing to concede the trend towards an increase in regional trading activities and that regionalism is a dominant economic force' (Stevens and Bird, 2004, p. 504).

This collection of regional studies offers a timely contribution to this scholarship. The chapters come from a wide range of countries and incorporate the five continents of the world. This is the first time an edited collection of this nature has included such a vast scope of advertising.

The book starts with an overview of trends and issues facing advertisers in a rapidly globalising world. In Chapter 1, Sinclair highlights the structures of the advertising industry and profound transformations undergoing societies in which advertising participates. He provides an overview of nationhood and introduces the role that minorities are playing in the growth of the advertising industry, especially in different regions and local markets. Sinclair highlights the structure of the industry and how holding groups and the consolidation of advertising agencies under common corporate owners has facilitated globalisation and developed a rhetoric of integrated marketing communications. Also discussed are the influence of new media, advertising and branding in a global world, as well as the impact of these trends on global advertising.

In Chapter 2, Brennan and Crawford investigate the dialectical relationship between globalisation and advertising from a bird's eye view. Arguing that advertising is in itself a product of and a contributor to globalisation, they paint a holistic picture of how clients, brands, media and consumers are evolving in a globalised context. Pointing out the ambiguities inherent in advertising practices, they also sketch the opportunities and challenges advertisers face in an ever more connected world, firmly grounding this analysis within a continuous historical framework. Also presented are up to date examples of global advertising across different cultural contexts, and how these illustrate the need for a more nuanced understanding of globalisation not as a monolithic process or endpoint, but rather a dynamic analytical lens with which some of the complexities surrounding advertising as a global practice can be dispelled.

Chapter 3 explores advertising in light of information technology development and viral advertising communication. It investigates and analyses digital advertising campaigns around the world to explore what constitutes 'viral' – what it means and what it takes to 'go viral'. Parker and colleagues explore the dynamics of digital advertising communication and its impact on globalisation as an individual and behavioural phenomenon on a global scale. In addition, the chapter provides an overview of the risks to advertising in a co-creative digital environment where the consumer can change and reconvey the message with a few clicks. The chapter also briefly covers advertising performance in the digital advertising space, investigating how digital advertising may be evaluated in terms of effectiveness and performance.

Chapter 4 takes us on a journey from the birth of the American nation and associates it with the 'spirit of American advertising'. Grow takes us on a thought-provoking journey through the development of American brands and the growth of a nation through advertising. It allows us a view into the magic of advertising and provides insight into how US advertising shapes modern values and lifestyles. The chapter is replete with insights into iconic brands and helps us understand how these brands have engaged the world in the global imaginations of lifestyle since the beginning of advertising. The chapter finishes with challenges to the industry and calls upon us as practitioners and academics to consider diversity, minorities and gender balance of the workforce. A final powerful truth is that 'despite the grandest dreams of American advertisers – and the illusions they have exported to the marketplace-life, liberty and the pursuit of happiness cannot be bought or sold'.

Examining the trajectories and styles of creativity in a sample of four Latin American countries, Chapter 5 argues that Latin America's geographical, cultural, and economic predispositions have uniquely shaped the region's creative advertising culture. Outlining the practice of advertising in relation to the evolution of the transnational agency and the industry's identity, Mensa Torras illustrates how Latin America's advertising has historically been 'global', experiencing significant impact from the US. Stressing the diversity of Latin

American culture and using the Cannes Award as a benchmark for creativity quality, the chapter illustrates the importance of cultural adaptation in effective advertising and the need for culturally relevant creativity.

Written from a seasoned practitioner's perspective, Chapter 6 explores two core notions, the global and the local, in relation to positioning the UK's advertising industry within the borderless world. Tracing the relevance and importance of the UK's geographical position in how advertising is practised on regional and global scales, Hook expresses uncertainty in the face of the unravelling Brexit phenomenon, arguing that access to talent is likely to be a problem with the internationalism that has given the UK advertising industry its competitive edge. Observing trends such as standardisation and optimisation as manifestations of advertising globalisation with a critical eye, Hook also points out how scalability as a focus in the practice of global advertising needs more nuanced interpretations.

Chapter 7 provides an insight into the challenges facing Europe at the moment. The premise of this is that advertising is increasing materialism and therefore contributing to environmental degradation. Through a series of 'green' case studies, Arroyo-Almaraz and Mamic show us what is being done to redress the concerns of the authors about ethical consumption and European policies in the modern era. Despite its power and the collective that is 'Europe', the European Union is confronting the realities of inequity, poverty and sections of their populations not being able to access the benefits of a globalised world. Both practitioners and academics are called to reflecting on the role of advertising in fostering these inequities.

Chapter 8 discusses the diversity of advertising practice in the regions of central and eastern Europe and presents an extensive review of the Polish advertising industry as a country embedded at the cross roads of East and West. Sketching general trends in the European advertising market before comparing and contrasting these general trends to the Polish context, Domanski illustrates how current digital advertising practices in the country are consistent with their global counterparts. Outlining major Polish advertising spending trends across media and across different industry sectors, the chapter ties in this discussion with discourses on globalisation and investment flows before ending with an emphasis on glocalisation as an effective hybrid advertising strategy.

Chapter 9 presents a wide reaching view of one of the most rapidly growing regions in the world. Olatunji's extraordinary breadth of knowledge provides an insight into an industry that is facing challenges from earlier colonial eras and now those of disparate economic and socio-cultural environments. While the focus of this chapter is on sub-Saharan Africa, there are insights and examples throughout that allow us to see the dynamics of advertising in the region as well as to understand the important brands and their contributions to their respective countries. An important contribution of this chapter is that it develops our understanding and perspective of globalisation and its outcomes from an African point of view.

Chapter 10 illustrates some of the complexities of advertising to the Middle East. Mohammed introduces us to Middle Eastern culture and some of the issues faced in global organisations working within the Arab Gulf countries. The ways that advertising is developed and adapted from the global world into the Gulf region shows a talent for interpretation that 'forces global corporations to take a uniquely local approach to the region'. His knowledge of both regional culture and advertising allows the reader to understand how advertising can be generally persuasive and yet culturally customised.

Sreekumar and Varman's chapter (Chapter 11) explores the relationship between globalisation and advertising using a combination of historical analysis of major advertising milestones and textual analysis of key advertisements since 1947. Critically reflecting on the impact of India's colonial history and the introduction of advertising to the country, the chapter provides a contextually rich account of how political turmoil, cultural diversity and national identity negotiate their relationship with globalisation as an ongoing process. Also briefly explored is the notion of the 'Indian consumer' as a post-colonial construct, and the possibility for dynamic futures of the Indian advertising industry.

In Chapter 12, Ling provides a comprehensive account of the colonial history of advertising in Singapore and firmly incorporates this account into his analysis of the industry's current state. Closely tracking the evolution of the media landscape and the transformation of international and local advertising agencies in Singapore from the nineteenth century to the twentieth, the chapter carefully analyses themes of continuity and disruption in how the Singaporean advertising industry has learnt to adapt to and create a vibrant unique consumer culture. Tying this analysis with cultural specificities in a diverse and modern Singapore, the chapter also discusses notable advertising campaigns in the wider context of regional growth and the country's idiosyncratic legal system.

Examining the characteristics of Chinese advertising over time while being cognisant of the speed and scope of change in the industry, Chapter 13 identifies the key macro influences in how the industry is practised and ties this extensive analysis with a wider discussion on the role of advertising in Chinese culture. Bilby and Kunal argue that China is playing an increasingly important role in the global advertising industry, and the chapter goes on to investigate concepts such as meaningful co-creation, celebrity endorsement, and cultural resonance with exemplary advertising campaigns. Asserting the importance of branding principles in the Chinese context as a result of increasing consumer sophistication, the chapter ends by painting a positive outlook on China's maturing and globally influential advertising industry

Chapter 14, by Dickenson and Crawford, introduces the Australasian advertising context. While Australia and New Zealand have a shared business ancestry, and therefore commercial culture, the differences between them are not insignificant. There are distinct national identities that lead to attention-grabbing advertising campaigns which can successfuly translate into either country or alienate the citizens of one by preferencing the other. Both Australia and New Zealand have dominated the creativity awards for many years, indicating that being at the end of the earth need not mean that the industry is in a backwater.

Chapter 15 concludes the edited collection and describes the lessons gleaned from the contributions. First, the chapter outlines the nature of the borderless world and the role that advertising plays in fostering the hybridisation of global cultures. Second, the chapter summarises the tensions and benefits of a digital world and highlights the paradoxes that beset advertising in digital mediums. The final section of the chapter puts forward some suggestions for how advertising is evolving to meet the challenges of globalisation. This chapter ultimately reminds us that we need to be acutely aware of the contexts in which advertising operates in order to understand the fundamental of a successful global campaign.

References

Ad Age (2016) 'Dove: Campaign for real beauty', *Top Ad Campaigns of the 21st Century*. Available at: http://adage.com/lp/top15/#realbeauty (accessed: 14 November 2015).

Banerjee, A. (1994) 'Transnational advertising development and management: An account planning approach and a process framework', *International Journal of Advertising*, 13, pp. 95–124.

Cayla, J. and Eckhardt, G. M. (2007) 'Asian brands without borders: Regional opportunities and challenges', *International Marketing Review*, 24, pp. 444–56.

Churkina, O. and Sandler, C. (2011) 'Glocalization: A measure of brands: Adapatation to local cultures'. In *Asia Pacific*, Melbourne: European Society for Opinion and Market Research (ESOMAR).

Clifton, R. (2009) *Brands and Branding*. London: The Economist/Profile.

Crawford, R. (2016) 'Opening for Business: A comparison of the J. Walter Thompson and McCann Erickson agencies' entries into the Australian market', *Journal of Historical Research in Marketing*, 8, pp. 452–72.

Crawford, R. and Dickenson, J. (2016) *Behind Glass Doors: The World of Australian Advertising Agencies, 1959–1989*. Crawley: UWA Publishing.

Fastoso, F. and Whitelock, J. (2010) 'Regionalization vs. globalization in advertising research: Insights from five decades of academic study', *Journal of International Management*, 16, pp. 32–42.

Ford, J. B. Mueller, B., Taylor, C. R., and Hollis, N. (2011) 'The tension between strategy and execution: Challenges for international advertising research', *Journal of Advertising Research*, 51, pp. 27–41.

Frith, K. T. (2003) 'Advertising and the homogenization of cultures: Perspectives from ASEAN', *Asian Journal of Communication*, 13, pp. 37–54.

John, F., Mariano, A. and Moore, L. (2012) *Research without Borders: The Globalisation of the Marketing and Research Functions in a Brave New World*. Atlanta: European Society for Opinion and Market Research (ESOMAR).

Keegan, W. J. (1969). 'Multinational product planning: Strategic alternatives', *The Journal of Marketing*, 33(1), pp. 58–62.

Kumar, N. and Steenkamp, J.-B. (2013) 'Emerging globalisation', *Admap*, December, pp. 37–9.

Levitt, T. (1983) 'The globalization of markets', *The Harvard Business Review*, May 1983.

Malcolm, R. (2009) '"Think Local, Act Global" guides Diageo's brand management', *Aadmap*, March, pp. 25–7.

Marketing Society (2015) 'Guinness: Made of More'. In Marketing Society UK Excellence Awards. Available at: www.marketingsociety.com/the-library/2015-winner-guinness-global-marketing-case-study#RXSoQ5A9CoMHI7bU.97 (accessed 7 March 2017).

Matanda, T. and Ewing, M. T. (2012) 'The process of global brand strategy development and regional implementation', *International Journal of Research in Marketing*, 29, pp. 5–12.

Neff, J. (2015) 'Dove: Campaign for real beauty', Available at: http://adage.com/lp/top15/#realbeauty (accessed 24 October 2016).

Okazakin, S. and Taylor, C. R. (2013) 'Social media and international advertising: theoretical challenges and future directions', *International Marketing Review*, 30, pp. 58–9.

Osegowitsch, T. and Sammartino, A. (2008) 'Reassessing (home-) regionalisation', *Journal of International Business Studies*, 39, pp. 184–96.

Precourt, G. (2011) 'Sir Martin Sorrell's five key drivers of the advertising business', *Event Reports, ARF Re:think*, March 2011.

Raynor, A. (2016) 'Authentic amplification or echo chamber? Generating brand engagement via social media'. In *Asia Pacific*, Melbourne: European Society for Opinion and Market Research (ESOMAR).

Ritzer, G. (2015) *Globalization: A Basic Text*. Chichester: John Wiley & Sons.

Roostal, I. (1963) 'Standardization of advertising for Western Europe', *The Journal of Marketing*, 27(4), pp. 15–20.

Rugman, A. (2003) 'The myth of globalisation', *Market Leader*, Spring.

Sinclair, J. (2007) 'Globalisation and regionalisation of the advertising industry in the Asia-Pacific', *Asian Studies Review*, 31, pp. 283–300.

Sinclair, J. and Wilken, R. (2009) 'Strategic regionalization in marketing campaigns: Beyond the standardization/glocalization debate', *Continuum: Journal of Media & Cultural Studies*, 23(2), pp. 147–57.

Stevens, M. J. and Bird, A. (2004) 'On the myth of believing that globalization is a myth: Or the effects of misdirected responses on obsolescing an emergent substantive discourse', *Journal of International Management* 10, pp. 501–10.

Tai, S. (1997) 'Advertising in Asia: Localize or regionalize?', *International Journal of Advertising*, 16, pp. 48–61.

Verrender, I. (2016) 'Is globalisation coming to an end?', Available at: www.abc.net.au/news/2016-06-20/verrender-is-globalisation-coming-to-an-end/7524732 (accessed 24 October 2016).

Walker Smith, J. (2012) '10 trend in global brands', *WARC Trends*, February, pp. 14–15.

White, T. (2014) 'Lay's global: How a great idea travelled around the world', *Institute of Practitioners in Advertising*, Entrant, IPA Effectiveness Awards.

Wilken, R. and Sinclair, J. (2007) 'Global vision, regional focus, "glocal" reality: Global marketers, marketing communications, and strategic regionalism'. In *Communications, Civics, Industry – ANZCA 2007 Conference Proceedings*, Melbourne. Available at: www.anzca.net/documents/182-global-vision-regional-focus-glocal-reality-global-marketers-marketing-communications-and-str-1.html (accessed 7 March 2017).

Yasue, M. and Gu Xiang Wen, G. (1998) 'Asian youth and implications for marketing strategies: Changes and differences in consumption attitudes and lifestyle attitudes.' In *Marketing in Asia*, Manila: European Society for Opinion and Market Research (ESOMAR).

1 Globalisation of advertising

An overview of trends and issues

John Sinclair

Throughout the final decade of the twentieth century, the concept of globalisation became ever more seen and heard as 'a key idea by which we understand the transition of human society into the third millennium' (Waters, 1995, p. 1). The need had arisen for an inclusive term able to encompass the huge economic, political, and sociocultural changes that were being experienced on a world scale. 'Globalisation' has since become a cliché of our times, associated primarily in everyday discourse with global economic and political interrelations, but there has also developed a vigorous discourse about globalisation in the sphere of culture, in the broad sense, and this includes the globalisation of advertising.

The advertising industry has become involved in globalisation because it is a service industry that supports the foreign investment of global advertisers and has an active role in stimulating global media development. But as well as being a force for globalisation in national media and consumer markets, the advertising agency business itself is highly globalised in its organisation. This chapter will outline how globalisation has arisen in the advertising industry, and how it is manifested in its structure today. The profound transformation of advertising in the digital age must also be considered, along with related changes in modes of belonging, such as nationhood and minority status. Finally, a more nuanced appreciation of globalisation is provided by looking at how it is mediated by differences within and between world regions.

Global trends in the advertising industry

The rise of globalisation

An integral part of the commercialised culture of the everyday globalised world are the brand names owned by global advertisers. Some global brands, such as Coca-Cola, have had an international presence for generations. They belong to companies which grew from local to national scale, mainly in the US and Western European countries. In the 1960s and 1970s, such firms would become known 'multinational' or 'transnational' corporations. However, many others achieved global reach within a decade or so. Notable amongst these has been the sudden rise of communication and information technology corporations. We now find Apple, Google, and Microsoft topping the list in annual surveys, pushing down the likes of Coca-Cola and McDonald's (Millward Brown, 2016). Either way, these are the corporate advertising clients we now call 'global'.

Looking at the globalisation of the advertising and marketing communication industries in historical perspective, this occurred as the US- and European-based consumer goods and services corporations spread themselves into foreign markets in the 1960s and 1970s. Correspondingly, advertising agencies were also setting up offices abroad, both to serve these existing clients, and to capture new ones. Furthermore, this 'transnationalisation' of the brand name advertisers, with their advertising agencies in step, created demand for advertising space and time in the media of those countries they entered. National governments were thus pressured to 'liberalise' their media in the 1980s, meaning privatisation and deregulation. At the same time, new technologies, notably international satellite television, were breaking down the borders of the national media systems. This in turn allowed several media corporations to internationalise themselves, such as Time Warner, Sony, and News Corporation, ushering in an age of global media. With the advent of the Internet, unprecedented new modes of media globalisation and advertising have seen the rise to global dominance of Google and a host of social media platforms, accessible to many more people by mobile communications.

Current global structures

The advertising industry can best be thought of as a set of relations between the advertisers, their agencies, and the media, a 'manufacturing/marketing/media complex' (Sinclair, 2012). As just suggested above, the globalisation of each of these entities has proceeded in relation to the others: the advertisers being the prime movers; the agencies at their service, but also having their own interests to pursue; and the media developing in pursuit of advertising revenue. Looking now at the advertising agency business in particular, we see how certain key trends were set in train in the 1980s and continue to be formative today: first, the incorporation of international agencies into holding companies at a global level; second, the integration of other marketing services into these same groups; third, the separation or 'unbundling' of advertising's two traditional functions of creating advertising campaigns and placing them strategically in the media; and, finally, the continued influence of 'global alignment'.

For globalisation to occur in a meaningful sense, there needed to be a discourse about globalisation that could facilitate and legitimise the process, and a structural change which would make the world advertising industry truly internationalised (much more than just US agencies serving US clients in foreign markets). These conditions came together in the 1980s, with the discourse from a US management guru, Theodore Levitt, and the structural transformation brought about by the leading British advertising agency of the 1980s, Saatchi & Saatchi. Saatchi & Saatchi built itself into a global corporation by taking up Levitt's doctrine (Mattelart, 1991) and sought to bring about 'the world of a few mega-agencies handling the megaclients' (Magnet, 1986, p. 39). By raising huge amounts of capital from the London Stock Exchange, Saatchi & Saatchi made a series of takeovers of companies bigger than themselves, both in the UK and the US. The holding company structure enabled them to integrate a number of independently operating international agencies under a single strategic, management, and financial umbrella. A similar path was followed by another UK agency, WPP, which took over some of the oldest and most revered agencies in the US, such as J. Walter Thompson. As of 2015, WPP was the world's largest holding group, and, although Interpublic and another US holding group, Omnicom, maintained a massive global presence, and Saatchi & Saatchi had become part of the French holding group, Publicis, the top five was rounded out by the perennially largest agency in Japan, Dentsu (Advertising Age, 2015).

Under the holding group model, a number of international advertising agencies function independently from each other, but under a common corporate owner at a higher level of management. However, as noted above, these holding groups are not restricted to advertising agencies; they also incorporate companies in related marketing 'disciplines' such as public relations, market research, direct mail, and similar marketing services. We thus come to see that the holding groups are engaged in much more than the business of advertising: they embody the rhetoric of 'integrated marketing communications'. The horizontal integration of the advertising agencies is basic to the management of 'client conflicts', and this was one of the main factors that led to the formation of the holding groups in the first place. Advertisers will not tolerate having an agency that is also working for a competitor. The holding group solution can be illustrated in the case of WPP's management of the Colgate and Unilever accounts. Both are competing global clients, but WPP is structured to cater for them both, with Young & Rubicam handling Colgate, while Ogilvy & Mather takes care of competing brands for Unilever.

Vertical integration provides clients with other marketing services under WPP's same 'mega-group' structure. If clients need public relations services, they can be referred to different companies in that field too, such as Burson-Marsteller, which often operate on a global basis. Similarly, market research can be provided by Millward Brown, while there are other companies again in the same stable offering non-advertising services in branding and design, direct marketing and promotions, and specialist areas such as healthcare and multicultural marketing.

Also integrated with the holding groups are specialist media-buying and planning, or 'media' agencies. Along with the rise of the holding companies, the 1980s saw the 'unbundling' of advertising's traditional functions of placing and making advertisements, formerly handled by one 'full-service' agency. This is the third point listed above: the business of strategically purchasing media space and time became hived off from the 'creative' business of devising and executing advertising campaigns, into quite separate agencies. Client conflict can be just as much an issue to be managed in media-buying as in creative campaigns. This is because media-buying is not only a matter of getting media space and time for the best price, but involves the crucial matter of media planning. Like a creative campaign, media planning involves strategies which a client does not want to risk being leaked to competitors. Specialist media-buying and planning agencies are profitable for the holding groups, because a group can funnel the total media-buying requirements of its several creative agencies through its handful of media-buying agencies to obtain considerable buying power with the media.

The final key structural trend to be considered is global alignment. Although long-standing agency–client relationships were formed in the early days of agency expansion, once again it was the 1980s, with the global brands discourse introduced by the Saatchis, which was the crucible of change. The Saatchis encouraged their clients, such as British Airways, to consolidate their accounts with the one agency network on a worldwide basis to expedite the running of global campaigns, and also to cut costs. This became a movement towards global alignment that accelerated through the 1990s. Global alignment impacted heavily upon the independence of local agencies, because, in order for them to gain access to global clients, they had to join a global group with which those clients were globally aligned.

Impact of 'new' media

The relatively comfortable relationship between advertisers, agencies and media throughout the golden age of mass media in decades past (in which the media offered content that could attract audiences so as to sell access to those audiences to advertisers via the agencies) was the standard 'business model'. However, this model has come under pressure from the Internet, particularly the rise of search advertising. As a fundamental function of Internet usage, searching through 'search engines' has emerged as an integral advertising platform. The search engine's basic business model rests on its ability to offer and sell advertising, but not on any platform other than on its own. Where traditional media attracted audiences with the offer of information or entertainment content, search engines attract users to the service itself, and match search queries to ads. In both cases, the audiences or users collected are then 'sold' to advertisers, but in distinct ways. We have seen how traditional media depend on large advertisers, who place their advertising via an advertising agency. Search advertising has in principle diminished the need for any such intermediary. In the process, it has simultaneously enabled the rapid rise to power of Google, by far the most successful search engine in the field. The mega-groups have retaliated, not only by opening up their own 'digital agencies', but by staking out their claims in the new specialised commercio-technical areas which the Internet has opened up: that is, the generation, placement, distribution, measurement and general management of online advertisements. These activities now populate a new digital space, between the agencies and the Internet, and form a third area of commercial service provision for the agencies, the first two being, as has been noted, the placement and the creation of advertisements. Advertising practice has become highly technical in this new age of the algorithm.

Current trends in advertising, media and society

Advertising, branding and the nation

Advertising is a major vehicle of branding. With the rise of the press, then radio and television coming to dominate social communication in the twentieth century, branding found its supreme vehicle in advertising. Advertising thus impelled the commercial growth of these media, just as branding is a force behind the new social media today. Advertising enables brands to acquire cultural meanings, such as hierarchies of status, associations with certain kinds of people, and even something like their own personalities.

An influential analysis of branding comes from Adam Arvidsson, who has shown how consumers, rather than being the passive dupes of advertisers, actually participate in the making of a brand, albeit unequally. His insight is that brands capitalise upon 'people's ability to create trust, affect and shared meanings: their ability to create something in common ... it is the meaning-making activity of consumers that forms the basis of brand value' (Arvidsson, 2005, pp. 236–7). As common meanings created collectively by people (whether a nation or a sub-culture) is one of the main things we mean when we talk about 'culture', Arvidsson contends that brand marketers pick up on such meanings and exploit them by associating them with particular products and services.

When we talk about national identity, we not only mean the identity of the nation in relation to other nations, but also the identity of those persons who see themselves as belonging to the nation, and for whom that is a dimension of their personal identity. In this second sense, and in line with the view that consumers make meaningful choices for themselves, it can be argued that they choose national belonging rather than have it imposed on them. Such allegiances can be expressed in making purchases of certain brands, particularly those that are represented to consumers as embedded in an everyday, popular national culture that they identify with as their own. This leads Martin Davidson to claim that 'it is in consumerism that we most express our sense of social belonging.... Culture is the society we build with our brands' (Davidson, 1992, p. 124).

National belonging can be seen as a form of resistance to globalisation: 'In the face of globalisation commonly shared things anchor people to place.... The ability of things to connote shared histories is potent' (Edensor, 2002, p. 116). However fraught and tenuous the idea of national culture has become in the era of global flows, and although some brands encourage us to think of ourselves as 'global citizens', cultural belonging continues to be associated with place and nationhood (Morley, 2000). Externally, many nations now cultivate a brand identity, each seeking to position itself vis-à-vis other nations in the global marketplace, competing for trade, tourism and investment, or protecting the unique 'nation of origin' status of their exports (Moor, 2007). Modern nation states are intrinsically interested in pursuing and promoting images of national unity and belonging, and in cultivating support for their policies at home and abroad. They do so increasingly through 'nation branding' – 'Cool Britannia' is an exemplary case. That is, the nation itself now presents itself as a brand, both internally and externally. Internally, in the interests of governance and as the custodian of the national culture with which it legitimises its authority, the nation state addresses its citizens as members of the 'imagined community' of the nation, and hence as participants in its supposed 'deep horizontal comradeship' (Anderson, 1983, p. 6).

To the extent that 'the market rather than the state has become the key reference point for national identity' (Foster, 1999, cited in Edensor, 2002, p. 111), the 'official nationalism' of the nation state is now infused with what has been called the 'commercial nationalism' of the market (James, 1983, pp. 79). This notion also addresses people in their capacity as members of the nation, not as citizens but as consumers, and calls upon the same 'trust, affect and shared meanings' (Arvidsson, 2005, p. 236) involved in national belonging. The ascendance of the values of the market over those of the nation state also entails a shift from the formal, official markers of nationhood towards those that are more grounded in popular culture and its commercialisation by the media. Thus, in addition to diffusing popular traditions and narratives of national belonging, and the 'shared meanings' of nationhood expressed in televisual and media culture in general, branded goods, 'as advertised on television' and elsewhere, also become mediators of membership of the nation.

Advertising and minorities

We should also be aware that the global flows of persons in the form of migration, displacement, tourism and other forms of 'deterritorialisation' mean that contemporary nation states and markets alike are confronted with culturally diverse and highly fluid populations. In these circumstances, myths of national belonging and their expression in communities of consumption can exclude at the same time as they include – the mainstream, dominant culture is affirmed, while minority cultures and subcultures are 'othered'. In terms of marketing and branding, minorities within a given national market mostly lack the scale and distribution necessary to attract the attention of marketers, although members of the same minority living in different countries, as in the case of diasporas, can form transnational markets for certain branded goods and services. Western Union for example, is literally transnational in the sense of cutting across national boundaries.

National networked free-to-air commercial television, in its dual historical role of nation-building and the forming of national markets for advertisers, has created contemporary developed nations as 'imagined communities of consumption' (Foster, 1991, p. 250). The marginalisation of minorities on national network television, and the fact that they can and do compensate with recourse to alternative national and/or global services, in their own languages, and ever more on line, means that they are set apart from the majority society. This in turn means that they are less accessible to advertisers, except for quite specific minorities with critical mass who are targeted by a relatively small number of quite specific advertisers. At first sight, such haven from the pervasive commercialisation of capitalist modernity might seem to be a desirable condition, but, if we accept Davidson's argument that consumerism facilitates one's capacity to express a sense of social belonging' (Davidson, 1992, p. 124), then that condition compounds the cultural alienation from the nation in which immigrant minorities may find themselves. To be at the margins of the world of goods created by the national commercial culture is to live a restricted form of the consumer-citizenship which links the mainstream to their contemporary nations, and thus leaves minorities with a diminished cultural belonging.

Advertising, globalisation and world regions

Standardisation, localisation and 'glocalisation'

In the process of becoming ever more globalised, the practices of marketing in general and advertising in particular have had to learn how to come to terms with the realities of cultural and other differences. While past decades saw campaigns for products such as Marlboro run on a uniform, 'standardised' basis in every country where they were sold – 'one sight, one sound, one sell' (Mattelart, 1991, p. 55) – cultural adaptation has become a fundamental strategic principle for marketers in the age of globalisation. Nevertheless, standardisation had considerable influence amongst global marketers in the 1980s. Not only did it fit neatly with the rhetoric and organisational transformations of the emerging global era, but it was, and is, seen to have economic advantages. So, if corporations have a strong economic disincentive against cultural adaptation, why would they want to engage in cultural adaptation?

One major reason was the hilarious or simply bizarre 'lost in translation' failures of certain celebrated global campaigns during the 1980s and early 1990s. But as well as obvious linguistic and cultural differences, including religious strictures and variations in tastes, marketers were also encountering practical differences in national regulatory regimes and distribution systems. Such experience turned attention to alternative ways of approaching global marketing. One of the clearest examples was Nestlé's pursuit of a more localised or 'multidomestic' strategy of differentially formulating products such as their instant coffee in accordance with the taste preferences of various national markets. So, although standardisation has continued to be attractive to global marketers for economic reasons, the realities of cultural and other differences have forced them to develop adaptive strategies to cope with market-by-market variations.

The result of all this has been a kind of a continuum in marketing theory and practice between standardisation and localisation, but some middle ground was being cleared by the beginning of the 1990s with the concept of 'glocalisation'. This had its origins in the strategies of Japanese marketers in Asia, notably Sony, who pursued 'global localisation', rather than 'global standardisation' (Iwabuchi, 2002). Glocalisation subsequently came to be embraced in global marketing as the practical wisdom of creating the right balance between minding the bottom line of standardisation while meeting the demands of localisation. In practice, this means maximising the organisational and economic advantages of standardisation, while adapting to cultural and other differences between markets to the necessary degree. Adaptation can be deployed at a number of levels: the subnational as well as the national, and perhaps even the world-regional. Furthermore, to the extent that adaptation is being made on cultural–linguistic grounds, rather than, for example, to meet national regulations, then geocultural or geolinguistic regions come into consideration: that is, nations or even groups within nations which are not geographically connected. We can call this 'strategic regionalism': marketing a product to several countries on a regional basis with minimum variation (Sinclair and Wilken, 2009).

Globalisation and world regions

Globalisation is not, as the word implies, a total and uniform process, equally affecting every part of the globe. Although the concept of 'globalisation' might signal the territorial ambitions of the manufacturing/marketing/media complex and reflect the fact of their presence in ever more parts of the world, it remains very much a figure of speech, a strategic exaggeration in the ideological rhetoric of globalism. Just as advertisers have found they have to adapt on a regional basis, our conceptual understanding of globalisation needs to be mediated by an understanding of differences in world regions. This is not the place to attempt an outline of each and every world region, so let it suffice to consider the case of Asia, which has some very interesting characteristics.

Taken as a whole, broadly defined world region, Asia encompasses three of the world's top ten national markets, namely China, Japan and South Korea, with India not far behind (Statista, 2016). Asia is dominated by one of the world's major marketing mega-groups, Dentsu of Japan. China and India in particular are both undergoing exceptionally rapid economic growth and seeing the emergence of new categories of consumers, notably the much-vaunted 'middle class' of those societies. This growth continues to attract global advertisers and agencies, and, at the same time, Chinese and Indian brands have begun to venture on to the world market. Yet Asia is defined more by its geographical unity than anything else, for, in most relevant aspects, the diversity of Asia is arguably greater than any other world region, presenting advertisers and their agencies, and media, with complex barriers, not only between nations, but within them. Significantly, it was Asia where the concept and practice of 'glocalisation' was invented.

Until recent decades, Asia had attracted little interest from the global manufacturing/marketing/media corporations, relative to their activities in other regions. However, rapid growth in both China and India in particular has recently brought a great deal of corporate attention. We now find that the most pervasive advertisers in the major markets of the region are the North Atlantic-based FMCG (fast moving consumer goods) marketers, notably Unilever and

Procter & Gamble. However, Asian automotive and electronic manufacturers also figure largely, and domestic FMCG companies are prominent in both China and India (Adbrands, 2016). As to advertising agencies, global agencies have been setting up in Asia for some time, mainly through joint ventures with local partners, and this combination of global FMCG marketers and agencies has stimulated the growth and proliferation of the different national media systems. Beyond this, it is difficult to generalise about Asia as a region, as each national market has its own distinctive characteristics.

China presents formidable natural barriers against building a national market, even for Chinese brands. For one thing, the sheer physical size of its territory and population pose a significant challenge for the logistics of distribution of goods and services, let alone the advertising of them. Thus, from a demographic and sociological point of view, there is extreme internal differentiation within China as a consumer market: there is no 'Chinese market' as such. China overtook Japan as Asia's largest, and the world's second-largest, national advertising market in 2013. South Korea is worthy of note because, like Japan, it has shown itself relatively resistant to penetration by the global manufacturing/marketing/media complex.

Conclusion

The advertising industry became implicated in the global transformations characterising the closing decades of the last century, and established its own internationalised and complex structure in the form of the holding group. Although this model has endured, the industry has also had to respond to the advent of the Internet , which has brought the challenges of search advertising, social media, and the digitisation of advertising management and targeting. Globalisation has not meant that advertising campaigns have become standardised around the world as early advocates hoped. On the contrary, advertising has had to reconcile itself with national belonging and other cultural differences between and within national markets. While the discourse of globalisation (both pro and anti) has created the impression that the influence of global corporations is a total and direct phenomenon, rather than partial and complexly mediated, attention to the peculiarities of world regions shows how advertising practice is mediated by transnational, regional, national, and sub-national levels.

References

Adbrands (2016) *Top Advertisers by Country*. Available at: www.adbrands.net/country_index.htm (accessed 10 November 2016).
Advertising Age (2015) *AdAge Agency Family Trees*. Available at: http://adage.coverleaf.com/advertisingage/20150504?pg=72#pg72 (accessed 10 November 2016).
Anderson, B. (1983) *Imagined Communities: Reflections on the Origin and Spread of Nationalism*. London: Verso.
Arvidsson, A. (2005) 'Brands: A critical perspective', *Journal of Consumer Culture*, 5(2), pp. 235–58.

Davidson, M. P. (1992) *The Consumerist Manifesto: Advertising in Postmodern Times*. London: Routledge.

Edensor, T. (2002) *National Identity, Popular Culture and Everyday Life*, Oxford: Berg.

Foster, R. J. (1991) 'Making national cultures in the global ecumene', *Annual Review of Anthropology*, 20, pp. 235–60.

Iwabuchi, K. (2002) *Recentering Globalization*. Durham, NC: Duke University Press.

James, P. (1983) 'Australia in the corporate image: A new nationalism', *Arena Journal*, 63, pp. 65–106.

Magnet, M. (1986) 'Saatchi and Saatchi will keep gobbling', *Fortune*, 23 June.

Mattelart, A. (1991) *Advertising International: The Privatisation of Public Space*. London: Routledge.

Millward Brown (2016) *2015 BrandZ Top 100 Global Brands*. Available at: www. millwardbrown.com/brandz/top-global-brands (accessed 10 November 2016).

Moor, L. (2007) *The Rise of Brands*. Oxford and New York: Berg.

Morley, D. (2000) *Home Territories: Media, Mobility and Identity*. London: Routledge.

Sinclair, J. (2012) *Advertising, the Media and Globalisation: A World in Motion*. London and New York: Routledge.

Sinclair, J. and Wilken, R. (2009) 'Strategic regionalization in marketing campaigns: Beyond the standardization/glocalization debate', *Continuum: Journal of Media and Cultural Studies*, 23(2), pp. 147–56.

Statista (2016) *Advertising Expenditure in the World's Largest Ad Markets in 2015*. Available at: www.statista.com/statistics/273736/advertising-expenditure-in-the-worlds-largest-ad-markets/ (accessed 10 November 2016).

Waters, M. (1995) *Globalization*. London and New York: Routledge.

2 Globalisation, branding and advertising's stakeholders

Linda Brennan and Robert Crawford

As an ever-evolving industry, advertising has both shaped the globalised world and been shaped by it. Global advertising emerges from the interplay of actors working at multiple levels within and across different countries and regions. Ideas traverse international boundaries almost instantaneously, facilitating rapid adaptation and integration into cultural and social structures.

Globalisation is hardly a new phenomenon. Since the dawn of time, people have travelled across continents, taking their culture(s) with them. Long distance, cross-cultural trade continued to spread innovation and change from one group of people to another. Religious missionaries similarly contributed to this process, spreading ideas across the globe whilst establishing new networks. Intercultural contact has likewise contributed to globalisation of ideas. More recently, globalisation has been shaped by colonialism and the dominance of the northern hemisphere in terms of economic, political and cultural influences.

As a result of these flows, globalisation is a complex process that has been taking place over eons and it is not feasible or necessary to pin it down as a concept or an effect. Globalisation is not internationalisation. Nor is it Westernisation, although it is often perceived as being a new form of colonialism. We argue in this chapter (and across this collection) globalisation comes about as a result of technological changes as well as flows of people and information throughout the ages. Technology is changing the way nations, politics and power are engaged with by citizens who are operating in a borderless world. Increasingly, these global citizens are affecting the countries that they visit and where they may be working and living, even if only temporarily. Thus, they are changing the nature of the nations and the regions in which they find themselves. To this end, regions are growing in importance and influence, as borders between co-located countries become increasingly porous.

The title of this book, *Advertising in a Borderless World*, reflects advertising's expansion across national borders as well as its incorporation of regional cultures and industries. The European Union, for example, established Europe as an entity where the open flow of people and ideas between countries is valued as much as its constituent nation states' distinctiveness. However, Britain's 2016 vote to exit the union challenged this balance, bringing about a period of significant uncertainty into how business is performed in Europe. Importantly, while firms might be multinational or global, business takes place at a local level and people in specific locations are at the core of the transactions that take place. Advertising seeks to respond to both the desire to be global and the desire to be different. People want to share in global values and lifestyles while maintaining their individual and social system identities. Globalisation covers transnational, international, macro-regional, national and micro-regional (municipal and local) boundaries. This system of entities incorporates international organisations, non-government organisations, professionals and consumers with access to the Internet. Each of the different levels has their own perceptions about the impact of globalisation on their daily lives. Advertising in the global context allows people, wherever they are located, to perceive other realities and creates different forms of reality, some of which can be translated across international borders and some of which are not readily transferred because of the dynamics of the global market space. By examining the changing roles and functions performed by clients, brands, the media and consumers, this chapter will illustrate the connections between the global, local and regional contexts and demonstrate their impact on the way that advertising is conducted.

Clients in a globalised world

In recent decades, the spread of commerce and commercial firms across the globe has been identified as a defining characteristic of globalisation. Multinationals have been instrumental to this process. Defined simply as a firm 'that owns or controls value-creating assets in more than one country' (Fitzgerald, 2015, p. 15), multinationals have been active drivers of 'economic, social, and technical transformations' (Jones, 2010, p. 6) across the globe. As clients, their impact on advertising strategies and practices has been and, indeed, remains profound.

While globalisation became one of the buzzwords of the late twentieth century, the expansion of commercial industries across national borders is far from a recent concept (Jones, 2010). The first multinationals were already in full-swing by the late nineteenth century. Following the hiatus caused by the world wars, the multinational firm re-emerged, with American-based companies leading the way. By the end of the twentieth century, multinationals had progressed from being mere exporters of goods and services, to being highly integrated and interdependent organisations where 'production, technology, finance, product development ... [and] marketing' (Fitzgerald, 2015, p. 12) were no longer the exclusive domain of the head office.

As globalisation 'envisages producers adopting best practice, while consumers enjoy low prices and imported goods and services' (Fitzgerald, 2015, p. 9), it has placed multinationals in a unique position. On the one hand, international competition and expansion have driven them to enhance their practices; on the other, they are able to operate as powerful clients that exert significant influence over their agencies. Operating as a service industry, advertising agencies have been actively involved in these processes – both directly and indirectly. J. Walter

Thompson established its global empire in the interwar period to service the needs of the General Motors account (Merron, 1999). Coca-Cola's desire for international consistency in its global strategy likewise led McCann-Erickson to open branches across the globe in the 1960s and 1970s (Alter, 1994). The arrival of multinational firms and multinational agencies inevitably affected local practices. Multinational firms setting up operations in new countries often demanded the same level of service from their local agencies as they received elsewhere in the world. Multinational agencies similarly promised to deliver world-class service to local advertisers. Such expectations and the establishment of new standards of service ensured that advertisers – multinational or otherwise – would maintain a tight grip on their agencies.

As multinationals extended their operations into new markets across the globe, they increasingly confronted the issue of standardisation. The degree to which international offices should utilise campaigns or strategies has been keenly debated. Views vary from agency to agency and, indeed, over time. Coca-Cola, for example, ran highly centralised campaigns from the 1960s through to the 1980s. The only exceptions were Australia and Japan, where local content restrictions required the local offices of the firm's agency, McCann Erickson, to create locally produced campaigns. McCann-Erickson's Australian offices often circumvented these rules by reshooting international campaigns frame by frame (Crawford and Dickenson, 2016, p. 36).

Contemporary advertising practice sees clients opting for less rigid approaches than their predecessors. Most brands currently operate in the middle ground between centralisation and decentralisation (Delener, 1996, p. 174). Nevertheless, the debate remains an ongoing one. So, for every study that reveals the centralising shift in advertiser operations (Mitchell and Bright, 1995), there are others that declare 'We don't create global strategies, ideas to benefit people with "global" in their job titles or roles, but local markets and their customers' (Weigel, 2012, n.p). Conceding that 'Most likely there is no right structure for managing a global brand', Chuck Kapelke contends that the chosen approach should be one that 'facilitates constant multi-directional channels for communication and cross-pollination of ideas and practices' (Kapelke, 2013, p. 8). Such openness is in part informed by the realities of executing a successful multinational campaign. 'There are quite simply, very few case studies of success by truly multimarket campaign', observes Peter Field (2008), adding 'multinational campaigns are difficult to get right and often result in inefficient "lowest common denominator" thinking'. Of course, the challenges of operating globally have not dented advertiser aspirations. Outlining its approach to the award-winning 'You're Not You When You're Hungry' campaign for Snickers, AMV BBDO revealed that its client still harboured lofty ambitions: 'Our challenge was to deliver a big, populist idea that would drive salience amongst the male and the female, the young and the old. In essence, we needed a campaign for everyone, for every country' (Effie Worldwide, 2011).

Brands

Alongside the globalisation of advertising has been a concomitant growth in global brands, notably brands that are able to connect to markets wherever they are located. The concept of branding has evolved from early identifiers using written words and symbols – for example, dynasty and emperor names on sculpture and pottery in China (Lion *et al.*, 1960), hot iron and ear marking on cattle (Roper and Parker, 2006), letters on clothing (Carstairs, 2006) or tattoos on skin (Bengtsson *et al.*, 2005). Branding initially served to ensure that ownership of property was clearly identified while discouraging theft. Such brands eventually became useful in indicating qualities (and quality). The Ming Dynasty (1368–1644) saw pottery produced on an industrial scale, which facilitated the gifting of such wares, particularly to diplomats and courtiers. Such pottery featured the dynasty and the emperor's marks but rarely that of the artist (Lion *et al.*, 1960). Consequently, the artistry and quality of the pottery came to represent the dynasty and/or the emperor's rule. More than a mere a sign and a symbol, branding from its inception was also founded on the desire to be of consequence (Bastos and Levy, 2012) and to indicate identity (de Mooij, 2013).

Yet, despite their longstanding history, global brands are notoriously difficult to define. First, brands are combinations of signs, symbols and attributes that facilitate connections between consumers and producers (see Figure 2.1). Second, brands may be globally recognisable but only relatively locally available (e.g. Qantas, the National Basketball Association). Third, to be considered global a brand must first be international (sold to different countries) and then multinational (sold in many different countries). However, then the dilemma arises: when a brand's key characteristic is its country of origin, is it truly a

Figure 2.1 Elements of a brand that have to translate across global boundaries.

global brand? For example, Qantas is an Australian airline with a key brand symbol of a kangaroo. Is this a global brand or is it merely a brand that has global awareness?

When it comes to global branding, the process of branding is not straight-forward: brands are made up of a number of elements that must be translated, transformed and transported throughout the global markets. 'Cookie-cutter' advertising seldom works as a global strategy (Flynn, 2011), as the point of branding is to differentiate one's product in the market. Differences between markets demand that the strategies be (at least) adapted for the market. As brands are made up of functional, technical and emotional components, there is a lot to adapt. The functional components of a brand include trademarks (protection from theft), packaging and labelling (identity) and attributes (qualities and quality). Technical components consist of symbols and marks (logos), words (brand name), differentiating factors and uniqueness (e.g. formulae), design elements and communication potential (e.g. moving images versus sound only). John Philip Jones (1998, p. 20) observes that brands were originally used in advertising to protect a monopoly or at best an oligopoly of market competitors, asserting legal rights to the product and therefore the consumers' desires to pur-chase their products. Brand loyalty therefore became an extremely important element in building brand equity and brand value. On the other hand, Judie Lannon (1999, p. 37) suggests that 'everything that a human does has some kind of symbolic value' and brands help people to convey that value both to them-selves and to their world. In this way, brands deliver value to the organisation and the consumer: providing one with economic benefits and the other with social and emotional benefits. In global advertising, market dynamics and struc-tures, consumers, values and cultures differ nationally and regionally. Creating advertising to suit these dynamics is challenging. On the one hand, high levels of inclusiveness can lead to homogeneous messaging that targets no one in par-ticular. On the other, being too divergent can exclude major constituents in the market space. Similarly, an overemphasis on local nuances might restrict under-standing to an overly narrow audience.

Possibly the most important component of a brand comprises the emotional connecting devices. Figure 2.2 illustrates devices such as icons that convey brand meaning (e.g. the Nike swoosh, McDonald's golden arches, Mercedes' three-pointed star), establish associations of ideas with the brand (e.g. connota-tions, implicit meanings, metaphors and analogies) and express the overall brand promise. The emotional connections define the brand narrative and the relation-ship that the consumer builds with the brand's persona, including the brand's identity. Because brands evolve over time and are usually grown within their home markets, the brand persona might not be readily translatable across cul-tural boundaries. Indeed, the advertising literature is replete with international branding faux pas (James, 2014), although these brands were perfectly accept-able in their home countries at the time of inception. For example, Gerber's use of a picture of a baby on the packaging of its baby-food container for African markets was consistent with its strategy in other continents. However, the firm

1	2	3	4	5
APPLE	GOOGLE	MICROSOFT	COCA-COLA	FACEBOOK
Value: $154.1 B Technology	Value: $82.5 B Technology	Value: $72.2 B Technology	Value: $58.5 B Beverages	Value: $52.6 B Technology
6	7	8	9	10
TOYOTA	IBM	DISNEY	MCDONALD'S	GE
Value: $42.1 B Automotive	Value: $41.4 B Technology	Value: $39.5 B Leisure	Value: $39.1 B Restaurants	Value: $36.7 B Diversified
11	12	13	14	15
SAMSUNG	AMAZON	AT&T	BMW	CISCO
Value: $36.1 B Technology	Value: $35.2 B Technology	Value: $32.6 B Telecom	Value: $28.8 B Automotive	Value: $28.4 B Technology
16	17	18	19	20
ORACLE	INTEL	NIKE	LOUIS VUITTON	MERCEDES BENZ
Value: $28 B Technology	Value: $27.7 B Technology	Value: $27.5 B Apparel	Value: $27.3 B Luxury	Value: $26 B Automotive

Figure 2.2 Top 20 brands September 2016.

Source: adapted from Interbrand, 2015 p. 9.

was surprised when illiterate and non-English speaking customers shunned the product and inferred that the food may have been made from babies (Haig, 2005). It had overlooked the fact that Western firms operating in the region generally featured the ingredients on their packaging. Car brand names are particularly problematic it seems, especially in Latin countries. For example, the Chevy Nova translates as 'It does not go' in Spanish and in Puerto Rico, Toyota's Fiera translates as 'ugly old woman'; furthermore, the Ford Pinto translates as small penis in the Brazilian patois (based on Portuguese). Creating a brand that can connect to multifarious global markets requires something beyond the product itself.

Claire Holmes (2016) suggests that the brands that lack a clear sense of self struggle to connect with audiences. A clear brand story is therefore needed to align the whole organisation. Such narratives will connect people to the brand regardless of where head office is or where the marketing decision-making is taking place. The ability to stand out from the crowd is increasingly difficult in a globalised world, with many 'me too' brands competing for consumer attention. Those brands that successfully cultivate their uniqueness in a positive way not only lead their category but are also more profitable than their competitors

(Walshe, 2016). When it comes to managing brands, agencies often assume the role of brand guardians (Yakob, 2016) when designing global strategies. However, agencies all too frequently struggle to be simultaneously global and local. Media convergence and the growth of programmatic advertising make it difficult for a brand to be locally differentiated and remain 'on message' in every market. Keeping the brand story coherent across different cultures, markets, media and platforms can be challenging. Binns and Gans (2015) thus contend that:

> Today's brands need to be adaptable to proliferating channels – one's Twitter presence ... may not (and probably shouldn't) be identical to its press persona, but they should be consistent in voice. The way a brand behaves in Nigeria may be different from how it behaves in the US, but it still needs to share a common essence.

The essence of the brand is its identity – the 'thing' that is communicated and communicable to the market, wherever it may be located.

The congruence between the brand's identity and the consumer's identity creates the connection between them. However, in global brands, the ability to connect to the consumer across national and regional boundaries is contingent on the brand's acceptability in the market place. What is relevant in Manhattan might be less relevant in Toronto or simply irrelevant in Johannesburg. Local and regional brands have a competitive advantage in their regional markets. They are more salient, but to be a global brand they need a strong brand proposition. This is where differentiation and monetisation become important (Walshe, 2016). Being different is not an end in itself: brands also need to find a way to make it pay. This requires a combination of a strong brand with powerful advertising that will enhance global relevance and global acceptability. This is a difficult task, particularly when confronted with local and regional barriers to brand development.

Neither branding nor advertising on their own can sufficiently engage a global audience. It is their combination that makes the difference. Holmes (2016) cites the example of Pepsi, which has devoted large amounts to advertising and communications yet has failed to cast off the perception that it is a mere alternative to Coke. Where Coke's message of freedom and joy is clear, consistent and relevant to its consumers (Volkmer, 2013), Pepsi confuses its consumers by changing campaigns and sending mixed messages that lack a common thread (Holmes, 2016). Coke connects with consumers in a number of ways. Its 'Share a Coke" campaign saw logos being replaced with friends' names and created an online referral campaign. This established a personal and social connection with the brand, thereby increasing its social value. This is a good example of how to use local social networks to build the global brand community. Of course, the reasons people like certain brands more than others remains an imprecise science. In a 2015 *Fortune* article, Kevin Lane Keller said of Microsoft "I can see why people have stopped hating them, but can't see why people would start loving them" (as cited in Badenhausen, 2015). Identifying and distilling those intangibles that underpin a brand's popularity is therefore a difficult task, but essential for any firm harbouring global ambitions.

In the past, fast moving consumer goods dominated the brand landscape. However, brands such as Kelloggs have been moved aside for newer more intangible brands. New technology brands are often abstract ideas and services that are not necessarily product-led. Such global brands sell aspiration, innovation and modernity. Young consumers seeking to demonstrate their ideal-selves to their world look to Apple products and the brand to express themselves. Google, Apple, Facebook and Amazon rely on constant innovation to stay ahead of competitors and to enhance their brand (Buckley, 2015). Modern brands have embraced online brand communities and seek to be transparent in order to build trust. The idea behind the brand is essential but consumers want more than products, they want experiences as well. In a world where a product will be updated in a few months, functionality seems to matter less than image (World Advertising Research Council, 2015). In 2016 quality issues plagued both Samsung and Apple as they rushed to market with new phones (Gibbs, 2016; Smith, 2016). However, the prospect of exploding phones or failing batteries was not enough to upend either brand's global dominance.

While there is such a thing as a theory of branding (Christodoulides, 2009) and a notional process for undertaking it (El-Amir and Burt, 2010), the decision to 'brand' a product is often organic, insofar as it is not a clear decision with stages or steps, let alone a coherent strategy (Hatch and Rubin, 2006). It is something that grows over time into the qualities that become the brand. For example, the Eiffel Tower has come to represent Paris and, with it, France and all things French. It is an icon and a brand at the same time. Brands are not inherently designed around consumer insights. A brand can start from a domestic or local base and spread around the world. Toyota and Coca-Cola both commenced operations as local brands selling to domestic markets before evolving into international and then global brands (Friedman, 1992; McEnally and De Chernatony, 1999).

Brands are inherently multidimensional in form and function. Advertising therefore seeks to convey the brand in a way that facilitates consumer engagement with the brand at emotional (heart) and cognitive (head) levels. The connection of both elements is integral to engagement. A brand's components thus create a story (narrative) that allows the brand's identity and personality to be perceived by the consumer. The consumer's response to the brand narrative is to engage with the brand, either by buying the product or connecting in some other way. This is an essential aspect of the modern brand, as Patrick Hanlon (2016) reveals: 'Brands have evolved. Today, "brands" are the moments and experiences shared between a user and a product.... Brands are no longer what we tell people we are, but what our community says about us'. For global brands, the brand community has no firm boundaries between segments. However, a brand's multidimensionality also creates vulnerabilities. Each dimension must be carefully aligned to ensure engagement with the brand across all the markets.

Brands are increasingly required to be more than an identifier or connection point for the consumer. Although the correct mechanism for measuring brand equity remains contentious, brands are required to deliver shareholder returns on investment (Baalbaki and Guzmán, 2016; Muravskii *et al.*, 2016). Global brands often have a locally based head office to which they are accountable and to which profits are repatriated to shareholders. However, the rise in global citizenship has pressured global brands to assume greater responsibility for their actions (Byford and Holt, 2013). The case that resulted in Apple being ordered to pay back taxes to Ireland of more than US$14.5 billion illustrates these pressures (Kanter and Scott, 2016). On the other hand, the Irish government's tax breaks for Apple illustrate the economic contribution that such brands make to the local economy. When it comes to global brands, there is a lot at stake: economically, politically and socially.

Although a brand must achieve economic goals, they also deliver benefits that are not necessarily financial. As Blake Morgan (2015) points out, the Dove Campaign for Real Beauty had a profound impact on women: 'Woman after woman in the audience raised her hand to explain the tangentially related benefits of the Dove Campaign for Real Beauty'. Brands that do well perform functions that meet human needs (Kay, 2014) and are genuinely useful to their markets. In Dove's case, the needs fulfilled were social and emotional. Baskin (2013) describes the campaign as:

> a work of genius.... It attaches an incontrovertibly legitimate point of view (POV) to its brand and, by donating money to leadership programs for girls and young women, it gives itself something to talk about with its customers other than scents and packaging.

Such intangible elements are translatable and transportable, offering more than the product or potential profits. They are also embedded in the consumer's imagination and enable them to transport themselves within the brand narrative to wherever and whatever they want to be.

Media

In their article 'The death of advertising', Roland T. Rust and Richard W. Oliver presented an alarming prognosis on the state of advertising:

> Advertising is on its deathbed and it will not survive long, having contracted a fatal case of new technology. Advertising's heir will be customer communications, a broader and more flexible topic which will be able to incorporate the dramatic changes introduced by the information superhighway.
>
> (Rust and Oliver, 1994, p. 76)

While to claim that advertising is dead may seem somewhat exaggerated some 20 years later, it is clear that advertising's case of 'new technology' has fundamentally transformed its form and function, especially when considered alongside the shifts in leadership of the world's Top 20 brand list.

Media revolutions have been integral to advertising's development. Improvements to printing presses saw advertisements progressively taking more space on each page. This provided the opportunity to spend more effort on creating arresting copy and visual imagery. Radio posed a fundamental challenge to print. As a medium, it prioritised the aural over the visual, requiring advertising professionals to rethink their communication strategies. Sponsored programmes and spots emerged as new advertising tools. Described by some as 'radio with pictures' (Meyers, 2013), television was perhaps less revolutionary in form than its predecessor. However, television's impact would be more profound, as it emerged as the most dominant advertising medium over the second half of the twentieth century. From the forgettable 15-second spot for carpet shampoo to the multimillion dollar epics aired at half time in the Superbowl, television attracted the lion's share of advertising expenditure not to mention attention from the consuming public and agency staff alike. Significantly, the growing popularity of pay television hinted that audience fragmentation might present a challenge to the giant networks that dominated the broadcast medium (Webster, 2005).

The emergence of digital media marked the end of television's halcyon days. However, the change was neither instantaneous nor linear. In the 1990s, it was something of an unknown entity. Many commercial firms were sceptical of the new medium, let alone its commercial applications. As the number of consumers going online steadily increased, established media outlets extended their operations into the digital realm. This combination persuaded advertisers and their agencies to pay more serious attention to the medium's advertising potentials. While advertising on popular sites was no different to advertising in popular newspaper or on popular programmes, there were new platforms which opened new opportunities and also required new ways of thinking. Google's emergence as a major advertising platform characterised this shift. Beginning as a mere search engine (Seymour *et al.*, 2011), Google realised that its capacity to order information placed it in a powerful gatekeeper role. Its sheer popularity led advertisers to see that Google was an important advertising platform and they were willing to pay for premium listings on the website. As online traffic increased, Google's power went from strength to strength. When BMW's German site attempted to manipulate the Google algorithm in 2006, the search engine flexed its muscles by downgrading the advertiser's site and effectively concealed it from online audiences (BBC News, 2006). Social media platforms offered a different type of platform that challenged advertising's traditional broadcast approach. Additionally, the rise of digital has meant that media buying is becoming more sophisticated with programmatic buying and this is making changes to how advertising is applied right throughout the advertising ecosystem (AppNexus, 2015).

The rise of digital media platforms has inevitably generated discussion about the nature of the new medium and how it operates. Convergence, for example, has been identified as a defining characteristic of the new media landscape. Arguing that convergence is better understood as 'a process' rather than as 'an endpoint', Henry Jenkins explains that 'the proliferation of channels and the portability of new computing and telecommunications technologies' has seen the media expand dramatically in both size and scope (Jenkins, 2004, p. 34). While the prospect of extending their reach has excited advertisers and their agencies, a degree of ambiguity can nevertheless be detected in their approach. A 2013 survey of London agencies found that, while they viewed media convergence as a positive development that enhanced campaign effectiveness, they believed that their clients lacked an understanding of convergence or how it was affecting their business (Mediaocean, 2013). For their part, agencies are often still learning on the job. To this end, it seems that 'the adoption of new technologies – and advertising in them – has expanded at a faster rate than knowledge about how to leverage them' (Taylor *et al.*, 2013, p. 200).

Advertising expenditure reveals that the digital revolution is still a work in progress. While advertising expenditure on digital media in countries such as Australia, Britain and Denmark exceeds the amount being spent on television, the American market will only see this trend taking place in 2017 (eMarketer, 2016). In most other countries, television remains the dominant medium. At the global level, television attracted 42 per cent of the global ad spend in 2015 while digital platforms accounted for 24.6 per cent (Carat, 2016). Digital media will continue to make inroads into television's dominance but rumours of television's death as an advertising medium are still exaggerated. However, television consumption is undergoing significant changes (see, for example, Lewis *et al.*, 2016). While viewing levels remain relatively consistent, the fragmentation of audiences poses a very real challenge to advertisers (Sharp *et al.*, 2009). As audiences view television programmes across different media platforms, the mass audience has effectively dissipated. The challenge of locating and reaching these scattered audiences has now become a priority for the advertising industry. It has also required advertisers and agencies to rethink their communication strategies. Netflix, for example, has emerged as one of the key television networks in the United States yet it proudly boasts that it does not carry advertisements. Product placements in many of its programmes nevertheless hint at the opportunities for advertisers in this field. Netflix's *House of Cards*, for example, has seen Samsung products integrated into storylines, while a Samsung promotion offered customers free subscriptions to Netflix (Peterson, 2015). Despite its aversion to broadcasting commercials, Netflix is also emerging as a major user of native advertising, strategically positioning stories in other media outlets that seek to generate interest in Netflix programmes that deal with similar issues or themes (Staunstrup, 2015). The proliferation of such networks (as well as other online platforms) will presumably see advertisers increasingly involving themselves in the production of content (Precourt, 2016).

Observing that much of the processes of the media revolution are 'predominantly processes of reforming and rearranging existing content and practices', Jim Macnamara nevertheless notes that 'New forms of media and communication practice with characteristics, properties and potentialities unlike their predecessors are emerging' (Macnamara, 2014, p. 8). Media platforms that facilitate active audience engagement reflect the rise of what Jenkins (2009) labels 'participatory culture' and its acceleration in the digital age. Although audiences had never been passive, social media created the opportunity for consumers to share their personal views and engage with advertisers and their brands in active, instantaneous and very public ways. Comments left on social media sites may vary between the angry and the inane, but advertisers cannot afford to ignore them (Sexton, 2015). Moreover, conversations and shares can provide unique insights to advertisers and their agencies. Speaking in 2015, Allison Barnes, Coca-Cola's digital anthropologist, revealed how Coke sought to listen to conversations across different social media platforms with a simple aim: to 'go and see what they're sharing and just match our marketing with that' (Advertising Research Foundation, 2015). A campaign that successfully goes viral similarly requires an understanding of audiences and their capacity to contribute. Such campaigns not only need to be interesting and emotive, they also need to be produced so as to facilitate sharing (Garey and Johnstone, 2015). The progressive integration of interactivity into the very structure of new campaigns marks a fundamental shift in the way that advertising is both conceptualised and executed. To this end, Marshall McLuhan's maxim is perhaps more apt than ever before: the medium has indeed become the message.

The speed with which new media outlets are adopted by audiences has placed the advertising industry on the back foot. Wagler's (2013) study of mid-west American agencies outlined the ways in which they were seeking to keep abreast of changes – from reading technology blogs and lunchtime seminars to employing programmers and young people 'who already have the skills we are looking for in their DNA' (Wagler, 2013, p. 118). The challenges that confront them similarly require innovative thinking. Fragmentation remains an abiding issue and the proliferation of media platforms will continue to exacerbate it. Identifying where audiences are located has become an increasingly demanding task. Once located, advertisers and their agencies need to think more broadly about their audience's context and the ways that this may affect their interaction with brand or advertisement (Poltrack and Bowen, 2011). As contexts vary significantly across media, space and time, finding the right message seems more elusive than ever before. The media's increasingly global reach also taps into an ongoing issue: to what degree should appeals be standardised (Zarantonello *et al.*, 2014).

While it is difficult to predict where the next media platforms will take advertising and the industry, broader trends in the development of media reveal that agility is integral to media strategy. In a world where advertisers and agencies are engaged in 'real-time, always-on brand conversations', the task of producing 'more work, across more channels, faster, and with the same or smaller budgets' (Priest, 2014) is acute. Coca-Cola's 'liquid and linked' marketing strategy is an attempt to meet this challenge. Understanding liquid as 'the need for a brand to be aware of the constant changes in the marketing and media landscape and be able to adapt' and linked as the notion that 'all brand messages, in whatever consumer touchpoint, need to belong to an overarching brand strategy' (Cox *et al.*, 2011), Coke's strategy seeks to establish a level of coherence amidst a fragmenting and evolving media landscape. Negotiating these divergent forces will be a hard task, but ultimately one that the advertising industry will need to master if it is to remain alive and relevant.

Consumers

The pace of globalisation and interchanges between populations has given rise to the concept of a global consumer (Durvasula and Lysonski, 2016). However, the global consumer still acquires within their home country and educes the relevant social norms from their social ecosystem. Thus, their identity as a consumer is derived from local, national and international influences. Global brands can serve the function of being the means by which consumers can see themselves as having a modern self image and to promote themselves to others as having a global cosmopolitan identity (Halkias *et al.*, 2016). Consuming global brands offer consumers an opportunity to belong to global society and to become global citizens. However, advertising's contribution to this process is complicated.

Rather than looking to advertising to be informed, consumers are seeking information and consumer support through social networks. They are also seeking subscriptions to their digital content to avoid advertising (Deloitte, 2016), and using ad blockers to avoid advertising in many forms (Williams, 2016). There has been a concomitant rise in activities designed to work around ad blocking, including a rise in native advertising, programme product placements, and mainstream entertainment (e.g. TV programmes, movies, games). However, some publishers are struggling to maintain their business models, and are still selling advertising in its previous mass-media monologic form. This has led to some creative thinking about how to intrude on users' 'free' online time. In 2016, Facebook apologised to consumers and advertisers alike for cheating on the viewing time of video download (Machkovech, 2016). As the Internet expands the availability of source content, consumers are searching for easy options to verify the information they find. They are also looking for simplified ways of searching and filtering their information. Yet online consumption continues to grow, revealing that advertising still has a place. The advertising industry can take solace in the fact that online ads are clicked on because consumers are usually interested in the content (40 per cent) (An, 2016).

A major challenge for advertisers in the globalised world is to locate consumers and to provide relevant and targeted information to them. Consumers expect everything to be available online and goods and services to be quicker and cheaper digitally (Miles, 2016). Few consumers search for advertising about a particular product – they will be online engaging with their social network, being entertained or keeping up to date with 'news'. Consumers do this by engaging with multiple devices and applications and will probably be distracted when they encounter advertising material (Smyth, 2014). Advertising has to adapt to multiple devices, a difficult task in the face of rapid technological changes. New devices are proliferating. The rapid growth in fitness bands and wearables, for example, reveals that the device can be more important than functionality.

Although people possess multiple products and applications, most do not actually use all of their devices even if they are wearing/carrying them all at once (Krebs and Duncan, 2015). Advertisers operating globally must have an understanding of the technological capabilities within the global market place. A dynamic, interactive ad design may work well in London or Tokyo. However, it may flounder in Monrovia or Lima where consumers may have a limited supply of data (Bode, 2016) or simply cannot access the ad on older devices. Content might be king when it comes to keeping people's attention and engaging them with the brand (Miles, 2016) but it counts for little if it cannot be seen.

The consumer's desire to be entertained (Deloitte, 2016) in any place and at any time poses a different challenge to advertising. Advertising has responded to this shift by attempting to go 'native'. Rather than interrupting viewers' entertainment, advertising is seeking to contribute to it. A good example was Beats, which seamlessly embedded its material in Miley Cyrus video clips at the same time as she was being 'famous' for twerking on the Video Music Awards (Buckley, 2015). Kay (2014) suggests that native advertising is hardly new and that it has always sought to keep the consumer entertained: 'Native advertising ironically bears the greatest resemblance to how TV advertising began with the rise of the soap opera, the sponsored post of the day' (Kay, 2014 p. 3). Ironically, native advertising challenges global advertising, as native advertising must be locally and individually relevant. With mass customisation of communication still in its infancy (although algorithms and artificial intelligence are gaining capacity to communicate 'one on one' with consumers) (CB Insights, 2016), this tension will remain.

With more than 75 per cent of the population of consumers being outside of the traditional western and northern markets, the image of the global consumer has evolved (see Figure 2.3). Ageing populations present another change, as does the growth of the middle classes in places such as India and China. Advertising practice therefore needs to change to reach these new market spaces (Bilby *et al.*, 2016). There is also a view that globalisation is contributing to an identifiable global consumer culture, one where ethnic identity contributes to flows of culture both to and from other countries (Cleveland *et al.*, 2015). However, Tod Wasserman (2015) counters that the global consumer is a myth. Wasserman predicts that consumers will opt for smaller locally produced brands over the seemingly soulless corporations as they search for sustainable, fair and responsible consumption alternatives. To this end, status is derived from being a responsible social and global citizen.

In 2013, 232 million people lived outside their country of origin (Euromonitor International, 2015). China and India account for 30 per cent of the world's population (Gorti *et al.*, 2015) and the consumer profile of these nations is changing rapidly as the economy changes and the process of modernisation continues. Migration in these markets and in others has also seen the growth of Islam and associated products and services (Euromonitor International, 2015). Importantly, East and West (as well as North and South) differ in terms of what they value from brands (Mizera and Cotugno, 2015). Such differences make it

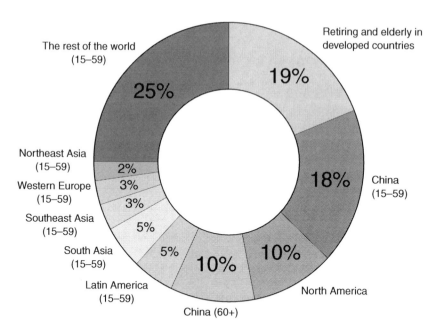

Figure 2.3 Where the consumers are.

Source: adapted from McKinsey, 2016.

increasingly difficult to fully segment and target markets. To this extent, markets are not really global: they have local and regional cultural considerations that must be accounted for.

Conclusion

As a result of political and economic environments and, more recently, of rapid technological advances, the advertising ecosystem comprising agencies, advertisers and consumers or buyers is characterised by its complexity and fluidity. Global advertising has been forced to respond to these changes taking place across local, international and regional environments. Media has also changed in response to technological developments. We therefore see more and more advertising taking place online, yet we cannot ignore the fact that television and entertainment remain the mainstays of consumer choices about buying products. Brands serve multiple purposes, economic and emotional: for the company and the consumer. For consumers, a brand helps delimit choices and makes decision-making easier and products 'safer' to buy. Building a global brand starts with building brand trust.

Despite global flows, consumption is local in essence and consumers rely on their social systems for access to norms and aspirations. The nature of the global consumer is changing, with ageing populations throughout the world and rising middle classes in developing nations. However, the sense that globalisation is giving rise to a homogeneous global audience needs to be treated with caution. Despite global advertisers wanting to use digital technology to reach wider and wider markets, people acquire their consumer culture from their social eco-system, which is locally derived. Global brands still need to be locally relevant to be desirable. Trends and cultures shift over time, especially as populations flow throughout the world. Rather than becoming more homogeneous, it seems that markets are becoming more diverse than ever before. While there is an overall drive towards modernisation, concepts of modernity and identity are very much locally determined.

To revisit Rust and Oliver's (1994) prediction, it seems that claims of adver-tising's death have been exaggerated. As it responds to the changes and chal-lenges set by clients, brands, media and consumers, advertising is not only reconfiguring the way it works, it is simultaneously a contributor to and a product of the globalised and borderless world.

References

Advertising Research Foundation (2015) *Re:Think 2015: Digital Anthropology Research-ing Audiences Online*. Available at: www.youtube.com/watch?v=U_QuhL5r45o (accessed 10 November 2016).

Alter, S. (1994) *Truth Well Told: McCann-Erickson and the Pioneering of Global Advert-ising*. New York: McCann-Erikson.

An, M. (2016) *Why People Block Ads (And What It Means for Marketers and Advertis-ers)*. Available at: https://research.hubspot.com/reports/why-people-block-ads-and-what-it-means-for-marketers-and-advertisers (accessed 10 November 2016).

AppNexus (2015) *Reaching Full Potential: Examining Attitudes to Programmatic across the Global Advertising Ecosystem APAC Report*. World Advertising Research Council and Circle Research.

Baalbaki, S. and Guzmán, F. (2016) 'A consumer-perceived consumer-based brand equity scale', *Journal of Brand Management*, 23(3), pp. 229–51.

Badenhausen, K. (2015) *Apple and Microsoft head the world's most valuable brands*. Available at: www.forbes.com/sites/kurtbadenhausen/2015/05/13/apple-and-microsoft-head-the-worlds-most-valuable-brands-2015/#6da8f1452875 (accessed 10 November 2016).

Baskin, J. S. (2013) *The Opportunity for Dove to Get Real With Its Branding*. Available at: www.forbes.com/sites/jonathansalembaskin/2013/03/07/the-opportunity-for-dove-to-get-real-with-its-branding/#26ed13cd3f63 (accessed 10 November 2016).

Bastos, W. and Levy, S. J. (2012) 'A history of the concept of branding: Practice and theory', *Journal of Historical Research in Marketing*, 4(3), pp. 347–68.

BBC News (2006) *BMW given Google 'Death Penalty'*. Available at: http://news.bbc.co.uk/2/hi/technology/4685750.stm (accessed 10 November 2016).

Bengtsson, A., Ostberg, J. and Kjeldgaard, D. (2005) 'Prisoners in paradise: subcultural resistance to the marketization of tattooing', *Consumption Markets & Culture*, 8(3), pp. 261–74.

Bilby, J., Reid, M. and Brennan, L. (2016) 'The future of advertising in China', *Journal of Advertising Research*, 56(3), pp. 245–58.

Binns, D. and Gans, S. (2015) *Activation: Structuring Brands for the Speed of Life*. Available at: http://interbrand.com/views/activation-structuring-brands-for-the-speed-of-life/ (accessed 10 November 2016).

Bode, K. (2016) *Why Are People Using Ad Blockers? Ads Can Eat up to 79% of Mobile Data Allotments.* Available at: www.techdirt.com/articles/20160317/09274333934/why-are-people-using-ad-blockers-ads-can-eat-up-to-79-mobile-data-allotments.shtml (accessed 10 November 2016).

Buckley, P. (2015) 'Statics and flows: The creation of brand fame in the digital age', *Market Leader*, Quarter 4, pp. 1–7.

Byford, V. and Holt, G. (2013) *Google, Amazon, Starbucks: The Rise of 'Tax Shaming'*. Available at: www.bbc.com/news/magazine-20560359 (accessed 10 November 2016).

Carat (2016) *Carat Ad Spend Report*. Available at: www.carat.com/global/en/news-views/carat-global-ad-spend-report (accessed 10 November 2016).

Carstairs, C. (2006) ' "Roots" nationalism: Branding English Canada cool in the 1980s and 1990s', *Histoire Sociale/Social History*, 39(77), pp. 235–55.

CB Insights (2016) *AI in Ads: 13 High-Momentum Companies Using Machine Learning in Marketing, Ads, and Sale*. Available at: www.cbinsights.com/blog/artificial-intelligence-advertising-sales-marketing-startups/ (accessed 10 November 2016).

Christodoulides, G. (2009) 'Branding in the post-internet era', *Marketing Theory*, 9(1), pp. 141–4.

Cleveland, M., Laroche, M. and Takahashi, I. (2015) 'The intersection of global consumer culture and national identity and the effect on Japanese consumer behavior', *Journal of International Consumer Marketing*, 27(5), pp. 364–87.

Cox, K., Turner, D., Crowther, J. and Hubbard, T. (2011) Integrated communications: One size doesn't fit all'. *Market Leader*, Quarter 4, pp. 35–7.

Crawford, R. and Dickenson, J. (2016) *Through Glass Doors: Inside the World of Australian Advertising Agencies, 1959–1989*. Perth: University of Western Australia Press.

Delener, N. (1996) 'Beware of globalization: A comparative study of advertising agency–client relationships', *Journal of Professional Services Marketing*, 14(1), pp. 167–77.

Deloitte (2016) *Media Consumer Survey 2015: Australian Media and Digital Preferences*, (4th edn). Available at: www2.deloitte.com/au/en/pages/technology-media-and-telecommunications/articles/media-consumer-survey-2015.html (accessed 10 November 2016).

Durvasula, S. and Lysonski, S. (2016) 'Finding cross-national consistency: Use of G-theory to validate acculturation to global consumer culture measure', *Journal of Global Marketing*, 29(2), pp. 1–14.

Effie Worldwide (2011) *2011 Gold Effie Winner 'You're Not You When You're Hungry'*, North America: Effie Awards. Available at: http://current.effie.org/downloads/2011_5627_pdf_1.pdf (accessed 7 March 2017).

El-Amir, A. and Burt, S. (2010) 'A critical account of the process of branding: towards a synthesis', *The Marketing Review*, 10(1), pp. 69–86.

eMarketer (2016) *Digital Ad Spending to Surpass TV Next Year*. Available at: www.emarketer.com/Article/Digital-Ad-Spending-Surpass-TV-Next-Year/1013671 (accessed 10 November 2016).

Euromonitor International (2015) *Cultural Diversity and its Impact on Global Consumer Markets*. Available at: www.euromonitor.com/cultural-diversity-and-its-impact-on-global-consumer-markets/report (accessed 7 March 2017).

Field, P. (2008) 'Multimarket campaigns', *Admap*, 490, pp. 16–18.

Fitzgerald, R. (2015) *The Rise of the Global Company: Multinational and the Making of the Modern World*. Cambridge: Cambridge University Press.

Flynn, T. (2011) *Why Cookie-Cutter Marketing Formulas Don't Work*. Available at: www.lessingflynn.com/blog/2011/06/27/why-cookie-cutter-marketing-formulas-dont-work#sthash.rCAwCgUa.dpbs (accessed 10 November 2016).

Friedman, T. (1992) 'The world of the world of Coca-Cola', *Communication Research*, 19(5), pp. 642–62.

Garey, E. and Johnstone, J. (2015) *Like, Share and Retweet: How to make your Insights go Viral*. Paris: Qualitative Paris.

Gibbs, S. (2016) *iPhone 7 Review: How Good Can a Phone Be If the Battery Doesn't Last Even a Day?* Available at: www.theguardian.com/technology/2016/sep/23/iphone-7-review-poor-battery-life (accessed 10 November 2016).

Gorti, V., Jain, R., Sexton, D. and Sen, K. (2015) *Measuring Pricing Power of a Global Brand in an Asian Market*. Singapore: European Society for Opinion and Market Research (ESOMAR) Asia Pacific.

Haig, M. (2005) *Brand Failures: The Truth About the 100 Biggest Branding Mistakes of All Time*. London: Kogan Page Publishers.

Halkias, G., Davvetas, V. and Diamantopoulos, A. (2016) 'The interplay between country stereotypes and perceived brand globalness/localness as drivers of brand preference', *Journal of Business Research*, 69(9), pp. 3621–8.

Hanlon, P. (2016) *What is a Strategic Brand Narrative*. Available at: www.forbes.com/sites/patrickhanlon/2016/04/26/what-is-strategic-brand-narrative/#387812a564af (accessed 10 November 2016).

Hatch, M. J. and Rubin, J. (2006) 'The hermeneutics of branding', *Journal of Brand Management*, 14(1–2), pp. 40–59.

Holmes, C. (2016) 'Grow brand value', *Admap*, March 2016, pp. 40–42.

Interbrand (2015) *Best Global Brands 2015: Brands at the speed of life*. Available at: http://interbrand.com/best-brands/best-global-brands/2015/ (accessed 10 November 2016).

James, G. (2014) *20 Epic Fails in Global Branding*. Available at: www.inc.com/geoffrey-james/the-20-worst-brand-translations-of-all-time.html (accessed 10 November 2016).

Jenkins, H. (2004) 'The cultural logic of media convergence', *International Journal of Cultural Studies*, 7(1), pp. 33–43.

Jenkins, H. (2009) *Confronting the Challenges of Participatory Culture: Media Education for the 21st Century*. Cambridge, MA: The MIT Press.

Jones, G. (2010) 'Globalization' In G. Jones and J. Zeitlin (eds), *The Oxford Handbook of Business History*. Oxford: Oxford University Press. pp. 141–68.

Jones, J. P. (1998) *What's in a Brand?: Building Brand Equity Through Advertising*. New York: Tata McGraw-Hill Education.

Kanter, J. and Scott, M. (2016) *Apple Owes $14.5 Billion in Back Taxes to Ireland, E.U. Says*. Available at: www.nytimes.com/2016/08/31/technology/apple-tax-eu-ireland.html?_r=0 (accessed 10 November 2016).

Kapelke, C. (2013) 'Launching global brands: Extend your reach', *ANA Magazine*, Spring 2013, pp. 18–30.

Kay, G. (2014) 'The post-disruptive advertising era', *Admap*, October, pp. 1–7.

Krebs, P. and Duncan, D. T. (2015) 'Health app use among US mobile phone owners: A national survey', *JMIR mHealth and uHealth*, 3(4), pp. 1–12.

Lannon, J. (1999) Brands and their symbols. In Jones, J. P. (ed.), *How to Use Advertising to Build Strong Brands*. Thousand Oaks, CA: SAGE. pp. 37–53.

Lewis, T., Martin, F. and Sun, W. (2016) *Telemodernities: Television and Transforming Lives in Asia*. Durham, NC, and London: Duke University Press.

Lion, D. G., Moreau-Gobard, J.-C. and Imber, D. (1960) *Chinese art: Bronzes, Jade, Sculpture, Ceramics*. New York: Universe Books.

McEnally, M. R. and De Chernatony, L. (1999) 'The evolving nature of branding: Consumer and managerial considerations', *Academy of Marketing Science Review*, 1999, pp. 1–26.

Machkovech, S. (2016) *Facebook Apologises for Feeding Inflated Video-View Numbers to Advertisers*. Available at: http://arstechnica.com/business/2016/09/facebook-apologizes-for-feeding-inflated-video-view-numbers-to-advertisers/ (accessed 10 November 2016).

Macnamara, J. (2014) *The 21st Century Media (R)evolution: Emergent Communication Practices*. New York: Peter Lang.

Mediaocean (2013) Media Convergence challenges Marketers. Available at: www.mediaoceanuk.com/news/media-convergence-challenges-marketers (accessed 11 November 2016).

Merron, J. (1999) 'Putting foreign consumers on the map: J. Walter Thompson's struggle with General Motors' international advertising account in the 1920s', *Business History Review*, 73(03), pp. 465–502.

Meyers, C. (2013) *Radio with Pictures: How the Ad Industry in the 1940s Debated the Transition from Radio to TV*. Chicago: Society for Cinema and Media Studies.

Miles, J. (2016) 'Protect the brand from commoditisation', *Admap*, January, pp. 1–5.

Mitchell, P. and Bright, J. (1995) 'Multinational headquarters control of UK subsidiaries' advertising decisions', *International Journal of Advertising*, 14(3), pp. 183–93.

Mizera, S. and Cotugno, A. (2015) 'West and East: A guide to migrating brands across the globe', *WPP Atticus awards Highly commended branding and identity*: World Advertising Research Council.

de Mooij, M. (2013) *Global Marketing and Advertising: Understanding Cultural Paradoxes*. Thousand Oaks, CA: Sage Publications.

Morgan, B. (2015) *Was Peter Drucker Wrong? The Modern Purpose of a Brand*. Available at: www.forbes.com/sites/blakemorgan/2015/12/28/was-peter-drucker-wrong-the-modern-purpose-of-a-brand/#5d25b79458d7 (accessed 10 November 2016).

Muravskii, D., Alkanova, O. and Smirnova, M. (2016) 'What was brand equity anyway, and how did they measure it?' In C. Campbell and J. J. Ma (eds). *Looking Forward, Looking Back: Drawing on the Past to Shape the Future of Marketing*. New York: Springer, pp. 311–14.

Peterson, T. (2015) *Netflix Isn't Closed*. Available at: http://adage.com/article/media/netflix-s-house-cards-tout-anheuser-busch-samsung/297318/ (accessed 10 November 2016).

Poltrack, D. F. and Bowen, K. (2011) 'The future is now', *Journal of Advertising Research*, 51(2), pp. 345–55.

Precourt, G. (2016) *Seven Remarkable New Media Trends for 2016*. California: IAB 2016 Annual Leadership Meeting.

Priest, I. (2014) *IPA ADAPT: Partnership is at the Heart of Agility*. Available at: www.campaignlive.co.uk/article/1296834/ipa-adapt-partnership-heart-agility# (accessed 10 November 2016).

Roper, S. and Parker, C. (2006) 'Evolution of branding theory and its relevance to the independent retail sector', *The Marketing Review*, 6(1), pp. 55–71.

Rust, R. T. and Oliver, R. W. (1994) 'The death of advertising', *Journal of Advertising*, 23(4), pp. 71–7.

Sexton, D. E. (2015) 'Managing brands in a prickly digital world', *Journal of Advertising Research*, 55(3), pp. 237–41.

Seymour, T., Frantsvog, D. and Kumar, S. (2011) 'History of search engines', *International Journal of Management & Information*, 14(4), pp. 47–58.

Sharp, B., Beal, V. and Collins, M. (2009) 'Television: Back to the future', *Journal of Advertising Research*, 49(2), pp. 211–19.

Smith, C. (2016) *Galaxy S7 Edge Explodes in the Philippines*, Available at: http://bgr. com/2016/09/26/galaxy-s7-edge-explosion/ (accessed 10 November 2016).

Smyth, C. (2014) 'Building brands: We're not re-inventing the (brand) wheel', *Admap*, June, pp. 1–5.

Staunstrup, P. (2015) *Netflix Showing the way in Native Advertising*, Available at: http:// staunstrup.se/en/native-advertsing/netflix-showing-the-way-in-native-advertising/ (accessed 10 November 2016).

Taylor, J., Kennedy, R., McDonald, C., Larguinat, L., El Ouarzazi, Y. and Haddad, N. (2013) 'Is the multi-platform whole more powerful than its separate parts?', *Journal of Advertising Research*, 53(2), pp. 200–211.

Volkmer, K. (2013) *What Makes Coca-Cola an Iconic Brand*, Available at: www.the-makegood.com/2013/07/17/what-makes-coca-cola-an-iconic-brand-and-how-do-i-build-one-end-may/ (accessed 10 November 2016).

Wagler, A. (2013) 'Embracing change: Exploring how creative professionals use interactive media in advertising campaigns', *Journal of Interactive Advertising*, 13(2), pp. 118–27.

Walshe, P. (2016) '10 traits of megabrands', *Admap*, February, pp. 1–5.

Wasserman, T. (2015) 'The myth of the global consumer', *Campaign US*, October, pp. 1–8.

Webster, J. G. (2005) 'Beneath the veneer of fragmentation: Television audience polarization in a multichannel world', *Journal of Communication*, 55(2), pp. 366–82.

Weigel, M. (2012) 'Global planning: Winning the post-geographic age', *Admap*, March 2012, pp. 1–5.

Williams, B. (2016) *FB Reblock: Ad Blocking Community Finds Workaround to Facebook*. Available at: https://adblockplus.org/blog/fb-reblock-ad-blocking-community-finds-workaround-to-facebook (accessed 10 November 2016).

World Advertising Research Council (2015) *What We Know About Building Brands*. WARC Exclusive. Available at: www.warc.com (accessed 7 March 2017).

Yakob, F. (2016) 'Point of view: The cult of branding', *Admap*, March, pp. 13–13.

Zarantonello, L., Schmitt, B. H. and Jedidi, K. (2014) 'How to advertise and build brand knowledge globally', *Journal of Advertising Research*, 54(4), pp. 420–34.

3 Digital advertising and the new world of 'viral' advertising

Lukas Parker, Dang Nguyen and Linda Brennan

Introduction

This chapter explores digital and viral advertising in a globalised context. In the field of advertising, digital communication as a means to connect with global audiences is a relatively new development, although its existence can be traced back as far as the mid-1990s. Theories of communication, designed in a monologic age may be less relevant to digital and dialogic media. Digital advertising is intrinsically linked to word of mouth advertising, or 'buzz marketing', although a digital ad might not be a viral one. Viral advertising is particularly known for its exponential self-replicating speed of transmission and virus-like spread from consumer to consumer, person to person. Increasingly, consumers are using social networks to engage in brand-related activity including the consumption and creation of content about brands and also spreading messages from or about the brands (Araujo *et al.*, 2015). This chapter discusses the characteristics of modern viral advertising, as well as viral advertising's place in globalisation. The chapter then goes on to provide examples of campaigns that have been successful in overcoming international and cultural borders.

Digital advertising is, by its very nature, global. This is because the source of the advertising or advertisement cannot control to whom, where or how their message is conveyed (Kaplan and Haenlein, 2010). This has positive but also potentially negative consequences. One key characteristic of digital advertising is its lack of controllability. As soon as a potentially viral advertisement has left its source, the sender has lost the ability to maintain the integrity of the message and the context it in which it will be received. This opens up the ability for potential transmitters to alter the message and co-create their own message – be that positive or negative. Spoof advertising replicates readily in the digital environment where ad aficionados adapt the image or text to suit their own purposes (see, for example, www.adbusters.org/spoofads/absolut-craze/).

Viral advertising and viral marketing, terms which are used interchangeably, are commonly thought of as electronic *word of mouth* (Kaplan and Haenlein, 2011). Viral marketing can be defined as 'the act of propagating marketing messages through the help and cooperation from individual consumers' (Liu-Thompkins, 2012, p. 59). It relies on consumers to spread the message rather than the traditional mass media. Viral advertising, however, supersedes notion *word of mouth* marketing in that it has the possibility of influencing and reaching a much larger audience at a greater than exponential rate (Kaplan and Haenlein, 2011). Moreover, given that concepts of online and offline are increasingly blurred, word of mouth transcends the original medium of transmission (one-to-one versus one-to-many or many-to-many). This is particularly evident in an age where the majority of Internet interactions occur on mobile devices (Pew Research Center, 2013). Most digital advertising aspires to be viral in nature. However, transmission of the ad, once it leaves the hands of the advertiser, is in the hands of the sharing audience, who will pass on the ad according to their own agenda and using whatever device is being accessed at the time. Sometimes it goes well as in the Snickers campaign (Kiefaber, 2015), where it won the consumer over and got a strong level of engagement, but sometimes it does not go as well as the advertiser had hoped: going viral for the wrong reasons is bad for the brand (Burke, 2015). However, as Lyngsfeldt (2015) points out, 'User generated content (UGC) from peers is on the rise and is the most effective marketing weapon in the marketing toolbox for brands who know how to use it effectively,' so advertisers need to learn to play the viral advertising game.

Viral advertising has changed the speed, spread and dispersion of word-of-mouth messages, particularly with the current popularity of social networks such as Facebook, Instagram, Snapchat, Twitter, WeChat and Weibo, and their predecessors including MySpace, Orkut and Friendster. However, although we tend to associate viral advertising with modern social networks, the viral advertising phenomenon arose before the advent of modern social networks. Email was the first common means of transmitting viral messages (Phelps *et al.*, 2004). In fact one of the earliest cited viral campaigns is that of Hotmail (a web-based email service), that in the mid-1990s by inserting the simple tagline 'Get your free e-mail at Hotmail' at the foot of every email sent by its users. At the time this campaign was successful building exponential growth in users of the service and all it required was a simple, textual tagline and one that the user did not have to add themselves. Over two decades later, it is still difficult to predict what will go viral when it comes to advertising, let alone harness it. In addition, consumer tastes and the media used by advertisers have evolved and remain highly fluid. This means that advertisers need to keep their ideas fresh and familiar with the various characteristics and personalities of current social networks and their users.

Further, the media channels used for transmission of viral advertising have not remained static, and they are not the same for all audiences. Facebook can claim to be the largest social network at present with around 1.7 billion monthly active users (Facebook, 2016), although there is evidence that the service is becoming out of favour among younger generations, particularly Millennials (born in the early 1980s to early 2000s) (Heine, 2013). Among these demographics, services such as Instagram and Snapchat are becoming increasingly popular. Moreover, other networks such as Twitter, which have smaller user bases (around 310 million by early 2016 estimates) (Statista, 2016), have only recently started exploring alternative commercialisation models within their plat-forms, and coming to terms with content promotion. Whether or not these can be monetized at the rate that Facebook has managed is yet to be seen. However, in 2015 Apple patented technology to ensure that they would 'own' the sharing space and, according to Edwards (2015) 'They're gobbling up everything they can learn about you and trying to monetise it. We think that's wrong'. Control-ling the sharing ads across platforms has become the newest form of making money. Apple's overarching capacity to cross platforms and devices is a unique advantage in this space, although Google is following closely. Additionally, while Twitter is useful as a means of spreading the message, paid advertising is neither prevalent nor welcome, and, unless it is entertaining, it is not spread widely by users and is therefore likely to disappear quickly in such an ephemeral medium. According to Craig Elbert, Bonobos's vice president of marketing '[Twitter] is still in the process of proving out return-on-investment.... We're continuing to test' (Marshall and Koh, 2015).

Although social networks are usually understood on a global scale, it is notable that the realities of social networking tend to be localised and social network usage varies from country to country. For instance, Sina Weibo, China's microblogging response to the popularity of Twitter and Facebook, had 100 million daily users in 2015, with 85 per cent of them being on a mobile device (China Internet Watch, 2015). China's rigorous content filtering practices and local appetite for home-grown technological platforms mean that advertisers need to be savvy about the technical idiosyncrasies of these platforms, as well as the specific media affordances that facilitate diverging digital cultures. As such, the genre of advertising changes according to the country's culture and accept-able standards (de Mooij, 2013). As more and more people access social net-works through mobile phones, cross-platform services such as WeChat become more and more popular, blurring the distinction between private and public com-munication. Platforms of this nature allow users to instant message with texts, voice recordings, videos or stickers while enabling broadcasting functions similar to that of social networking sites (e.g. Moments on WeChat, which can be linked to Facebook and Twitter). Infringing upon the dating industry territory, these platforms also allow for random pairing of service users through a 'message in a bottle' mechanism. With applications of this nature packing as many communication functions and scenarios as they can get into their technolo-gies, advertisers need to stay on top of new cultural and social realities that might ensue. For example, artificial intelligence is needed just to engage with the consumer, as they can be anywhere, any time and be interacting on any platform with myriad others involved (Chaffey, 2016). This can be expensive to design and even more expensive to staff the insights team required to turn data into advertising strategy (Accenture Interactive, 2016).

Although it is common for users to have a presence on multiple social net-works, consumers tend to use networks that are popular with their peers. More-over, consumers commonly use different networks for different purposes, for example Twitter for news, Facebook for keeping up with the family, Snapchat for communicating with peers, LinkedIn for business networking and Instagram for sharing photos or following celebrities. The maxim holds that advertisers need to be where their audiences are, and customers are always on the move.

Viral advertising and globalisation: communities persist

The complex patterns of virality on social networks have been well documented in network science (Berger and Milkman, 2010; Hansen *et al.*, 2011; Mills, 2012; Sampson, 2012). To date, the most popular approach to conceptualise meme virality, for example, is that of epidemiology (Weng *et al.*, 2013). In other words, memes are currently understood as spreading through social networks in a similar manner to diseases. Contagions differ across different phenomena, however. Within network science, the spread of diseases, and, by extension, digital memes, are considered as simple contagion as opposed to complex contagion, which characterises the spread of behaviours (Backstrom *et al.*, 2006; Centola, 2010). Weng *et al.* (2013) pointed out that network structure plays an important role in predicting the spreading pattern of viral content, particularly memes. Specifically, the role of communities has recently been recognised as powerful in predicting the virality of memes based on early spreading patterns. Simple contagion models explain the initial spread of messages (one-to-one) but complex contagion incorporates popularity or selectivity (of both sender and message content) and spreads many-to-many.

Indeed, the community construct has been key to viral advertising and viral marketing since the inception of the area, not least because of the way it resonates with classical marketing philosophy (i.e. customer-centricity). Far from being geographically bounded, communities are now widely understood as 'borderless'; they form organically through common causes, or can be ascribed as such through network analysis methods such as link clustering (Ahn *et al.*, 2010). What is immediately visible to the naked eye with these new conceptualisations is the rise of transnational social movements and consumer cultures, with some of the former not being possible at all without the mediation of new information and communication technology, and the latter being reinforced with the aid of technology. Our collective understanding of globalisation therefore slowly takes a subtle shift: with the increasing salience of concepts such as network and community, the globalisation conversation takes on a more nuanced tone. Narratives following that of Thomas Friedman's (2005) 'flat world', while gaining significant popularity in the early years of the new millennium, seem to be on the wane. There is increasing recognition of cultural and political differences, and persisting as well as newly formed patterns of inequality, on a global scale. One of the most sobering and fundamental empirical arguments against the idea of the world getting smaller and flatter, and therefore a level playing field for businesses and advertisers, is that concerning digital connectivity. Graham (2015), for example, argued that, while technology enthusiasts such as Jimmy Wales of Wikipedia are eager to claim universal Internet connectivity in the foreseeable future, the vision remains impossible without lowering the costs of access for the poor. For example, initiatives by technology companies such as Free Basics by Facebook may contribute to closing the gap of access. Therefore, it is worth taking a step back and reflecting upon the potential and impact of digitally enabled practices of advertising as an influence for globalisation. While viral advertising clearly changes the way advertising, as a force for globalisation and cultural transformation, operates, networks by design connect as well as bypass nodes.

Across the globe, people interact with each other, form groups, create group identities, reframing their self-identities in relation to others and persist in maintaining said identities. From the 'associational life' in the US to *shequ* in China, communities form the basis of social life. Globalisation since its inception has always carried with it a philosophy of community integration – hence the popularity of terms such as 'global village' or 'global theatre'. While the merits and deficits of globalisation are debatable, digital advertising provides a means by which communities can connect with each other to generate new meanings and new forms of engagement with each other, both within extant communities and in the formation of new communities that transcend borders and boundaries. These communities then change the nature of the societies in which participants are embedded by transferring cultural memes across communities.

Recognition of the different communities being brought together on one seemingly global platform increases the possibilities of advertising, but also demands different approaches to getting the message across. Advertising practice matured in a monologic communication culture, whereas digital is the ultimate form of dialogic communication. As such, previous modes of 'broadcast' and 'transmission', and their concomitant theories of 'reach' and 'exposure', can no longer be the benchmark of advertising effectiveness (IAB Europe, 2016). Thus, advertising no longer sets the agenda; for the first time in history advertising may be catching up with and trying to interpret a global digital culture whose values are sometimes radically different from that manifested and perpetuated by advertising. Advertisers adapt digital trends, sometimes to their advantage, by crafting digital campaigns using the mechanisms of content sharing and discussion, creating and managing online communities evolving around their brands, and monitoring online conversations for reputation management. Advertisers also impose existing commercial structures online, partnering with technology companies to negotiate content priority (e.g. Google Adwords), fine-tuning their targeting practice with real-time and more detailed profiling data about their audience than ever (e.g. Facebook ads). However, the digital space is also occupied by digital natives who are not happy with the commercialisation of their domain and have invested much web-citizen time, expertise and money in finding ways to avoid digital advertising (Williams, 2016). To quote a user:

> Let's hope that in 5–7 years AdSense will be over and, with it, 90 per cent of blogs and websites. The next step will be start paying for the use of Facebook and the few services that could survive.
>
> (https://adblockplus.org/blog/fb-reblock-ad-blocking-community-
> finds-workaround-to-facebook)

The challenge for the future will be monetisation of the internet without advertising when it plays such a key role in many technology companies' business models, and as such inserting itself into the structure of what scholars such as Castells (2010) have labelled 'information economy'.

Different social networks are possible in different countries and across different age groups and indeed, using different platforms and means of communication. These communities are connected by multifarious motivations, and can connect regardless of geographic location. However, in a sense, there has always been a 'geographical stickiness' (Graham, 2013) to the way information is exchanged online, where age-old preferences and practices simply do not go away. For example, China rejects Facebook and builds its own social network, Sina Weibo, whose operation is under the Chinese government's scrutiny. Chinese people who persist in their use of Twitter, which is also formally blocked in China, consist of a very specific group of activists and radicals whose content reach tends to not be their own target audience (Yang, 2014), but rather international audiences who are not blocked from using such sources. Local start-ups are also quick to develop and market their own products, whose success is different in different countries. For example, LINE is most popular in Japan, Taiwan, Thailand and Indonesia, whereas Korea prefers KakaoTalk, and Vietnam favours its home-grown Zalo; each has its own form of gaining ad revenue. For instance, LINE tries to conform to a small group membership model (Japan Buzz, 2016), thereby supporting its community members by screening them from mass marketing. KakaoTalk has 34 per cent of its ad revenue from mobile marketing as opposed to online ads (Tun, 2015), and while Zalo has more than 30 million users, Do (2015) suggests that 'Facebook and Google capture a considerable portion of the ad market while Vietnam's local content players are struggling to keep up while the advertising pot grows bigger'.

Ephemeral media such as Snapchat remains largely an American phenomenon, while Whatsapp is most popular in South Africa. Far from levelling the playing field for advertisers in a homogenising global market, doing digital marketing with a global outreach means having an increasingly sophisticated understanding of different local markets while recognising and taking advantage of global trends. It is in this sense that cultural awareness, and potentially cultural sensitivity, becomes an increasingly important criterion for viral advertising campaign development. While you may hide behind a test-market in ad land, you cannot hide your mistakes in the digital world (Fromowitz, 2013).

The characteristics of viral advertising

Kaplan and Haenlein (2011) state that advertisers need to consider three criteria when developing a campaign: the right people (messengers) need to receive the right message in the right circumstances (environment) (See Figure 3.1). Messengers are key in that they are the key drivers of the spread of the message. It is therefore wise for advertisers to consider carefully the right people to start the

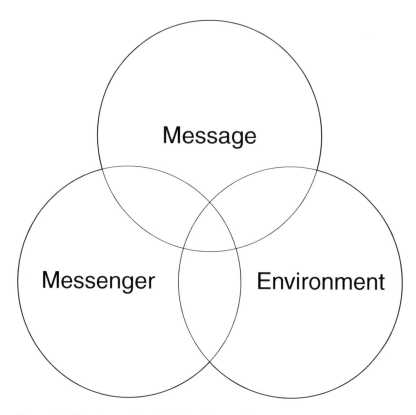

Figure 3.1 Criteria to make viral advertising work.

Source: Kaplan and Haenlein, 2011.

spread of the 'virus'. Market mavens are typically the first to receive the message and gain satisfaction from sharing it within their social circles (Lee *et al.*, 2015). Mavens are connected to the market and are typically proactive in the spreading of viral messages; similar to innovators in the diffusion of innovation (Rogers, 1962). Once these messages are forwarded and then shared by *social hubs*, people with very large numbers of social network connections or followers, the exponential amplification and dispersion of a viral message begins.

Before a maven considers initiating the spread of virus, the message must be attractive and importantly add value to their position as expert in the social network. Messages must be memorable, interesting or connect emotionally (Araujo *et al.*, 2015; Berger and Milkman, 2012; Dobele *et al.*, 2007) with the messengers. Humour, sex, fear, disgust, joy, surprise: all are potential emotional triggers, for the receiver of the message to want to resend or share the message in their social groups. If the message is not compelling, it is unlikely to be spread very far. Likeability has been found to be the key to consumers sharing content (De Angelis *et al.*, 2012; King *et al.*, 2014), particularly video advertising content (Shehu *et al.*, 2016). Moreover, Araujo *et al.* (2015) found that in specialised social networks such as Twitter informational cues are an important for consumers deciding whether to share (reTweet) brand messages. However in terms of virality, spread is directly related to attractiveness of the message to the sender and the receivers in terms of improving their network. The sender wants to look attractive by sharing; the receiver wants to connect to an attractive person via a message.

Lastly, for messengers to want to share an advertising message with their friends the environmental conditions must be right. This means that the message must be in alignment or at least relate to (or even oppose) the current zeitgeist – it must capture that moment. In addition to the external environmental factors at play, the social group of the messenger is also considered. Messengers will only pass on or share the message, advertising or otherwise, when they think it's not something that everyone knows about (Kaplan and Haenlein, 2011). 'Everyone' in this case means the social network connections of the potential messenger. Messengers derive satisfaction from being the first amongst their connections, from receiving positive feedback from connections or from their connections resending or sharing the message (Beverland *et al.*, 2015).

An example of these characteristics was evident in the success of the 'Dumb Ways to Die' viral video/advertisement (https://youtube/IJNR2EpS0jw). The campaign, commissioned by Metro Trains in Melbourne, Australia, was launched in November 2012 to promote rail safety. The campaign revolved around a three-minute YouTube video that showed simple cartoon characters suffering humorous and outlandish deaths set to a catchy, infectious tune. The campaign was extraordinary in terms of its visibility and virality – over 27 million hits in the first two weeks of its release and is Australia and New Zealand's most shared advertisement of all time (Ward, 2015). The video had over 142 million views as of October 2016. Internet users created hundreds of their own mashups of the video, spoofs, remixes and karaoke versions. McCann, the ad's creator, also released a karaoke version of the song, a string of follow-up videos and mobile game apps around the same theme. The campaign is an example of a message targeted at a narrow geo-demographic – public transport users in Melbourne, Australia – yet resonating well beyond its original intended audience.

Consumer ownership and repurposing of message – co-creation

Consumers pass on viral messages, but they can act as co-creators of the message. Advertisers rely on consumers' active cooperation and co-creation for the success of a viral campaign (Beverland *et al.*, 2015; Yadav *et al.*, 2016). Beverland *et al.* (2015) proposed that consumers use viral content as an extension of their desired self (or selves) and their identity goals. The case of the ALS (Amyotrophic Lateral Sclerosis, or motor neurone disease) 'Bucket Challenge' typifies the co-creation of a campaign in a positive way. The multimodal video meme (Rossolatos, 2015) was a sensation in August and September 2014: participants were videoed dousing themselves with buckets of water and ice over their heads, in order to 'challenge' others to either make a video themselves or donate to ALS. Participants included people from various backgrounds, ranging from high profile celebrities and politicians, to people from the poorest regions of the globe with limited access to online social networks (Koohy and Koohy, 2014). Consumers and participants were both sharing the message but also creating their own versions of the message and therefore taking ownership of the campaign themselves. Notably, there were considerable numbers of high profile celebrities involved in co-creating the message and 'challenging' other celebrities to support the cause. This campaign was moderately transmissible among a group of globally influential celebrities, but challenge was more likely to be spread by richer celebrities, perhaps in part reflecting greater social influence (Ni *et al.*, 2014); further highlighting the importance of identity goals in the transmission of viral content.

The Ice Bucket Challenge campaign resulted in US$98.2 million being donated directly to the cause, which was 35 times more than for the same period in the previous year (Koohy and Koohy, 2014). Ni *et al.* (2014) suggest that possible factors accounting for the speed and extent of the Ice Bucket Challenge pandemic may include the online social media mode of transmission and the short serial interval for taking up the challenge. The Ice Bucket Challenge spread quickly across the world as nominees became immediately 'infectious' and responded quickly once nominated. The campaign had a huge impact within a few weeks and then rapidly disappeared from public discourse, highlighting the transient nature of a typical viral meme. While the challenge continues to be used as a fundraising activity (Woolf, 2016), as a meme it has declined in shareability, thereby illustrating that, much like a biological virus, people become immune once exposed to the campaign.

In another example of viral advertising, in March 2015 visitors at the South by Southwest festival in Austin, Texas, who used the Tinder mobile dating social network were exposed to an innovative, geographically bound viral campaign. The campaign for Ex Machina, a movie that tackles existential concepts as well as artificial intelligence, involved a computerised woman called Ava chatting directly to Tinder users. The 'woman' on Tinder echoed the plot of the film by asking users what made them human, whether they had been in love, and, after a while, would send through a link to an Instagram page for the film (Nudd, 2015). This was when the users would eventually catch on to the fact that they had been speaking to a computer, not a woman. Once the word spread, the campaign and the conversations went viral, which created a lot more publicity around the film than the initial advertising device itself. The campaign was not a typical viral campaign involving the direct passing on of the advertiser's message, nor did it co-opt receivers of the message to co-create their own message. However, the campaign also raised questions about whether 'tricking' users is a good way to promote a film.

'Harnessing' digital to go viral: making communities work in your favour?

Can advertisers craft an advertising campaign that becomes 'viral'? The answer is, they can try! There is no guarantee that a 'viral' advertising campaign on paper will become a viral advertising campaign in actuality – in the same way that not every advertising campaign is born to be successful. However, doing virality carries risks, especially to the brand. Apart from having less control over campaign outcomes by relying on external and unpredictable factors, digital advertising can be unsuccessfully viral. That is, viral advertising can backfire and often does; and, when it does, the consequences tend to be memorable and hard to contain.

One of the most classic 'genres' of viral advertising gone wrong is when corporations and brands attempt to hijack topical issues trending on social media. There are three key recurring problems when brands engage with their audience on social media: zeal for brand personification, opportunistic mentality and lack of strategic planning. Any engagement needs to be clearly 'on message', 'on brand' and relevant for the audience, so reactive ideas to pick up on a meme or a trend need to be screened for relevance and adherence to the strategic planning for the brand. The rules are simple: don't press send without doing your homework into the connection between the meme and the brand.

A recent example of this 'genre' of backfire is the case of DiGiorno Pizza hijacking the #WhyIStayed hashtag on Twitter (see Figure 3.2). Trending as a hashtag for victims of domestic violence to share their personal experience of abuse and create solidarity against victim-blaming narratives, #WhyIStayed was (in)appropriated by DiGiorno Pizza when they sent out a tweet that was completely out of context:

> ***DiGiorno Pizza (@DiGiornoPizza):*** #WhyIStayed You had pizza.
> *9/8/14, 11:11pm*

Figure 3.2 DiGiorno's apology (Twitter).

>*Keosha Varela (@K_J_Writes):* So Many courageous ppl sharing their stories re: #whyistayed and #whyileft. Domestic Violence is often a hidden issue, bring it to light.
>*1h*

>*Adrienne Airhart (@craydrienne):* I couldn't face the fact that I was a text-book statistic: if (step)daddy hurts you, so will hubby. #whyistayed
>*1h*

The tweet was met with anger from the Twitter community and was promptly deleted, followed by a general apology (and a series of direct apologies to those who had found the tweet offensive).

While DiGiorno Pizza was quick to address the mistake in a frank and direct manner, (which should be textbook crisis management), the brand flooding Twitter feed with apologetic tweets only seemed to paint them as panicky and reactive. This can be understood in light of the three recurring problems with social media engagement outlined earlier. First, the incident can be framed as a consequence of brands personifying themselves with a 'voice' in order to stay relevant in social media conversations. Indeed, it is not difficult to come across social media 'gurus' giving advice on how brands should not be brands when they are on Facebook or Twitter; they are encouraged to have a personality to which their customers can relate. The person in charge of the Twitter account in DiGiorno Pizza's case, therefore, is not a social media specialist, nor a content curator. To his or her audience, he or she is a personified version of DiGiorno Pizza – a personality with a voice and many an opinion on different issues. While the personification of brands is usual in advertising, it is a tricky concept to follow through upon when the brand itself does not appear to know which personality it should adopt and perform. It is also unknown whether a coherent and consistent personality can be engineered in reaction to a wide variety of complex social issues pertinent to conversations happening on a range of social media platforms.

Second, the key philosophy driving not only this incident, but also numerous similar social media blunders, into a corner, is opportunism. Again, opportunism is not inherently bad; the risks associated are, however, much higher when a brand's communication is driven by such a philosophy. As DiGiorno Pizza admitted themselves, they were sloppy and hasty in trying to participate in a trending topic, to be part of the conversation, to engage with the community. Social listening means observing trends with clear objectives, carefully thought through guidelines for reaction or participation, and critical assessment of a brand's potential contribution to the story. Taking advantage of opportunities is important but any opportunity needs to contribute to the brand and its reputation.

Third, and consequently, reacting fast in the fast-moving environment that is social media does not mean strategic planning goes to waste. On the contrary, strategic planning is key to preventing and fixing mistakes effectively. It is understandable that brands are eager to engage with the dynamic digital culture happening in front of them – 'fear of missing out' happens to brands as much as it does to people. A clear strategy that is frequently and critically assessed and fine-tuned is necessary for brands to remain at the top of their game.

Another caveat is to think about what makes an online community. It is difficult to pin down precisely what a community is – when it comes into being and when it ceases to exist. However, a brand cannot legitimately use an irrelevant community and expect to be welcomed. Using the previous example, can all the domestic abuse victims participating in the #WhyIStayed be considered a community whose ephemeral congregation is of significance to DiGiorno? (Wellman, 1999, 2001) has documented the demise of all encompassing, socially controlling communities and the rise of fragmented personal communities that change in day, week and month. He termed this the rise of 'networked individualism', where relationships are narrowly defined and network members quickly shifting (Wellman, 2001). It is important to note that this is a macro-level observation whose implications for advertising might not be as straightforward as labelling any given group of randomly or momentarily congregated people as community for the sake of segmentation parsimony. Strategic thinking has a role to play in helping brands and advertisers to move away from the reactive and opportunistic mentality that largely drives social media failures. Had DiGiorno considered the brand community, consulted their strategic plan and been responsive to their market instead of reactive to the Twitterverse, they may have had less to apologise about.

Evaluation of campaigns: effectiveness and performance

Some of the key measures of a digital marketing campaign's performance include number of views, click through rates, hits for specific content, the number of shares in social media (e.g. 'likes' on Facebook or 'reTweets' on Twitter). Each of these measures show consumer engagement on different levels, from interest through to endorsement of the advertiser or advertising message, and are borderless in terms of being able to be measured. Furthermore, other related consumer (re)actions can also be measured, such as the number of reviews for a product, the number of members for a campaign webpage quantify. Beyond online data related to online traffic/behaviour, consumer surveys can assess the degree of product or brand knowledge, though this type of measurement is more complicated and requires more resources. Whilst not exhaustive, Table 3.1 shows some of the metrics and measures that can be used to assess the performance of a digital campaign.

Furthermore, while these measures are used extensively, there is a tendency to measure what can be measured rather than what can improve brand performance. Elements that are not measured which are pertinent to the digital world are: creativity, behaviour change, message uptake, media and marketing ROI, connectivity, relevance, credibility, and of course sales effects, all of which have been shown to affect the outcomes of digital campaigns.

As with most conventional campaigns behavioural measures are very important because changes in consumers' behaviour/decisions are often what is

Table 3.1 Campaign effectiveness and performance measurements

Measure	Indicates	Considerations
Views	Exposure	Does not show engagement with the message. May be asserted as viewed even though it has been running in the background or scrolled through.
Click-through	Interest and purchase/ response behaviour	Accidental click through
Shares	Attitudes, likeability	Likes, shares and retweets need to be taken within context, because they can indicate either positive or negative attitudes. 'Like' may mean many things and does not necessarily mean 'I like this idea'.
Number of reviews for a product/brand	Attitudes	More likely to show very positive or very negative reviews, rather than more nuanced assessment.
Klout scores	Engagement	The scores only measure some social networks and the algorithm has changed over time.
Consumer surveys	Knowledge, attitudes, intentions, reported behaviours, etc.	Difficult to access or discern participants who were exposed to the viral advertisement.

sought by advertisers. These can include number of sales, requests for information, samples or test-drives. Apart from conventional behavioural measures, consumers' brand engagement and influence can be measured through *Klout* scores (see https://klout.com/corp/score) (Ashley and Tuten, 2015; Turban *et al.*, 2016). Klout measures over 400 variables from over ten social, social media and social blogging networks and ranks participants on their reach, influence and the influence that their connections have.

Conclusion

Digital media are accelerating the rate of globalisation, as they change the many facets of what it means to be a global brand, and by extension the practice of advertising itself. However, it must be recognised that it is a complicated journey because cultural and social influences affect the way people and brands connect in the digital realm. As can be seen from the examples presented in this chapter, digital advertising, particularly viral advertising, has been trying to catch up with an ever-evolving digital culture that varies across different contexts. Importantly, the digital world is one that is actively seeking to avoid advertising, and digital natives are getting better at creating an online environment where they consume advertising only if they want to and if it is relevant to their lived experiences. At the heart of this digital culture, we can not only see the idiosyncratic media affordances that come with the different digital platforms available, but also consumers' need to be engaged and entertained on their own terms. As advertisers deal with this dynamic globalised and digital world, as well as the significant loss of control over what effective audience engagement can be, they not only need to be on top of the latest trends and technologies, but also be embedded in the various digital cultures in which they operate.

References

Accenture Interactive (2016) *How To Maximize New Advertising Models*. Available at: www.accenture.com/au-en/insight-navigating-digital-media-market-maximize-models-summary (accessed 11 November 2016).

Ahn, Y. Y., Bagrow, J. P. and Lehmann, S. (2010) 'Link communities reveal multiscale complexity in networks', *Nature*, 466, pp. 761–4. doi:10.1038/nature09182.

Araujo, T., Neijens, P. and Vliegenthart, R. (2015) 'What motivates consumers to re-tweet brand content?' *Journal of Advertising Research*, 55(3), pp. 284–95. doi:10.2501/jar-2015-009.

Ashley, C. and Tuten, T. (2015) 'Creative strategies in social media marketing: An exploratory study of branded social content and consumer engagement', *Psychology & Marketing*, 32(1), pp. 15–27. doi:10.1002/mar.20761.

Backstrom, L., Huttenlocher, D., Kleinberg, J. and Xiangyang, L. (2006) 'Group formation in large social networks: Membership, growth, and evolution'. Paper presented at the Proceedings of the *12th ACM SIGKDD international conference on knowledge discovery and data mining*. Ithaca, NY: Cornell University.

Berger, J. and Milkman, K. L. (2010) 'Social transmission, emotion, and the virality of online content', *Wharton research paper*, 106. Philadelphia, PA: University of Pennsylvania.

Berger, J. and Milkman, K. L. (2012) 'What makes online content viral?', *Journal of Marketing Research*, 49, pp. 192–205.

Beverland, M., Dobele, A. and Farrelly, F. (2015) 'The viral marketing metaphor explored through Vegemite', *Marketing Intelligence & Planning*, 33(5), pp. 656–74. doi:10.1108/mip-08-2014-0146.

Burke, S. (2015) 'Read with caution: 15 of the absolute worst marketing campaigns from 2014', *Spokal*. Available at: www.getspokal.com/read-with-caution-15-of-the-absolute-worst-marketing-campaigns-from-2014/ (accessed 11 November 2016).

Castells, M. (2010) *The Rise of the Network Society* (2nd edn). Chichester: Wiley-Blackwell.

Centola, D. (2010) 'The spread of behavior in an online social network experiment', *Science*, 329(5996), pp. 1194–7. doi:10.1126/science.1185231.

Chaffey, D. (2016) 'Digital marketing trends 2016–2017', *Smart Insights*. Available at: www.smartinsights.com/managing-digital-marketing/marketing-innovation/digital-marketing-trends-2016-2017/ (accessed 11 November 2016).

China Internet Watch (2015) *Weibo MAUs Reached 222 Million in Q3 2015*. Available at: www.chinainternetwatch.com/15740/weibo-q3-2015/-ixzz4LZTxBdT8 (accessed 11 November 2016).

De Angelis, M., Bonezzi, A., Peluso, A. M., Rucker, D. D. and Costabile, M. (2012) 'On braggarts and gossips: A self-enhancement account of word-of-mouth generation and transmission', *Journal of Marketing Research*, 49(4), pp. 551–63. doi:10.1509/jmr.11.0136.

Do, A.-M. (2015) 'Vietnam's chat app Zalo challenges Facebook with 30 million registered users', *TechniAsia*. Available at: www.techinasia.com/zalo-30-million-registered-users-vietnam (accessed 11 November 2016).

Dobele, A., Lindgreen, A., Beverland, M., Vanhamme, J. and van Wijk, R. (2007) 'Why pass on viral messages? Because they connect emotionally', *Business Horizons*, 50(4), 291–304. doi:10.1016/j.bushor.2007.01.004.

Edwards, J. (2015) 'Apple invented a new type of viral advertising that can track users in social media', *Business Insider, Australia.* Available at: www.businessinsider.com.au/apple-patent-for-viral-advertising-in-social-media-2015-6 (accessed 11 November 2016).

Facebook (2016) *Facebook Reports Second Quarter 2016 Results* [Press release]. Available at: https://investor.fb.com/investor-news/press-release-details/2016/Facebook-Reports-Second-Quarter-2016-Results/default.aspx (accessed 11 November 2016).

Friedman, T. L. (2005) 'It's a flat world, after all', *New York Times Magazine.* Available at: www.nytimes.com/2005/04/03/magazine/its-a-flat-world-after-all.html?_r=1 (accessed 11 November 2016).

Fromowitz, M. (2013) 'Cultural blunders: Brands gone wrong', *Campaign.* Available at: www.campaignasia.com/article/cultural-blunders-brands-gone-wrong/426043 (accessed 11 November 2016).

Graham, M. (2013) 'Geography/internet: Ethereal alternate dimensions of cyberspace or grounded augmented realities?', *The Geographical Journal*, 179(2), pp. 177–82. doi:10.1111/geoj.12009.

Graham, M. (2015) *Internet For All Remains an Impossible Dream, No Matter What Jimmy Wales Says.* Available at: https://theconversation.com/internet-for-all-remains-an-impossible-dream-no-matter-what-jimmy-wales-says-48423 (accessed 11 November 2016).

Hansen, L. K., Arvidsson, A., Nielsen, F. Å., Colleoni, E. and Etter, M. (2011) *Good Friends, Bad News Affect and Virality in Twitter Future Information Technology.* Heidelberg: Springer Berlin.

Heine, C. (2013) 'Are marketers worried about millennials fleeing Facebook? ANA confab attendees respond in 15 seconds or less', *Adweek*, 15 October. Available at: www.adweek.com/news/technology/are-marketers-worried-about-millennials-fleeing-facebook-152956 (accessed 11 November 2016).

IAB Europe (2016) *Nielsen Report: Digital Ad Ratings™ Global Benchmark and Findings.* Available at: www.iabeurope.eu/research-thought-leadership/nielsen-report-digital-ad-ratings-global-benchmark-and-findings/ (accessed 11 November 2016).

Japan Buzz (2016) *Advertising on Line Japan.* Available at: www.japanbuzz.info/advertising-on-line-japan (accessed 11 November 2016).

Kaplan, A. M. and Haenlein, M. (2010) 'Users of the world, unite! The challenges and opportunities of social media', *Business Horizons*, 53(1), pp. 59–68. doi:10.1016/j.bushor.2009.09.003.

Kaplan, A. M. and Haenlein, M. (2011) 'Two hearts in three-quarter time: How to waltz the social media/viral marketing dance', *Business Horizons*, 54(3), pp. 253–63. doi:10.1016/j.bushor.2011.01.006.

Kiefaber, D. (2015) 'Here's the amateur Snickers ad that just won its creator $50,000: Hunger brings out the devils (both of them!)', *Adweek*, 23 September. Available at: www.adweek.com/adfreak/heres-amateur-snickers-ad-just-won-its-creator-50000-167053 (accessed 11 November 2016).

King, R. A., Racherla, P. and Bush, V. D. (2014) 'What we know and don't know about online word-of-mouth: A review and synthesis of the literature', *Journal of Interactive Marketing*, 28(3), pp. 167–83. doi:10.1016/j.intmar.2014.02.001.

Koohy, H. and Koohy, B. (2014) 'A lesson from the ice bucket challenge: Using social networks to publicize science', *Front Genet*, 5, p. 430. doi:10.3389/fgene.2014.00430.

Lee, S. H. M., Leizerovici, G. and Zhang, S. (2015) 'The satisfaction and stress of being a market maven: A social network perspective', *Journal of Consumer Behaviour*, 14(5), pp. 325–34. doi:10.1002/cb.1523.

Liu-Thompkins, Y. (2012) 'Seeding viral content: The role of message and network factors', *Journal of Advertising Research*, 52(4), pp. 59–72. doi:10.2501/JAR-52-4-000-000.

Lyngsfeldt, T. (2015) 'User generated content beats traditional advertising', *AdNews*, 23 March. Available at: www.adnews.com.au/opinion/user-generated-content-beats-traditional-advertising (accessed 11 November 2016).

Marshall, J. and Koh, Y. (2015) 'The problem with Twitter ads', *The Wall Street Journal*, 30 April. Available at: www.wsj.com/articles/the-problem-with-twitter-adsthe-problem-with-twitter-ads-1430438275 (accessed 11 November 2016).

Mills, A. J. (2012) 'Virality in social media: The SPIN framework', *Journal of Public Affairs*, 12(2), pp. 162–9. doi:10.1002/pa.1418.

de Mooij, M. (2013) *Global Marketing and Advertising: Understanding Cultural Paradoxes* (4th edn). Thousand Oaks, CA: Sage Publications.

Ni, M. Y., Chan, B. H., Leung, G. M., Lau, E. H. and Pang, H. (2014) 'Transmissibility of the Ice Bucket Challenge among globally influential celebrities: Retrospective cohort study', *BMJ*, 349, 16 December, g7185. doi:10.1136/bmj.g7185.

Nudd, T. (2015) 'Tinder users at SXSW are falling for this woman, but she's not what she appears: 'Have you ever been in love?' ', *Adweek*, 15 March. Available at: www.adweek.com/adfreak/tinder-users-sxsw-are-falling-woman-shes-not-what-she-appears-163486 (accessed 11 November 2016).

Pew Research Center (2013) *Mobile Technology Fact Sheet*. Available at: www.pewinternet.org/fact-sheets/mobile-technology-fact-sheet/ (accessed 11 November 2016).

Phelps, J. E., Lewis, R., Mobilio, L., Perry, D. and Raman, N. (2004) 'Viral marketing or electronic word-of-mouth advertising: Examining consumer responses and motivations to pass along email', *Journal of Advertising Research*, 44(4), pp. 333–48. doi:10.1017/S0021849904040371.

Rogers, E. M. (1962) *Diffusion of Innovations*. Gencoe: The Free Press.

Rossolatos, G. (2015) 'The Ice-Bucket Challenge: The legitimacy of the memetic mode of cultural reproduction is the message'. *Signs and Society*, 3(1), pp. 132–52. doi:10.1086/679520.

Sampson, T. D. (2012) *Virality: Contagion theory in the age of networks*. Minneapolis, MN: University of Minnesota Press.

Shehu, E., Bijmolt, T. H. A. and Clement, M. (2016) 'Effects of likeability dynamics on consumers' intention to share online video advertisements', *Journal of Interactive Marketing*, 35, pp. 27–43. doi:10.1016/j.intmar.2016.01.001.

Statista (2016) 'Number of monthly active Twitter users worldwide from 1st quarter 2010 to 3rd quarter 2016 (in millions)', *Statista*. Available at: www.statista.com/statistics/282087/number-of-monthly-active-twitter-users/ (accessed 11 November 2016).

Tun, Z. T. (2015) 'How KakaoTalk makes money', *Investopedia*, 23 June. Available at: www.investopedia.com/articles/investing/062315/how-kakaotalk-makes-money.asp (accessed 11 November 2016).

Turban, E., Strauss, J. and Lai, L. (2016) 'Customer engagement and metrics', *Social Commerce: Marketing, Technology and Management*. Basel: Springer International Publishing.

Ward, M. (2015) *Viral Video Chart: Australia And NZ's Top 10 Most Shared Ads of All Time*. Available at: https://mumbrella.com.au/viral-video-chart-australia-and-nzs-top-10-most-shared-ads-of-all-time-303408 (accessed 11 November 2016).

Wellman, B. (1999) *Networks in the Global Village*. Boulder, CO: Westview Press.

Wellman, B. (2001) 'Physical place and cyberplace: The rise of personalized networking', *International Journal of Urban and Regional Research*, 25(2), pp. 227–52. doi:10.1111/1468-2427.00309.

Weng, L., Menczer, F. and Ahn, Y. Y. (2013) 'Virality prediction and community structure in social networks', *Sci Rep*, 3, p. 2522. doi:10.1038/srep02522.

Williams, B. (2016) 'Adblock Plus and (a little) more', *ABP*, 11 August. Available at: https://adblockplus.org/blog/fb-reblock-ad-blocking-community-finds-workaround-to-facebook (accessed 11 November 2016).

Woolf, N. (2016) 'Remember the ice bucket challenge? It just funded an ALS breakthrough', *Guardian*, 27 July. Available at: www.theguardian.com/society/2016/jul/26/ice-bucket-challenge-als-charity-gene-discovery (accessed 11 November 2016).

Yadav, M., Kamboj, S. and Rahman, Z. (2016) 'Customer co-creation through social media: The case of "Crash the Pepsi IPL 2015"', *Journal of Direct, Data and Digital Marketing Practice*, 17(4), pp. 259–71. doi:10.1057/s41263-016-0008-7.

Yang, G. (2014) 'Internet activism and the party-state in China', *Daedalus*, 143(2), pp. 110–23. doi:10.1162/DAED_a_00276.

4 American advertising and the politics of consumption[1]

Jean M. Grow

> We hold these truths to be self-evident, that all men are created equal, that they are endowed by their Creator with certain unalienable Rights, that among these are Life, Liberty and the pursuit of Happiness.
>
> (American Declaration of Independence, 4 July 1776)

From its inception, American advertising has been suffused with the values that have defined the nation's political ideals: life, liberty, and the pursuit of happiness. In the early years of the American colonies, and as the newly founded democracy grew, advertising was a crucial economic driver. By the close of the nineteenth century, advertising had become an institutionalized force offering life and liberty through consumption. As the twentieth century unfolded, advertising was at the heart of the industrialized engine that built a robust U.S. economy by equating happiness with consumption. By the dawn of the twenty-first century, as American advertising agencies continued to open local agencies worldwide, American political ideals had become global aspirations. In the process, American advertising's hegemonic power has infused the aspirational values of life, liberty, and the pursuit of happiness into the global marketplace. Today, these aspirational values are rooted in, and perpetuated by, consumption; and, with the pervasive nature of technology, their influence bleeds across international borders.

Twitchell (2000) claims that advertising is, at its heart, a practice akin to religious devotion; Sivulka (1998) suggests that advertisers propagate desire; and Marchand (1985) argues that American advertising is the magic that shaped modernity. All of these are, in part, true. Advertising's propagation of desire did shape modernity, and its place in postmodern American culture does inspire a form of cultural devotion both at home and abroad. However, at its core American advertising is the iconic representation of the American political ideals of life, liberty, and the pursuit of happiness.

To contextualize American advertising, a brief overview of its early history, from the birth of the colonies to the close of the nineteenth century, is presented. Next, American brands built during the twentieth century, as well as the people and institutional forces that shaped them, are explored. The chapter closes by looking forward into the twenty-first century, concluding with some challenges American advertising faces.

The early years: a passion of independence

America's first newspaper advertisement was published in Boston in 1704. Yet, the heart of marketing and media was in Philadelphia, with Benjamin Franklin serving as the catalyst for American advertising and the propagation of American ideals. In 1729, Franklin published the *Pennsylvania Gazette*, which included pages of "new advertisements." Five years later, he launched America's first magazine, aptly named, *The General Magazine*. Franklin lived boldly, not unlike twenty-first-century entrepreneurs, promoting his inventions and ideology across the colonies and abroad, and laying the foundation for the inventors and advertisers who followed. Franklin's mind and skills as a communicator were essential in shaping the United States' Declaration of Independence in 1776 and Constitution in 1787, thus linking the birth of the American nation to the spirit of American advertising.

The eighteenth and early nineteenth centuries saw a proliferation of newspaper and magazine advertising along with a growing distribution of posters and pamphlets, largely produced in-house by the publishers. These print media advertised retail dry goods, imported merchandise, and acquisitions. Prior to the abolishment of slavery in the U.S., some privileged White Americans ran advertisements for slave auctions and ran notices seeking the return of run-away slaves. Early American advertising messages promoted life and liberty (for some) and set the stage for advertisers to embrace the pursuit of happiness in the coming decades.

In the mid-nineteenth century the advertising industry began to be formalized. In 1843, Volney Palmer opened the first advertising agency in Philadelphia. In 1858, N. W. Ayer & Son opened and established a commission structure for writing and placing ads, a structure which has lasted into the dawn of the twenty-first century. In 1887, James Walter Thompson established J. Walter Thompson and created the first account executive position, formalizing the relationship between advertising agencies and their clients, while, in 1889, retailer John Wanamaker hired a full-time copywriter and began producing all Wanamaker's advertising in-house. The tradition of in-house retail advertising departments continues today with robust departments at American retail brands such as Target and Kohl's.

The nineteenth century also saw the birth of brands. In 1837, Proctor and Gamble (P&G) opened its doors, while two years later Goodyear created "vulcanized" rubber for use in auto tires. Farmers' wives were introduced to Mason jars in 1858, Charles Fleishmann standardized yeast in 1868, and a year later Henry J. Heinz bottled horseradish, the first of his "57 Varieties" of condiments. Consumers' thirsts were quenched when, in 1870, Charles Hires combined roots and herbs and began brewing the first "root beer" soda. In 1874, Joseph Schlitz brewed the "Beer That Made Milwaukee Famous" (Schlitz) and two years later Anheuser-Busch created "The King of Beers" (Budweiser). The Quaker Oats icon appeared in 1885; at the same time Carnation condensed milk was claiming that it provided "sweet, freshness" in the can. In 1890, Aunt Jemima made her debut on boxes of pancake mix and in 1893 Rastus appeared on packages of Cream of Wheat. Both were black servants. These images, with their racist roots, remain today, although often with disclaimers such as: Aunt Jemima "stands for warmth, nourishment and trust – qualities you'll find in loving moms from diverse backgrounds" (Aunt Jemima, 2016). Many of these products eased the hardship of nineteenth-century American life with advertising copy used to pitch them as purveyors of liberty, thereby leading the way to happiness.

Hucksters were also a staple of the late nineteenth century. P. T. Barnum with his "masterful deceptions" (Twitchell, 2000, p. 16) was the finest of them all and an immense influence on American advertising. He understood the need to create an occasion to sell and created the "Greatest Show on Earth" to do just that. Advertising copy of the time, inspired by Barnum's work, hawked "limited edition," "collector's item," "discount price," and "everything must go." However, Barnum was not alone. The late 1880s brought a firestorm of patent medicine hucksters, including Lydia Pinkham, who produced the crème de la crème of patent medicines all branded using her name. Pinkham, and others, promised everything from a "cure for all female weaknesses" to "purifying the blood." They plied their wares using trading cards, a popular advertising medium during the late nineteenth century, which entertained consumers and provided them a modicum of momentary happiness.

In the post-Civil War era, a tired America was looking for a reprieve from the suffering of war. Brands began showcasing beautiful women in an art nouveau style, along with framing products as providing pleasure while easing life's burdens. As brands grew and their slogans proliferated, so did the need for trade-mark laws, which were initiated at the close of the nineteenth century and culminated in the Trademark Act of 1905. America's early advertising established the foundation for the nation's brands to become the symbolic purveyors of the American ideals of life, liberty, and the pursuit of happiness.

The twentieth century: industrialized liberty

At the opening of the twentieth century, industrialization was set to change the nature of American advertising, including the establishment of advertising as a profession. In 1904, John E. Kennedy introduced reason-why copy and shortly thereafter Claude Hopkins introduced scientific copy. As the first Ford Model-Ts rolled off the assembly lines in 1908, there were ready-made, working-class con-sumers to whom advertising copy provided the "reason-why" they needed a Model-T or a host of newly created consumer package goods (CPGs). In 1927, Alfred Sloan of General Motors introduced the concept of "planned obsoles-cence." His strategy was "a car for every purse and purpose" (Rothenberg, 1999), which fuelled demand for cars and CPGs, alike.

In 1917, advertising agencies formally banded together to advance their growing influence and created the American Association of Advertising

Agencies (AAAA) in New York City. The AAAA ensured that New York would become the hub of the American advertising industry. It also established a 15 percent commission on media placement, which remained the standard into the twenty-first century.

Mass production, driven by the industrial revolution, led to the emergence of retail chains (Sivulka, 1998). By 1913, Woolworth's department stores (now defunct) had over 600 locations across America. J. C. Penney had nearly 300 outlets by 1920. Grocery chain Piggly Wiggly had established a self-service shopping format by 1928, allowing consumers to select goods on their own. The growth of chain stores and the explosion of CPGs went hand in hand. In 1911, Woodbury soap provided "Skin you love to touch." In 1912, Morton Salt sold table salt by telling consumers, "When it rains it pours." Shortly after, Nabisco launched its crème-filled chocolate sandwich-cookies called Oreos, while Hellman's introduced its "Blue Ribbon" mayonnaise. In 1920, Baby Ruth candy bars, named after U.S. President Grover Cleveland's daughter, hit the stores along with Eskimo Pie ice cream treats and Wonder Bread. Betty Crocker arrived in 1921; her iconic image, created in 1924, has since been revised eight times to reflect a changing America. By 1945, Betty Crocker was the second most recognizable woman in the U.S., behind First Lady Eleanor Roosevelt (Betty Crocker, 2015).

The introduction of commercial radio in 1922 was a seismic shift for American advertising. It opened the door to American homes and offered an intimacy not possible with print media. Branded sponsorship of programming fuelled radio's growth. In 1924, Goodrich Tires sponsored the first hour-long radio show in the same year the National Broadcasting Company (NBC) launched 19 stations nationwide. Brands such as Palmolive, Eveready, and Dodge sponsored radio programs introduced with jingles that would become their brand monikers. There was also *Amos 'n' Andy*, a radio drama set in New York's Harlem neighborhood featuring two Black men with voice-overs by two White actors, and sponsored by Pepsodent "for white teeth." Advertising like this demonstrated the racist American culture of the time that was played upon by American advertisers. In 1928, the Lucky Strike Cigarette Dance Orchestra debuted on over 39 NBC stations. One year later, the American Tobacco Company spent US$12.3 million on advertising, signaling the beginning of massive spending on cigarette advertising that would dominate American media for the next 60 years (Garfield, 1999). By the end of the 1920s, radio had become central to American life, as family and friends gathered around the radio to listen to their favorite shows sponsored by what would become their favorite brands. A decade later, radio surpassed magazines as "the number-one source of advertising revenue, a gap that kept widening until the introduction of television" (Sivulka, 1989, p. 186).

Throughout the great depression of the 1930s and leading up to World War II, the advertising industry continued to expand modestly, with its growth reflecting the nation's own population growth. Expansion into the Midwest led Leo Bozell and Morris Jacobs to launch Bozell & Jacobs in Omaha in 1921, followed by a second agency in Chicago in 1935. Chicago-based Leo Burnett would soon become famous for its brand characters including: Tony the Tiger in 1951,

Charlie the Tuna in 1961, Ronald McDonald in 1963 and the Pillsbury Dough Boy in 1965 (Enrico, 1999). *Advertising Age*'s launch in 1930, in Chicago, demonstrated the emerging power of the Midwest advertising market. Finally, in 1932, George Gallup joined Young & Rubicam as director of research and the public opinion poll was born. Gallup's contributions, including the Gallup Poll, reverberated across America's advertising landscape and to this day impact politics and advertising.

During both World War I and World War II, traditional advertising spending declined while solicitations for war bonds, Red Cross donations, and armed forces recruitment went up. Patriotism defined the tonality. During World War II, women were portrayed as strong and heroic, symbolized by Rosie the Riveter. The non-profit Ad Council, established in 1942, created 423 campaigns including Rosie the Riveter and Smokey the Bear in 1944, Keep America Beautiful in 1953, and The Crying Indian in 1971 (Melillo, 2013). The depth and breadth of its work shaped and defined how many Americans came to see themselves. Its work provided tangible linkages between advertising branded messages and America's consumable political ideals.

If there is any event that launched American brands into the global marketplace, it was World War II. Companies such as Coca-Cola and R. J. Reynolds followed U.S. troops into battle. Coca-Cola opened bottling plants on every continent upon which the Allies fought. America rode to victory with GIs handing out Nestlé chocolates and Camel cigarettes, while toasting their victory with Coca-Cola. Nestlé surely did "make the very best chocolate." "I'd Walk a Mile for a Camel" had more resonance than ever. Coke provided memories of home and a modicum of happiness. With a global network of manufacturing and distribution centers set up, these brands were ready to expand into the fledgling global marketplace after the war. American brands had receptive new audiences who, in a post-war period, were enthralled with the ideals such brands symbolized: life, liberty, and the pursuit of happiness.

Between 1945 and 1960, America was in a post-war boom, and advertising answered the call. Cities across the U.S. were growing, driving suburban expansion with a baby boom that fuelled consumption rooted in "a desire for individuality that could only be satisfied by brand differentiation" (Rothenberg, 1999). For returning GIs, nothing fulfilled the dream of "the fabulous fifties" (Sivulka, 1998) more than marrying the woman of their dreams. DeBeers' 1948 tagline, "A diamond is forever," written by Frances Gerety, of N. W. Ayer, offered the promise of eternal happiness and cemented the diamond ring as the engagement ring. Advertising of the fabulous fifties also framed transportation as a luxurious liberty. Chevrolet's "See the USA in your Chevrolet" was the perfect companion to the 1950s lifestyle, complete with America's sprawling vistas and its burgeoning new suburban enclaves. If you could not afford a car, Greyhound happily encouraged travelers to ride a bus and "Leave the driving to us." Regardless of the vehicle, everyone could afford some mode of transportation – and a ticket to happiness.

The fabulous 1950s would not be complete without advertisers selling Americans the ideal of beauty, which was nothing other than another way to promote happiness through consumption. Automobile advertisements showed beautiful women adorning their cars as objects of desire. Clairol introduced women to beauty products with modern, in-home hair color. In 1956, Shirley Polykoff of Foote, Cone & Belding crafted the perfect headline, "Does she or doesn't she?" The inherent promise offered women the economical (in-home) fulfillment of advertisers' fantasies of beauty as crafted by Polykoff. The power once embedded in Rosie the Riveter was now supplanted in a bottle of hair color. Finally, as consumption grew throughout the 1950s and 1960s so too did advertising budgets with General Motors and P&G proving to be the two biggest spenders (Endicott, 1999).

The 1950s also saw another infusion of money into tobacco advertising. In 1955, Leo Burnett rebranded Marlboro, transforming it from a woman's brand to a man's brand, with the Marlboro man – the iconic representation of the American political ideals, which consumers across the world know today. If nothing else the fifties were an "era of motivational manipulation" (Garfield, 1999, p. 58).

Like radio, television profoundly shifted the way advertising was delivered. Between 1949 and 1951, ad spending grew ten-fold. Between 1951 and 1955 it grew nearly another ten-fold, reaching US$1 billion, which represented a quarter of all advertising spending. By 1957, there were 450 TV stations across America and by 1960 nearly 90 percent of all homes had a television set (Advertising Age, 2005). While television commercials' origins are in the 1950s, the cultural impact of television advertising and branded sponsorship has lasted for decades (University of Texas, 2015). In 1951, *I Love Lucy* debuted on CBS and not long after families gathered to watch brand sponsored shows such as the *Texaco Star Theatre*. In 1954, NBC's *The Tonight Show* debuted as a platform to introduce emerging cultural icons and brands. This was followed by another branded television show in 1955, Disney's *The Mickey Mouse Club*. In 1964, The Beatles appeared on *The Ed Sullivan Show* and provided a brief halo effect for its sponsor, Sears.

In 1967, the first National Football League (NFL) Super Bowl game was broadcast on television. In that moment, football and American brands found a marriage of convenience on a media platform that reached a large mass audience. Brands flocked to the Super Bowl. On the heels of the sexual revolution, Noxzema featured actress Farrah Fawcett slathering shaving cream on football icon Joe Namath's face in a 1973 Super Bowl spot. In 1980, a Super Bowl spot for Coke featured the Pittsburgh Steelers' "Mean" Joe Green's softer side as he handed a bottle of Coke and a smile to a young boy and made viewers weep. Apple debuted its new Macintosh computer with its 1984 commercial, a spot that ran just once during the 1983 Super Bowl. The spot marked Apple as the innovator in personal computing. After Apple's allegorical reference to Orwell's *1984*, the Super Bowl became a mecca for advertisers to showcase their creativity. Agencies used brands as vehicles for self-promotion, with many brands happily participating despite rising media costs for Super Bowl ad placement.

The creative revolution of the 1960s ushered out "the conformist '50s" and ushered in "the searching '60s" (Rothenberg, 1999, p. 130). The 1960s, like no other decade in the history of advertising, had a profound effect on the industry from the internal structure to its creative output. No other person was more prominent than the creatively brilliant Bill Bernbach. In his 1949 manifesto, Bernbach wrote, "Let us prove to the world that good taste, good art, good writing can be good selling" (Garfield, 1999, p. 18). And he did. As a founding partner and Chief Creative Officer of Doyle Dane Bernbach (DDB), Bernbach restructured the creative process by establishing "creative teams," pairing copywriters (the people who write the ads) and art directors (the people who design the visual components of ads) thereby establishing a model that remains largely unchanged to this day. In doing so, Bernbach prioritized creativity as never before. In 1960, DDB created the iconic Volkswagen "Think small" and "Lemon" ads and the industry was forever changed. Art, for the first time, became just as important as copy – if not more important. While Bernbach was a visionary, he was not alone. In 1961, Rosser Reeves introduced the American advertising industry to the unique selling proposition (USP), a strategic planning tool still in use today in various forms. In 1962, David Ogilvy, known as the father of advertising, published *Confessions of an Advertising Man*, which cemented his reputation as someone who could balance "the art of creativity with a certain amount of science" (Hays, 1999). Three years later, Ogilvy merged his agency with the British agency Mather & Crowley to form one of the first international agencies, Ogilvy & Mather. In 1966, Mary Wells Laurence established Wells, Rich, Greene and became the first woman to head a major advertising agency. Then, as now, her status was an anomaly: men dominated and still dominate American advertising creative departments and agency management positions.

The 1960s were also a time of social upheaval in the United States. The ads of that decade reflected the changing times and often provided a nod to social revolution or the happy consumption of sensual pleasures. In 1963, Avis boldly owned being in second place behind car rental competitor Hertz claiming, "We try harder." Pepsi launched "The Pepsi Generation" and with that the cola wars against rival Coca-Cola. President Lyndon B. Johnson's Daisy commercial shocked television viewers with an image of an exploding atomic bomb juxtaposed to an innocent child counting the petals on a daisy. The imagery helped catapult Johnson to re-election victory. All of these ads were produced by DDB, whose creative style dominated American advertising during the 1960s.

The 1960s also saw an explosion in fast food and cigarette advertising. In 1968, McDonald's introduced the Big Mac. That same year tobacco giant Phillip Morris partnered with Leo Burnett to launch two iconic campaigns: "You've come a long way, baby" for Virginia Slims and "Come to where the flavor is. Come to Marlboro country" for Marlboro. Throughout the 1960s, advertising messaging tapped into the emotions born of social upheaval by promoting desire and expanding on the possibilities of consumable happiness.

Despite shrinking advertising budgets during the 1970s, the creative traditions of the 1960s carried on, while the battle of brands began. In 1969, Coke responded to "The Pepsi Generation" with the "It's the real thing" campaign.

Shortly thereafter, 7 Up used Rosser Reeves's USP to reposition itself as the "Uncola." In 1974, Miller Lite launched the tagline "Tastes great, less filling," and in 1979 Budweiser answered with "This Bud's for you." Fast food advertising continued its growth in the 1970s. In 1971, McDonald's launched, "You deserve a break today." In 1973, Burger King answered with, "Have it your way." Perhaps inspired by the proliferation of fast food, Wells, Rich, Greene (WRG) developed "I can't believe I ate the whole thing," for Alka-Seltzer in 1971. While in 1977 WRG created the "I Love NY" campaign, with Milton Glaser designing a heart to replace the word love. The campaign led to New York City's revitalization and reinforced the city's reputation as the symbolic centre of America. The campaign has been copied by cities across the world ever since.

The late 1960s and the 1970s also saw a number of important legal and ethical challenges. In 1964, the Surgeon General issued a report on the hazards of smoking cigarettes. The U.S. Congress passed legislation in 1969 requiring warning labels on cigarette packaging and prohibiting broadcast advertising of cigarettes (Center for Disease Control and Prevention, 2015). This heralded the beginning of the end of traditional cigarette advertising, which culminated in the 1998 tobacco settlement requiring cigarette companies to cover medical costs for tobacco-related illnesses and to fund anti-tobacco education. In 1971, the AAAA launched the National Advertising Review Board, ostensibly to monitor and self-regulate questions of social appropriateness, while monitoring the industry's social responsibility. Then, in 1976, the Supreme Court granted advertising First Amendment protection to advertising messaging, which opened the floodgates to exaggerations in copy, commonly known as puffery.

The American advertising industry has historically portrayed American consumers through a culturally and ethnically narrow lens. It was not until the 1970s that African American models were included in mainstream advertising, albeit quite infrequently. The decade also saw the birth of multicultural advertising and the agencies that supported it. In 1971, Thomas Burrell found the first African American advertising agency, Burrell Communications in Chicago. In 1972, Sara Sunshine founded the first Hispanic agency SAMS (Spanish Advertising & Marketing Services) in Miami. These agencies, like those that followed, were segregated from the mainstream agencies reflecting the political doctrine of "separate but equal" that had legally supported segregation in American public education. When general market agencies attempted to portray multicultural Americans, which was rare, their attempts often fell flat. A classic example of this failure was the Ad Council's 1971 "The Crying Indian" ad, an extension of the "Keep America Beautiful" campaign. Rather than casting an American Indian, they used Italian-American actor Espera Oscar de Corti. Nearly 50 years later, minorities and women still struggle for accurate representation and fair employment in American advertising, which will be revisited at the conclusion of this chapter.

The 1980s and 1990s represent two decades of mergers and acquisitions, in part driven by a global recession in the late 1970s (Fitzpatrick, 1999). As advertising agencies merged creating global integration, three things happened:

- First, small boutique shops bubbled up, many far away from New York City. It seemed that the new hot creative city changed every other year. Agencies such as Fallon in Minneapolis, Wieden + Kennedy in Portland, or Chiat/Day in Los Angeles were drawing clients away from New York City.
- Second, account planning was introduced in the 1990s and formally brought the voice of consumers into the strategic planning process. Jay Chiat, co-founder of Chiat/Day, brought account planning to America when he hired a British planner in 1982. By the end of the twentieth century, account planning in the United States was as American as apple pie.
- Finally, American agencies began to expand into the global marketplace, buying up local agencies or opening up local branches under their American name.

Despite merged agencies and diminished budgets, exciting work was still being produced. For example, 1981 saw the launch of the iconic Absolut Vodka bottle campaign, which continues to this day. In that same year, the U.S. Army called American recruits to, "Be all you can be." In 1984, "Morning in America," heralded Ronald Reagan's re-election as the 40th President of the United States by encapsulating the political ideology of the America dream. Also in 1984, Wendy's asked, "Where's the beef?" and in the process suggested to consumers that they had the power to demand more from brands.

However, the most remarkable work of the 1980s and 1990s was Nike's "Just do it" campaign created by Wieden + Kennedy. First launched in 1988, the tagline soon became the core of the Nike brand and helped build an empire. Nothing expressed life and liberty like the stories of Nike athletes, in part because the campaign created a human persona for the Nike brand. With half of the U.S. population yet untapped in Nike's advertising, Wieden + Kennedy called on copywriter Janet Champ to create a campaign for women and girls. The result was the iconic "If You Let Me Play" campaign that energized girls and women around positive messages related to girls and sport. Today, Nike epitomizes the essence of what it means to be American – to bootstrap your way to the top. Like so many American brands today, no matter where in the world you see a Nike ad, its brand message is consistent – and consistently American: "Just do it."

Near the end of the century, the rise of technology infused new life and, for some, great fear into advertising (Wheaton, 2015). Some agencies saw technology as a threat to their profit margin, while others saw technology as providing new creative opportunities. The Internet, led by advancements in technology and the rise of social media and mobile apps that support digital branding have blossomed into twenty-first-century media staples. Thus, it is not surprising that we see digital advertising messages celebrating consumption while heralding the ideals of democracy through digital engagement.

Into the twenty-first century: consumable happiness

By the beginning of the twenty-first century, American brands and the advertising that supported them, became a focal point of conscious and unconscious patriotic expressions of American capitalism and democracy. In that sense, it was not a surprise that, following the terrorist attacks in New York on September 11, 2001, President George W. Bush suggested Americans demonstrate their patriotism by shopping. To coincide with renewed patriotism and purchasing power, Bush named Charlotte Beers, Chairperson of J. Walter Thompson, as Secretary of Public Diplomacy and Public Affairs. Bush well understood the politics of consumption and the consumption of politics. It was common to see many advertising messages of the time reflecting patriotic ideology.

Even as traditional media and consumer spending increased, American advertising was slow to embrace digital technology and social media in particular. With the launch of Facebook in 2004, YouTube in 2005 and Twitter in 2006, the advertising industry found itself playing catch up after these platforms themselves set the rules for advertising in the years that followed. Today, advertisers are still catching up, while consumers continue to play a dominant role in shaping the digital landscape and how brands respond to them within it.

Six campaigns in the twenty-first century represent iconic advertising industry favorites. In 2000, Alex Bogusky of Crispin Porter + Bogusky created the "Truth" campaign in support of the American Legacy Foundation's tobacco education efforts that promoted smoke-free and tobacco-free advocacy. "Truth" strategically placed body bags across American cities, bringing awareness to the number of deaths caused by tobacco. In the process, it garnered more earned media than any campaign that year. In 2001, Minneapolis's Fallon created the BMW Films. These short videos went viral, revealing the automobiles' extraordinary performance and with targeted precision entertained consumers. In 2004, Ogilvy launched Dove's "Campaign for Real Beauty," reminiscent of Nike's "If You Let Me Play" campaign from nearly ten years earlier. It challenged the objectification of women and the brand took on the mantel of women's advocate, with full-scale social media campaigns and branded programming in the years that followed. In 2007, Droga5 created the UNICEF Tap Project. This pro-bono work (American advertising agencies' version of corporate social responsibility) encouraged diners to pay for their otherwise free water, with all funds going to UNICEF. It raised US$2.5 million for global safe drinking water initiatives. With creativity that rivals advertising of decades past, *Advertising Age* named these campaigns as some of the best of the twenty-first century (Hanlon, 2015).

However, two additional campaigns warrant discussion, in large part because of their social media savvy:

• First, Barack Obama's 2007/8 presidential campaign with social content and digital marketing executed by Blue State Digital. While Shepard Fairey's Hope poster was iconic (see Figure 4.1), Blue State Digital's social

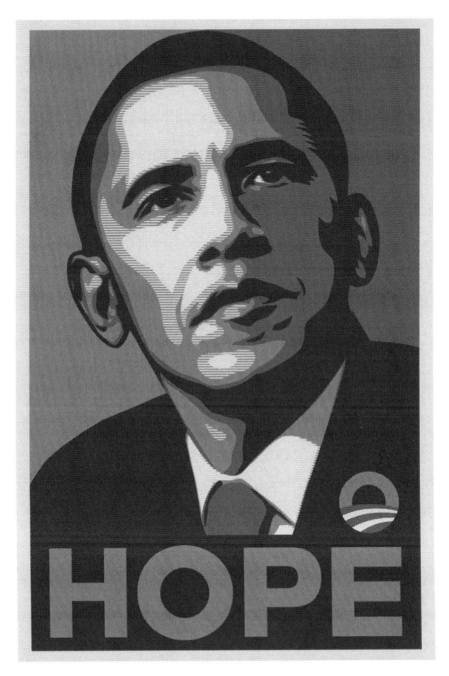

Figure 4.1 Shepard Fairey's Hope poster, created in response to Barack Obama's 2008 campaign for president, was embraced by the campaign and signified American political ideals while symbolically transferring them onto Obama.

engagement, driven by an army of savvy techies, exceeded anything previously imagined in terms of consumer engagement. Obama raised more money than any other presidential candidate in U.S. history, the majority from small donations via social media and email. He dominated YouTube and trounced his opponent on Facebook, handily winning the 2008 election.

* Second, the 2013 Oreo Super Bowl engagement. With the Super Bowl game delayed due to an electrical blackout inside the stadium, Oreo's digital agency, 360i, jumped into action. It tweeted "You can still dunk in the dark," and social media lit up with consumers' first taste of "real-time" marketing. 360i created a moment of happiness that as securely tied to the Oreo brand.

Each of these campaigns, with the exception of the Truth campaign, delivered its own twist on happiness. Additionally, each campaign was either strategically framed by digital technology or leveraged it tactically. BMW allowed consumers to happily have a voyeuristic drive in "the ultimate driving machine." Dove championed women to love their bodies and be happy in them. The Tap Project allowed diners to ratchet up their dining pleasure through altruism. Obama's campaign made hope a cause for happiness and led to his election as the 44th president of the United States. Oreo simply tapped into what it already owned (dunking an Oreo in milk), creating happiness in what was an otherwise frustrating moment. After all, isn't providing happiness the grand bargain advertisers have struck with American consumers?

Closing discussion

An interesting phenomenon emerges as we look across time. American advertising practitioners have a propensity to navel gaze, with seeming indifference to consumers' preferences. This might be "considered self-centered backslapping if not downright paradoxical" (Hanlon, 2015). Yet one twenty-first-century advertising practitioner, Alex Bogusky, stepped beyond the navel gazing. Bogusky who was named Co-Chairman of Crispin Porter + Bogusky in 2008 and "Creative Director of the Decade" by *Ad Week* in 2010 quit advertising the same year *Ad Week* sang his praises. In this reflective moment, Bogusky founded Common, an organization designed to creatively solve social problems through the development of products that take care of consumers while attempting to change the world. His journey reflects a broader social trend in America today, one which American advertisers would be wise to engage with.

Navel gazing will no longer work. There are powerful social shifts afoot, driven by consumers' desires for change, from workers' rights to ecological concerns to political extremism. These challenges have prompted the rise of CSR (corporate social responsibility) campaigns, which have become a staple in American advertisers' arsenal. At its best, CSR contributes positively to society, by playing a role in helping to keep corporations accountable. Crispin Porter + Bogusky's Truth campaign and Droga5's Tap Project are examples of CSR at its best. At its worst, CSR is co-opted to mask corporate ineptitude and greed, and advertising wastefulness. The Ad Council's 1971 "Crying Indian", with its miscast Indian, and Pepsi's 2010–12 "Refresh Project", with the funds promised to community projects often falling woefully short, are examples of CSR ineptitude. The success of CSR is always rooted in corporations' ability to use brands to celebrate the good work they do by subtly reinforcing American political ideals of life, liberty, and the pursuit of happiness – f or brands are the vehicles through which American corporations espouse their ideals. The advertising messages of CSR are also a reminder that we, practitioners and consumers alike, all play a part in the politics of consumption.

There is one final challenge that the American advertising industry surely must address: the lack of diversity across the advertising industry, particularly in creative departments. Women are woefully underrepresented in creative departments across America (Grow and Deng, 2014), as are people of color. Further, across all departments, American advertising agencies do not reflect the diversity of the general market (Bendick and Egan, 2009) – the America these agencies are hired to engage with and influence. Rather, ethnically diverse practitioners are found working within multicultural agencies, too often segregated from general market agencies. America is growing more diverse each day. Now is the time for the American advertising industry to step into the twenty-first century and hold the truths that America purports "to be self-evident, that all men [and women] are created equal" – regardless of their gender or the color of their skin.

In closing, American advertising is intrinsically bound to the nation's history and political ideals. At the same time global capitalism is largely framed by America's brands, which are both beloved and reviled. In some parts of the world, American brands are welcomed as iconic, aspirational markers of greatness and American advertising strategies are passionately embraced. Yet, in other parts of the world, American brands are loathed as iconic makers of globalization and hegemonic domination. In the end, American brands and the advertising that supports them are nothing short of memes for American political ideals. Despite the grandest dreams of American advertisers – and the illusions they have exported to the global marketplace – life, liberty, and the pursuit of happiness cannot be bought or sold.

Note

1 Acknowledgment: The author gratefully acknowledges the support of fellowship from the Women's International Study Center (WISC) in Santa Fe, New Mexico.

References

Advertising Age (2005) *1950s TV Turns on America.* Available at: http://adage.com/article/75-years-of-ideas/1950s-tv-turns-america/102703/ (accessed 11 November 2016).

Aunt Jemima (2016) *Aunt Jemima: Our History,* Available at: www.auntjemima.com/aj_history/ (accessed 11 November 2016).

Bendick, M. and Egan, M. L. (2009) *Research Perspectives on Race and Employment in the Advertising Industry.* Bendick and Egan Economic Consultants, Inc. Available at: www.bendickegan.com/publications.htm (accessed 7 March 2017).

Betty Crocker (2015) *General Mills: History of Innovation the History of Betty Crocker,* Available at: www.hist_betty-3.pdf (accessed 11 November 2016).

Centres for Disease Control and Prevention (2015) *History of the Surgeon General's Reports on Smoking and Health.* Available at: www.cdc.gov/tobacco/data_statistics/sgr/history/ (accessed 26 June 2015).

Endicott, R. C. (1999) 'Big spenders', *Ad Age Advertising Century,* p. 128. Available at: http://adage.com (accessed 7 March 2017).

Enrico, D. (1999) 'Top 10 icons', *Ad Age Advertising Century,* pp. 41–6. Available at: http://adage.com (accessed 7 March 2017).

Fitzpatrick, S. (1999) 'What price loyalty?', *Ad Age Advertising Century,* pp. 99–136. Available at: http://adage.com (accessed 7 March 2017).

Garfield, B. (1999) 'Top 100 advertising campaigns', *Ad Age Advertising Century,* pp. 18–41. Available at: http://adage.com (accessed 7 March 2017).

Grow, J. M. and Broyles, S. J. (2011) 'Unspoken rule of the creative game: Insights to shape the next generation from top advertising creative women', *Advertising & Society Review* 12(1) [Online].

Grow, J. M. and Deng, T. (2014) 'Sex segregation in advertising creative departments across the globe', *Advertising & Society Review,* 14(4) [Online] doi:10.1353/asr.2014.0003.

Hanlon, P. (2015) 'Ad Age's Top 15 Campaigns of the 21st century: Has the advertising industry become divergent?', *Forbes.* Available at: www.forbes.com/sites/patrick hanlon/2015/01/12/ad-ages-top-15-campaigns-of-the-21st-century-has-the-advertising-industry-become-divergent/ (accessed 11 November 2016).

Hays, C. L. (1999) 'David Ogilvy, 88, father of soft sell in advertising, dies', *New York Times.* Available at: www.nytimes.com/1999/07/22/business/david-ogilvy-88-father-of-soft-sell-in-advertising-dies.html (accessed 11 November 2016).

Marchand, R. (1985) *Advertising the American Dream: Making Way for Modernity 1920–1940,* Berkeley, CA: University of California Press.

Melillo, W. (2013) *How McGruff and the Crying Indian Changed America: A History of Iconic Ad Council Campaigns.* Washington, DC: Smithsonian Books.

Rothenberg, R. (1999) 'The advertising century', in *Ad Age Advertising Century,* pp. 9–16, 130–33. Available at: http://adage.com/article/special-report-the-advertising-century/ad-age-advertising-century-greatest-icon/140149/ (accessed 7 March 2017).

Sivulka, J. (1988) *Soap, Sex, and Cigarettes: A Cultural history of American Advertising.* Belmont, CA: Wadsworth.

Twitchell, J. (2000) *Twenty Ads that Shook the World: The Century's Most Ground-breaking Advertising and How It Changed Us All.* New York: Three Rivers Press.

Wheaton, K. (2015) 'C'mon, marketers! Why aren't you periscoping your meerkat sessions yet?', *Advertising Age.* Available at: http://adage.com/article/ken-wheaton/marketers-periscoping-meerkat-sessions/297947/ (accessed 11 November 2016).

University of Texas (2015) *Television History: A Timeline 1878–2005.* Available at: http://tarlton.law.utexas.edu/exhibits/mason_&_associates/documents/timeline.pdf (accessed 11 November 2016).

5 Latin America and its influence on global creative advertising

Marta Mensa Torras

Latin America and advertising

Latin America is geographically formed by the 20 'developing' countries located south of the United States (Dabène, 1999). Being 'under' has not only been a geographic feature, but also a condition for progress. Unlike North Americans or Europeans, Latin Americans are used to being in crises. Pablo Del Campo (2009), the Worldwide Creative Director of Saatchi & Saatchi, explained in an interview that 'in Latin America we live in a permanent crisis; we have good creatives because the idea of survival is fixed in us'. Latin Americans seem to be predisposed to be creative as they often lack the possibility of addressing all of their needs. As such, every day can pose new challenges. Consequently, Uncertainty Avoidance indexes – measuring individual future uncertainty – are high in Central and South America (see Figure 5.1). Countries such as Guatemala and Uruguay have a rate of 99 per cent, while the figures for El Salvador and Peru are respectively 94 per cent and 87 per cent (Hofstede Centre, n.d.). As Del Campo (2009) observes, such instability underpins creativity in Latin America. This creative potential has also been identified by Buitrago and Duque (2013) in their work on the Orange Economy, which focuses on industries that combine creativity and culture and which transform ideas into products, such as architecture, graphic design or advertising. Such activities generate wealth and have the capacity to rebuild a country. In the case of Latin America, this sector has grown significantly and it is currently estimated that the Orange Economy has generated US$174.75 million in the region. The largest contributor is Brazil with US$66 million, followed by Mexico with US$55 million (Buitrago and Duque, 2013).

Advertising in Latin America in the twenty-first century

Since the 1920s, the Latin American advertising structure has generally followed the same pattern as the US agencies (Sinclair, 2013). J. Walter Thompson opened offices in Argentina, Brazil and Uruguay in the late 1920s, thanks to General Motors, which was extending its operations internationally. N. W. Ayer arrived in 1931 to address the needs of Ford while McCann Erickson ventured into the region in 1935 to service Standard Oil's international needs (Woodard,

Figure 5.1 Latin American map with Uncertainty Avoidance (UA) and Masculinity (M) indexes, according to Hofstede Centre.

2002). Such pioneering brands preceded Coca-Cola, Gillette, Kraft, Kellogg's and Procter & Gamble. For these transnational agencies, the decision to establish offices in Latin America was not motivated by any real desire to reach the Latin American market, but rather the need to service their clients' needs.

In the 1980s, British and French agencies also moved into Latin America. However, they soon encountered the 'conflict of interest' problem when entering these markets. Clients did not wish to see their agencies working for their competitors – even if the agency was located in another region. Saatchi & Saatchi sought to resolve this problem by creating a group structure with different and independently operated offices (Sinclair, 2013). Thus, the agencies Del Campo Saatchi & Saatchi in Argentina and F/Nazca Saatchi & Saatchi in Brazil may have customers in the same category despite being in the same advertising group.

As the formative years of the advertising industry in Latin America were marked by transnational agencies, it is little surprise that Latin American countries have continued to emulate tactics and marketing strategies from the richest countries (Arellano, 2002). However, Eric Mayorga (2015) of the University of

Piura (Peru) contends that such efforts have 'been a mistake'. Mayorga argues that Latin American advertising agencies should start building an independent identity, given the region's idiosyncrasies, and assess their capabilities without deference to what is being done or not done in the United States or Europe.

In some regions of Latin America, such as Peru or Ecuador, being 'white' is associated with the United States or Europe and is synonymous with wealth and opportunity (Mayo *et al.*, 2005; Coe *et al.*, 2004; Kang, 1997). Consequently, many advertising models have white skin, blonde hair and blue eyes, and speak the local language with a foreign accent. Such attributes help make the ad more striking and give the message more credibility. For example, Saga Falabella, a Chilean mall in Peru, was accused of racism and discrimination for a Disney doll ad. The 2014 ad shows four girls with European, not Peruvian, characteristics. Consumer complaints about the models' unrealistic appearance were expressed on the Internet and quickly went viral. Facing such a consumer backlash, the brand removed the advertisement and apologised. On the other hand, there are other countries in Latin America, such as Argentina or Brazil, that try to create realistic portrayals. For example, Young & Rubicam made the campaign 'The Argentinians are the most beautiful ones'. The ad was a tribute to International Women's Day and the objective was to emphasise local beauty norms. The ad won an award at the Ibero-American Advertising Festival (FIAP) in 2002.

Today, the Latin American advertising market is estimated to be worth US$49.85 billion (Statista, 2015). Of this, 80 per cent is concentrated in Brazil, Mexico and Argentina (Wentz, 2010). In comparison to other regions in the world, Latin America's adspend is relatively low. Although it is 6.5 per cent higher than the Middle East and 5 per cent higher than Africa, it is still 23.6 per cent lower than Asia-Pacific (Sinclair, 2013). Such figures, however, should not overshadow the fact that the Latin American market is growing very quickly (Johnson, 2010), with advertising and marketing development being twice as high as other continents. According to the Global AdView Pulse report (Inform-aBTL, 2013), Latin America was the leader with respect to advertising growth in 2013, with an increase of 11.9 per cent investment in the region.

Latin America and the global advertising industry

Latin America currently houses some of the most open markets in the world and is also a major global supplier of energy, minerals and food (Barshefsky and Hill, 2008). Since the 1980s, opening markets and formal trade agreements between the United States and Latin American countries have increased trade. They have also provided several benefits on both sides (Tulchin, 2016). Thanks to the North American Free Trade Agreement (NAFTA), trade between the United States, Canada and Mexico has almost tripled. Mexico has become the third largest trading partner of the United States and the second largest purchaser of US exports (Piketty, 2013). Latin America supplies more oil to the United States than the Middle East, and the region has great potential to also become the largest supplier of alternative fuel sources, contributing to energy security for the United States (The Economist, 2010). Furthermore, Latinos represent 15 per cent of the US population, and almost 50 per cent of its population growth. Latinos also constitute an important part of the electorate (Barshefsky and Hill, 2008). Consequently, the United States is home to Spanish-speaking media outlets as well as advertising agencies exclusively aimed at the Latino market. For example, Lapiz is an advertising agency owned by the Leo Burnett network. It is responsible for developing communication strategies that exclusively target the Hispanic market in the United States. Such factors have contributed considerably to the growth and development of the advertising industry in Latin America.

Although Latin American advertising has established a global presence, certain aspects of globalisation that fail to recognise the region's characteristics and cultural values nevertheless pose a hindrance to local development. So-called 'canned ads' exemplify this situation. The phrase refers to commercials that arrive from foreign markets and are broadcast in Latin America without any change. Such commercials are usually part of international advertising campaigns and therefore pay little respect to local cultural values (Gregory and Munch 1997; Ricks, 1993; Tansey *et al.*, 1990). A further issue still is the fact that advertising agencies' strategies are often 'cut and paste' from other markets without regard to local requirements. Table 5.1 shows the leading advertising agencies in Latin America in 2014. Of the 43 listed agencies, only nine are local; the remainder are owned by multinationals from the United States or Europe: Ogilvy; DDB; BBDO; Young & Rubicam; TBWA, Leo Burnett; JWT; Saatchi & Saatchi; Publicis or McCann Erickson. At the Cannes Lions International Festival of Creativity 2015, Ogilvy & Mather was recognised as the Advertising Network of the Year and the best in Latin America. As Table 5.1 reveals, Ogilvy & Mather operates across the region with offices in Brazil, Argentina, Colombia, Mexico and Costa Rica.

Uniqueness

Latin America is home to over 620 million inhabitants, making it the third most populous geographic region in the world (United Nations, 2014). It is a multicultural terrain with a mosaic of identities and hybrid cultures, with indigenous and mixes of the European, African and Asian populations (Canclini, 2005; Hall, 1987). However, Latin Americans also share significant similarities. These include: the Spanish language,[1] indigenous dialects, the Catholic religion, social inequalities, sexism, soap operas, salsa, exoticism, resourcefulness,[2] micro climates, natural resources, colonialism, diminutives, gastronomy, optimism, hospitality, kindness, shamanism, superstition, mysticism (Katz, 2015; Zárate, 2011; Del Pozo, 2002; Dabène, 1999).[3] Of these characteristics, we have selected two that have a very constant presence in Latin American advertising, and, in our opinion, are the most significant: poverty and male chauvinism.

One in four people in Latin America are poor, which equates to some 164 million poor people in the region. The strongest concentrations of poverty are to

Table 5.1 Ranking of the best advertising agencies, according to Adlatina (2014)

Country	Number of agencies	Names of the agencies
Brazil	12	1 Ogilvy & Mather Brazil 2 FCB Brazil 3 Loducca 4 DDB Brazil 5 Almap BBDO Brazil 6 Young & Rubicam Brazil 7 JWT Brazil 8 Borghi/Lowe Brazil 9 Santa Clara Brazil 10 Lew Lara TBWA Brazil 11 Isobar Brazil 12 Leo Burnett Tailor Made Brazil
Argentina	9	1 Del Campo S&S 2 Ogilvy & Mather Argentina 3 Leo Burnett Argentina 4 Grey Argentina 5 Ponce Argentina 6 Y&R Argentina 7 DON Argentina 8 David Buenos Aires 9 TBWA Buenos Aires
Colombia	6	1 Ogilvy & Mather Colombia 2 Lowe/SSP3 Colombia 3 Geometry Global Colombia 4 Sancho BBDO Colombia 5 Y&R Colombia 6 Leo Burnett Colombia
Peru	4	1 McCann Erickson Lima 2 FCB Mayo Peru 3 Fahrenheit DDB Peru 4 Publicis Peru
Mexico	4	1 Ogilvy & Mather Mexico 2 Circus Mexico 3 DDB Mexico 4 BBDO Mexico
Chile	3	1 Prolam Y&R Chile 2 Simple Chile 3 BBDO Chile
Costa Rica	2	1 Ogilvy & Mather Costa Rica 2 Leo Burnett Costa Rica
Puerto Rico	2	1 DDB Latina Puerto Rico 2 JWT San Juan Puerto Rico
Paraguay	1	1 Oniria TBWA Paraguay

be found in Honduras (67.4 per cent), Nicaragua (58.3 per cent) and Paraguay (54.8 per cent) (ECLAC, 2014). Illiteracy is an issue that is seldom addressed by advertising in the First World, but in Latin America it is the norm. In Peru, seven out of ten children do not understand what they read. An advertisement for the BBVA bank by Volver D6 agency sought to deal with this issue by raising funds for BBVA Foundation's programme 'Reading is to be ahead'. Typefaces on the bank's automatic teller machines were modified so as to prevent the user from reading. By generating this situation of cognitive dissonance for the user, the experience sought to raise awareness of illiteracy. Another example of advertising raising awareness of social problems was the campaign 'The complaint of the uncomfortable children' for Our Mexico of the Future Foundation. The campaign sought to encourage audiences to consider the future of their country by having children recreate situations of extreme violence, corruption, insecurity and poverty.

Latin America has a very traditional social structure, more so in some countries than others. The view that the man of the house works outside the home and contributes economically, while the woman looks after the children and the home is shared across the region (Arellano, 2002). The three countries with the highest rates of 'masculinity' according to the Hofstede Centre study are Venezuela (73 per cent), Mexico (69 per cent) and the Dominican Republic (65 per cent) (see Figure 5.1 above). In these nations, the relationship between husband and wife is usually characterised by a dominant man and a submissive woman. For men, the concept of male chauvinism is strong and identifies their gender and role within the household (Gregory and Munch, 1997). Advertising has thus been used to promote greater respect for women. The Independence agency's 'Whistle your mother' campaign for Everlast is one such example. The brand wanted to fight street sexual harassment, where men use obscene vocabulary upon seeing a woman on the street. Unbeknownst to the men depicted in the campaign, the 'unknown' women were in fact their own mothers. After the mothers saw that it was their own sons who harassed them, they scolded them in public. The video went viral and spread to other Latin American countries including Mexico, Colombia, Ecuador, Chile, Argentina and the US Latino population. However, such campaigns should not overshadow the fact that the media and advertising industries have played a major role in promoting the image of women as sex objects (Castillo and Mensa, 2009; Reichert *et al.*, 2007; Shields, 1997, Busby and Leichty, 1993; Ferguson *et al.*, 1990). Things are not necessarily any better within the advertising industry, where the number of women and opportunities for them are restricted. As the creative departments of advertising agencies are 79.7 per cent male and 20.3 per cent female, it seems that women will continue to struggle to change sexist stereotypes in advertisements (Grow and Deng, 2014; Mensa and Grow, 2015).

Arellano (2002) has a very optimistic view of advertising as social development. He believes that marketing can play an important role in assisting the progress of a society which lacks productive and financial resources. Thus, marketing not only becomes an instrument of success for companies in the market, but it can also be an important tool for social development. In general, it seems that advertising is gambling on advertisements where values such as companionship, friendship and kindness are central. It appears that this trend has been motivated by the economic crisis of 2008, since it was not only a crisis of figures but of values, marked by deception, dishonesty and power (Schneider, 2013). Declaring 'We are polite, let us always be,' McCann's campaign for the Chilean-owned Wong supermarket chain illustrated how advertising could be used to reiterate social values. Another case was the Circus Grey campaign for the BCP bank in Peru, which sought to encourage greater social harmony. Faced with the finding that 72 per cent of Peruvians think that the worst enemy of a Peruvian is another Peruvian, the campaign sought to challenge this mentality using a mix of controversy and intrigue.

Latin American creativity

According to Peruvian Pepe Funegra, creative director of the agency Mother NY, 'Ideas are universal'. If ideas are universal, then it stands that creativity is also universal. Of course, the way or manner in which these ideas are projected is influenced by the environment or the cultural context in which the creative work is produced (Kharkhurin and Samadpour, 2008). For Cohen (2012), adaptation is one of the most important factors in the analysis of creativity issues, since it implies that individuality and environment interconnect. Culture, tradition, values, customs, norms, behaviours and beliefs all influence a person's creativity (Rudowicz, 2003; Runco, 2007). Therefore, depending on the country where the creative is located, the cultural environment will affect his or her creativity. In Latin America, some countries are renowned for their creativity. Such creativity is often measured by the number of prizes won at advertising festivals. At the Cannes Lion International Festival of Creativity, Latin America won 214 awards in 2015 (see Table 5.2). The countries with the largest number of medals were Brazil, Mexico and Argentina. What makes these countries the most

Table 5.2 Medal Board for Latin America in Cannes 2015

Country	Grand Prix	Gold	Silver	Bronze	Awards
Brazil	1	18	35	53	107
Mexico	1	2	8	16	27
Argentina	0	8	7	11	26
Colombia	0	4	7	6	17
Ecuador	0	3	3	7	13
Chile	0	4	2	6	12
Peru	0	0	1	5	6
Puerto Rico	0	1	1	0	2
Uruguay	0	1	0	0	1
Venezuela	0	0	0	1	1
Costa Rica	0	0	0	1	1
Paraguay	0	0	0	1	1

creative in Latin America? What is their personality like as a country? These are some of the issues to be resolved next.

Brazil: open-mindedness

Brazil is the fifth most populous country in the world with more than 200 million inhabitants. From a list of 143 countries, it is ranked ninth in the Happy Planet Index (Brazil, 2015). The region has a Happiness Index of 61.0 per cent, higher than Argentina (59.0 per cent) or Mexico (55.6 per cent). Brazilians won the Grand Prix Film at Cannes in 2015. It was the first time a Brazilian entry had been awarded the coveted prize. The successful campaign was created by agency F/Nazca Saatchi & Saatchi from São Paulo, which celebrated the 100th anniversary of photography. Why did it take Brazil 62 years to win a Grand Prix? According to Fábio Fernandes, Brazilian president and creative director of F/Nazca Saatchi & Saatchi, 'It is easier to win a GP with Guinness than with Skol'. That is to say, a global brand is more likely to win at festivals than a local one.

Brazilians are said to be open-minded and somewhat less formal and conservative than other Latin Americans (Brazil Country Review, 2015). Their daring may even outrage a nation with an ad. This was the case with the campaign for the Brazilian Association of Organ Transplantation by Leo Burnett Tailor. The campaign featured an eccentric Brazilian millionaire who decides to bury his half-a-million dollar Bentley. Such madness generated significant negative reaction. But, on the day of the car's supposed funeral, the millionaire drew attention to the idea that many people bury things more valuable than a car: their organs. Another aspect to note is that Brazilians value art. They have impressive contemporary art museums such as those in Rio de Janeiro or São Paulo, and architectural surprises with Oscar Niemeyer's designs. São Paulo, the largest city in Latin America, is home to one of the largest outdoor urban art museums. Graffiti or *pixações* are ubiquitous on the walls of the city, making São Paulo the world capital of graffiti. The commercial 'The Art of Waiting' by Grey highlights this respect and admiration for urban art. In it, a graffiti artist paints a wall while he is calling his phone company to cancel his contract. This process lasts two hours and 11 minutes. The ad, made for the Association for the Protection of Consumer Rights, aims to shorten this activity and make life easier for Brazilians. It also won an award at Cannes in 2015. However, this type of communication would not work in Peru, for example. A recent controversy was caused by the mayor of Lima, who decided to remove murals of high artistic quality on account of them having no connection with the history of the capital. Such an attitude would have little place in the artistic and open-minded spirit of Brazil.

Mexico: identity

In terms of land mass, Mexico is the third largest country in Latin America (after Brazil and Argentina). However, in terms of population size, (it has a population of more than 120 million), it is second only to Brazil. According to the Institute for Mexicans Abroad (IME, 2014) approximately 33.6 million Mexicans live in the United States, Mexico's northern neighbour. This makes the United States the country where most Mexicans live, after Mexico. The economic forecasts for Mexico are positive. The Mexico Business Forecast Report (2015) predicts that by 2024 the country will have a strong economy generating significant foreign investment.

Mexican advertising had long been undervalued. Puerto (2006) suggests that this lack of attention stemmed from the fact that foreign ideas were recycled or adapted locally. Observing that advertising which does not reflect the local values of a culture will go unnoticed and will be ignored by consumers, Gregory and Munch (1997) suggest that Mexican advertising was also in danger of being ignored by consumers. Only gradually did Mexicans come to recognise that authenticity was the key to being different. Enrique Laguardia, Mexican advertising creative, underscores the importance of authenticity when he explains that 'my country is a giant that is emerging. The most important is to improve Mexican advertising creativity from within' (Puerto and Jesús, 2006, p. 95). This embrace of Mexican creativity has meant that Mexico is now second in the region for creative awards. In 2016, Mexican advertising won its first Grand Prix at Cannes. The campaign, called 'Always intimate words', was designed by Leo Burnett Mexico for Procter & Gamble. Discussing this achievement, the agency's general creative director, Fernando Bellotti, explained that 'Mexico is showing and bringing its rich culture to advertising', emphasising that 'the advertising has a local flavour' (Adlatina, 2014). The commercial covers an important local issue: women in the Zapotec culture, who do not use certain words related to female sexuality because they are considered taboo. This is why some medical conditions are misdiagnosed because the patients do not have the words to identify their illness. The ad reflects a very particular and cultural aspect: this is the identity that advertising in Latin America should aspire to achieve.

Argentina: satire

With a population of around 40 million, Argentina has one of the largest economies in South America. A culturally rich country, Argentina has a high level of education and enjoys the lowest illiteracy rate in Latin America. Unlike other Latin American countries, Argentina looks more to Europe than to the United States. This is, in part, a reflection of the influx of Italian and Spanish migrants (Argentina Country Report, 2015).

Argentinian advertising has earned international attention for its creative quality and its 'disruptive style' (Martin Llaguno and Baquerín de Riccitelli, 2011). Argentinian agencies are big sellers when it comes to their advertising. They also engage in extensive consumer insights research, picking up on insights that other agencies do not. When they gain an insight, they often squeeze the most out of it, reaching into the depths of human psychology and behaviour. The 'Message in a Bottle' advertisement by Del Campo Saatchi & Saatchi for Andes beer illustrates this approach. Based on the idea that some things are difficult to say face to face, the beer label carried a QR code where consumers could upload a message to be given to another person (along with the beer itself). It seems Argentines are the only ones in Latin America who can make fun of anything, and we mean *anything*! The ad 'Requiem' by Young & Rubicam Buenos Aires played on death; 'I Will Survive' by Del Campo Saatchi & Saatchi challenged bullying; and 'Hurricane Laura', also by Del Campo Saatchi & Saatchi, made fun of the fact that hurricanes are named after women. This is in fact one of the notable aspects of Argentinean advertising: irony and double meaning. To this end, Natalia Iriarte, an Argentine national and the creative director of the Peruvian agency Dodoconyoyo, muses that advertising in Argentina 'reflects the loud personality of its people'.

Other Latin American countries

Other countries in the region, including Chile, Colombia and Peru, are gradually developing more creative work. The most important agency in Chile is Prolam Young & Rubicam, which won eight Lions at the Cannes Lions International Festival of Creativity in 2015. Their best advertising campaign was for UNICEF to combat cyber bullying. The ads showed a group of school children with their mobile phones photographing other children in situations that degrade their self-esteem with the copy 'One shot is enough'.

Colombia's Geometry Global agency won a gold award at Cannes in 2015 for an advertisement for Colombia's Ministry of Environment and Natural Resources that connected local culture and environmentalism. Lionfish are an invasive species in the Caribbean that were endangering the livelihood of local fishermen. Geometry Global created a campaign which encouraged Colombians to eat the fish and incorporate its consumption into their diets.

Although Peru has won few international accolades, it has made some important creative contributions to advertising. One example of award winning work by Peruvian agencies was done by Mayo in Lima. Mayo created billboards that generate water. As it rarely rains in humid Lima, this campaign attracted significant attention. In demonstrating that real problems such as lack of water could be resolved, it hoped to persuade aspiring engineering students to study at the University of Engineering & Technology (UTEC) in Lima.

In 2016, Publicis Venezuela surprised the world when it won an award for the Alzheimer's Foundation. The campaign sought to encourage people to donate by creating a bank account number that was impossible to forget: 0000–0000–00–0000000000. Such creativity is all the more impressive in light of Venezuela's recent political and economic instability.

Cuba presents a very different situation, not for its advertising, but for its absence. It is devoid of any ad agencies, creative directors or spots. Publicity is restricted to propaganda campaigns in favour of the military government. As Cuba opens up to the outside world, it will present a new opportunity for advertising and creative ideas.

Conclusion

The presence of transnational agencies has caused advertising in Latin America to struggle to find its own identity. Since the 1920s, the Latin American advertising agency structure has been heavily influenced by agencies and advertisers from the United States. More recently, the industry has been more open to local Latin American cultures. To enhance cultural adaptation, transnational advertising has increasingly considered the cultural values of each country and integrated local norms into agency structures as well as in advertising content. Transnational agencies in Latin America have consequently found that they could generate a higher level of culturally relevant creativity.

Importantly, the increasing opportunities for Latin American agencies to create advertisements for global brands such as Coca-Cola or Toyota has provided them with greater opportunities to contribute to international advertising. On the flip side, these locally produced campaigns for global brands present an opportunity to honour local customs and build brand loyalty. Of course, significant creative work has been done for local brands, indicating that creativity is not the sole preserve of the big brands.

As Latin America is a developing marketplace, advertising in the region could and should leverage digital platforms. In this new era, we not only talk about globalisation but also 'digitisation'.[4] By 2017, it is estimated that mobile phone usage in Latin America will grow an average of 70 per cent a year (Katz, 2015). The growth in digital technology in Latin America suggests new avenues for growth in Latin American advertising, which is not dissimilar to opportunities in other developing marketplaces elsewhere in the world. With an eye on the future, advertisers in Latin America need to turn robustly towards digital communications.

The quality of advertising in Latin America may not reach the same level as that in the United States, the United Kingdom or Germany, but the region's advertising does offer much to the broader advertising industry and, indeed, to academia. Writing in the *International Journal of Advertising*, Charles R. Taylor (2012) observed that academic research on advertising had focused almost exclusively on English-speaking markets, forgetting the rest of the world. Noting that Latin America was emerging but relatively unknown, Taylor comments that 'The complete lack of articles on Brazil is particularly notable given the growth of this market and the quality of advertising it is known for'. Martin Llaguno and Baquerín de Riccitelli (2011) similarly express concern for the lack of studies on advertising in Argentina. As this study has helped demonstrate, there is much to be learnt from the campaigns and creative practices emerging in Latin America – for practitioners and scholars alike.

Notes

1 Six cultural dimensions framed Hofstede's original work. Each dimension is ranked on a scale of 1–100 (with 50 as the average) media. Uncertainty Avoidance is one of these dimensions and identifies the degree to which people respond to ambiguity and try to

avoid uncertainty (Hofstede Centre, 2014). Some countries have a '?'. This means that Hofstede Centre does not have this information.
2 Portuguese is spoken only in Brazil. Not all Brazilians speak English. For most, it is easier to understand Spanish than English.
3 In Spanish 'recurseo' is to look for casual income outside the usual activity.
4 It is difficult, but at the same time important, to answer the question 'What unites Latin Americans?' We made a list using the brainstorming technique, but we know that the degree to which these characteristics apply varies across each Latin American country.

References

Adlatina (2014) *Online Newsletter Covering the Advertising Industry in all of the Latin American and Iberian Countries*. Available at: www.adlatina.com (accessed 11 November 2016).

Arellano, R. (2002) *Comportamiento del consumidor: Enfoque América Latina (Consumer behaviour: Latin America Focus)*. Mexico: McGraw-Hill.

Argentina Country Report (2015) *Argentina Country Review*. Houston, TX: Country-Watch, pp. 1–259.

Barshefsky, C. and Hill, J. T. (2008) *Relaciones Estados Unidos–América Latina: una nueva dirección para una nueva realidad (US–Latin American relations: A New Direction for a New Reality)*. New York: Council on Foreign Relations.

Brazil 2015 Country Review (2015) *Brazil Country Review*, pp. 1–217.

Buitrago, P. F. and Duque, I. (2013) *The Orange Economy: An Infinite Opportunity*. New York: Inter-American Development Bank.

Busby, L. and Leichty, G. (1993) 'Feminism and advertising in traditional and nontraditional women's magazines 1950s–1980s', *Journalism Quarterly*, 70, pp. 247–65.

Canclini, N. G. (2005) *Hybrid Cultures: Strategies for Entering and Leaving Modernity*. Minneapolis, MN: University of Minnesota Press.

Castillo, G. and Mensa, M. (2009) 'Estudio sobre la imagen de la mujer peruana en la publicidad gráfica del suplemento sabatino Somos' (Peruvian women's image: a content analysis of the roles by woman in print advertisements), *Journal of Communication*, 8, pp. 145–66.

Cepal (2014) *Panorama Social de América Latina (Latin America Social Outlook)*, Santiago de Chile: United Nations Economic Commission for Latin America and the Caribbean.

Coe, A., Hamilton, S. and Tarr, S. (2004) 'Product purchase decision-making behavior and gender role stereotypes: a content analysis of advertisements in *Essence* and *Ladies' Home Journal*, 1990–1999', *The Howard Journal of Communications*, 15, pp. 229–43.

Cohen, L. M. (2012) 'Adaptation and creativity in cultural context', *Journal of Psychology*, 30(1), pp. 4–18.

Dabène, O. (1999) *América Latina en el Siglo XX (Latin America in the Twentieth Century)*. Madrid: Síntesis.

Del Campo, P. (2009) *Advertising Age*, 80 (22).

Del Pozo (2002) *Historia de América Latina y del Caribe, 1985–2001 (Latin American and Caribbean History, 1985–2001)*. Santiago de Chile: Lom.

ECLAC (2014) *Economic Survey of Latin America and the Caribbean 2014: Challenges to Sustainable Growth in a New External Context*, Economic Commission for Latin

America and the Caribbean. Available at: www.cepal.org/en/node/32228 (accessed 7 March 2017).

The Economist (2010) 'A special report on Latin America: So near and yet so far'. *The Economist*, 9 September. Available at: http://adage.com/article/global-news/top-100-global-advertisers-world-opportunity/147436 (accessed 11 November 2016).

Ferguson, H. H., Kreshel, P. and Tinkham, S. (1990) 'In the pages of Ms: Sex role portrayals of women in advertising', *Journal of Advertising*, 19, pp. 40–51.

Gregory, G. D. and Munch, J. M. (1997) 'Cultural values in international advertising: An examination of familial norms and roles in Mexico', *Psychology & Marketing*, 14(2), pp. 99–119.

Grow, J. M. and Deng, T. (2014) 'Sex segregation in advertising creative departments across the globe', *Advertising and Society Review*, pp. 14–24.

Hall, S. (1987) 'Identity: the real me: Post-Modernism and the question of identity', *Ica Documents*, 6, pp. 44–6.

Hofstede Centre (2015). 'The Hofstede Centre'. Available at: https://geert-hofstede.com/the-hofstede-centre.html/ (accessed 11 November 2016).

IME (2014) *Statistics of the Mexican Population in the World*. Institute for Mexicans Abroad. Available at: www.ime.gob.mx (accessed 11 November 2016).

InformaBTL (2013) *Global AdView Pulse Report*. Available at: www.informabtl.com (accessed 11 November 2016).

Johnson, B. (2010) 'Top 100 global advertisers see world of opportunity', *Advertising Age*. Available at: http://adage.com/article/global-news/top-100-global-advertisers-world-opportunity/147436 (accessed 11 November 2016).

Kang, M. E. (1997) 'The portrayal of women's images in magazine advertisements: Goffman's gender analysis revisited', *Sex Roles*, 37, pp. 979–96.

Katz, R. (2015) *El ecosistema y la economia digital en América Latina (The ecosystem and the digital economy in Latin America)*. Madrid: Fundación Telefónica y Ariel.

Kharkhurin, A. V. and Samadpour, S. N. (2008) 'The impact of culture on the creative potential of American, Russian and Iranian college students', *Creativity Research Journal*, 20 (4), pp. 404–11.

Martin Llaguno, M. and Baquerín de Riccitelli, T. (2011) 'Radiografía del sector publicitario argentino: características sociodemográficas, organizacionales y actitudinales de la fuerza laboral de la comunicación comercial' (Argentine advertising industry: socio-demographic, organisational and attitudinal characteristics of the labour force of commercial communication). *Ecos de la comunicación*, 4(4), pp. 75–92.

Mayo, D., Mayo, C. and Mahdi, S. (2005) 'Skin tones in magazine advertising: Does magazine type matter?', *Journal of Promotion Management*, 11, pp. 49–59.

Mensa, M. and Grow, J. (2015) 'Creative women in Peru: Outliers in a machismo world', *Communication & Society*, 28(2), pp. 1–18.

Mexico Country Risk Report (2015) *Mexico Business Forecast Report*, (2), pp. 1–55.

Piketty, T. (2013) *Capital in the Twenty-First Century*. Cambridge, MA: The Belknap Press of Harvard University Press.

Puerto, F. D. J. C. (2006) 'Creatividad publicitaria y creativos en México: Una aproximación' (Advertising Creativity and Mexico Creative: An Approach). Unpublished Masters in Communication Thesis. México. D.F: Universidad Iberoamericana.

Reichert, T., Latour, M., Lambiase, J. and Adkins, M (2007) 'A test of media literacy effects and sexual objectification in advertising', *Journal of Current Issues and Research in Advertising*, 29, pp. 81–92.

Ricks, D. A. (1993) *Blunders in International Business.* Cambridge, MA: Blackwell Publishers.

Rudowicz, E. (2003) 'Creativity and culture: A two-way interaction'. *Scandinavian Journal of Educational Research*, 47, pp. 273–90.

Runco, M. A. (2007) *Development Trends and Influences on Creativity.* Burlington, MA: Elsevier Academic Press.

Schneider, B. (2013) *La empresa y la gerencia: Post-crisis de una época de cambios a un cambio de época* (The Company and Management: A Post-crisis Era to a New Era). Lima: El Comercio.

Shields, V. R. (1997) 'Selling the sex that sells: Mapping the evolution of gender advertising research across three decades', *Communication Yearbook*, pp. 71–109.

Sinclair, J. (2013) 'The advertising industry in Latin America: A regional portrait'. In: McAllister, Matthew P. and West, Emily (eds), *The Routledge Companion to Advertising and Promotional Culture.* London and New York: Routledge, pp. 115–30.

Statista (2015) *Facts on The Advertising Industry in Latin America.* Available at: www.statista.com/topics/1499/advertising-in-latin-america (accessed 11 November 2016).

Tansey, R., Hyman, M. R. and Zinkhan, G. M. (1990) 'Cultural themes in Brazilian and United States auto ads: A cross-cultural comparison', *Journal of Advertising*, 19(2), pp. 30–39.

Taylor, C. R. (2012) 'On advertising in the BRICs and other emerging markets', *International Journal of Advertising*, 31(2), pp. 227–30.

Tulchin, J. S. (2016) *América Latina x Estados Unidos: uma relação turbulenta* (*Latin America and the United States: A Turbulent Relationship*). Sao Paulo: Editora Contexto. United Nations (2014) *Informe la situación demográfica en el mundo* (*Demographic Situation Report in the World*). New York: United Nations.

Wentz, L. (2010) 'Why so many agencies are storming road to São Paulo', *Ad Age*. Available at: http://adage.com/article/global-news/brazil-drawing-ad-agencies-globe/147480 (accessed 11 November 2016).

Woodard, J. P. (2002) 'Marketing modernity: The J. Walter Thompson Company and North American advertising in Brazil, 1929–1939', *Hispanic American Historical Review*, 82(2), pp. 257–90.

Zárate, Y. (2011) 'Revisiting Latin American Communications and Culture', *Westminster Papers in Communication and Culture*, 8(1), pp. 1–6.

6 Not an island: the symbiotic connection of the UK and global advertising industry

Matthew Hook

From wild West End to global epicentre

Whilst Madison Avenue in New York may be the iconic place in the mythos of the global advertising industry, London's West End and in particular Soho must surely be a close competitor. The history of the two cities has been firmly entwined since the mid-twentieth century and in its own right London has left an indelible mark on both the shape of the advertising industry and its prevailing culture. The UK's most famous advertising luminary, Sir Martin Sorrell, is not only the CEO of the largest organisation by far in the history of the advertising industry, but is also a direct link back to the heady days of the 1960s–1980s when the British advertising made its global reputation through agencies such as CDP, Saatchi & Saatchi and BBH.

In this golden era, the twin roots were established that continue to nourish the UK's role in the advertising world today. One is a reputation for a cerebral approach to the business of advertising that continues to see strategic departments full of Brits in agencies all over the world. The other is an appetite for innovation in the business model of advertising, with a constant questioning of the role of the agency and of the operational model that sits behind it. Amongst other innovations, London is the ancestral home of the prevailing models of the acquisition-hungry holding company, the rise of communications planning as a discipline, and the success of the independent global media agency network.

Globalisation sits at the heart of a proper understanding of the UK's current place in the advertising world. In its own right, the UK economy is not as significant a proportion of global adspend and of the ambitions of global marketing organisations as it used to be. The globalisation of media is putting great pressure on some of the key domestic organisations as it is in many other markets globally. And the status of British creativity in advertising is not necessarily as elevated as it used to be, with the rapid ascent of other creative communities around the world, from Silicon Valley to Shanghai, and the migration of advertising away from the wry cultural observation (in which British advertising has always specialised) to a style that travels more easily across the world. For the moment, London remains one of the great cities of the global advertising economy, and indeed the rest of the UK also has a strong advertising and communications sector that represents an estimated value of US$6 billion to the UK economy.

Globalisation is a phenomenon under examination around the world, and no more so than in the UK, which is likely to have left the EU by 2018/19. However, as the advertising industry adapts to the requirements of a digital economy, driven by personal connectivity and the demands of modern business, an understanding of its role in the global advertising ecosystem is fundamental to understanding the dynamics of the UK advertising business.

The UK in global context – market, cluster, region and hub

The region in which the UK sits, largely described as either Europe or EMEA (Europe, Middle East and Africa) according to different global structures, is an extremely complex one, so the impacts of globalisation are multilayered and nuanced. Unlike some other large nations, the media landscape is relatively nationally homogeneous, and local media and marketing is a relatively small part of the picture (though Manchester and Edinburgh in particular are significant advertising hubs). However, this relatively simple national picture exists in a global context of markets, clusters, regions and hubs.

Europe is best understood not as one market (though some global organisations class it as such) but as 55+ independent markets, clustered and tiered in terms of a variety of dynamics including size, digital maturity, language and strength of culture similarity. Between markets there can be areas of extreme difference, such as attitudes to data policy (e.g. Germany has one of the world's most restrictive policies on the use of personal data for commercial purposes, possibly owing to its post-war political heritage), penetration of eCommerce (weekly usage anything between 2 per cent and 29 per cent across EMEA), and indeed the structure of agency relationships (e.g. very different models of remuneration and media-buying models) (see Figure 6.1). In all these areas, there is a gradual equalisation process, but the journey is not linear and current suspicion of the EU, for example, will add a new counter-balance to this trend.

The economic power and leverage of globalisation is an unstoppable force, that has seen the worlds of marketing communications, media ownership and advertising technology continue to internationalise over time. Thus in the UK, as in most markets, advertising industry remains a balanced hybrid between the local and the international. However, London's role as a hub for the region, and particularly as a bridge between US-centred global businesses and the rest of the world, continues to give the UK a more international perspective than the regional norm. Both the supply side (media owners and technology) and the demand side (advertisers) are still evenly balanced between global and domestically players – though this level of internationalisation varies considerably by business categories.

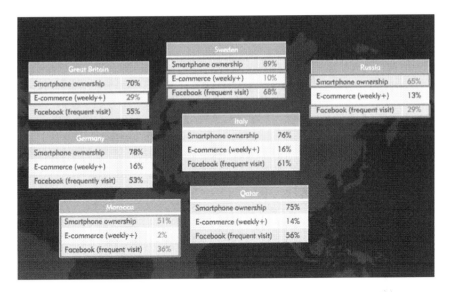

Figure 6.1 The Consumer Connections Study 2016, Carat.

Locally driven businesses

Those categories which depend on large amounts of physical infrastructure, or that have highly localised regulatory frameworks, continue to support primarily localised businesses, whose approach to marketing communications is therefore also localised. Retail, banking and utility firms are generally local in operation, and, whilst in some cases they may be part of global organisations (e.g. Asda, Aldi and Lidl as food retailers with overseas owners, Santander as a global banking brand), advertising still tends to be primarily localised.

Another major market phenomenon is that telecommunications remain focused primarily on maximising the opportunities for technology convergence within markets. As such, these advertisers primarily operate locally, as they invest deeply in the battle for share of household connectivity. This is likely to change rapidly in the next five years, as the industry internationalises, but for the moment this means some of the biggest players are primarily UK-focused. In particular, this category includes Sky, a prominent player in entertainment, broadcasting, sports and connectivity, and a clear spend leader in the UK market at present.

When adding in the UK government (still a prominent voice but increasingly focused on efficiency and on digital communications in the post-recession era), 18 of the market's top 30 advertisers are primarily or entirely local in their advertising communications.

Whilst the proportion of locally driven advertisers may be gradually decreasing, these businesses experience a significantly higher level of creative freedom

Table 6.1 Adspend in the United Kingdom

Advertiser	2015 Expenditure
British Sky Broadcasting Ltd	£223,914,187
Procter & Gamble Ltd	**£208,937,129**
BT Ltd	£162,540,474
Unilever UK Ltd	**£140,009,567**
Virgin Media	£122,370,645
Reckitt Benckiser (UK) Ltd	**£100,263,883**
Asda Stores Ltd	£85,213,470
Lidl UK Gmbh	**£84,534,834**
Tesco Plc	£78,241,575
Mcdonalds Restrs Ltd	**£73,516,786**
Dfs Furniture Co Ltd	£71,712,316
Aldi Stores Ltd	£69,801,901
Sainsburys Supermarkets Ltd	£67,200,927
Jd Williams & Co Ltd	£66,999,178
Dsg Intl Holdings Plc	£64,667,096
Marks & Spencer	£64,209,716
Nestlé	**£63,769,778**
Vodafone Ltd	**£59,259,070**
Wm Morrison Supermarkets Plc	£57,497,487
Boots The Chemists Ltd	£56,639,422
Loreal Paris	**£54,740,036**
Amazon (UK) Ltd	**£52,243,199**
Argos Ltd	£51,339,150
Microsoft Ltd	**£47,946,214**
Shop Direct Home Shopping Ltd	£46,230,027
Mars Confectionery	**£45,939,906**
British Gas Plc	£45,657,168
O2/Telefonica	**£45,212,061**
Talktalk Group	£43,580,169
Specsavers Optical Group Ltd	£40,906,557

Source: Nielsen, 2015.

and the ability to calibrate budgets to local growth opportunities rather than global prioritisation. The net result is that local advertisers punch above their weight in investment levels, particularly in adspend growth and also in creative recognition.

International advertisers

In almost any category where there are strong, internationally integrated players, the UK is a Top 5 market by sales value. This means that categories such as FMCG, fashion, alcoholic drinks, technology, leisure and entertainment are mainly dominated by international players. For most of these advertisers, marketing has some kind of multimarket structure in place, and, whilst media investment continues to be predominantly localised, 'creative' is often primarily defined at a global, regional and cluster level. This is generally accompanied by a shared multimarket point of view on best practice. This creates some tensions at the local level, but is overall perceived by international businesses as reducing organisational duplication and driving best practice in both efficiency and growth.

The UK has a unique role to play in marketing operations for these international businesses, and this has a big impact on the nature of the advertising business in market. Relatively few of the biggest global spenders are actually headquartered in the UK, but those that are include some of the most iconic international advertisers, such as Diageo, British Airways and Vodafone. However, even for global businesses that are not UK-based, the London advertising industry tends to take a central role in the global management of marketing. International businesses based or regionally hubbed in places such as Geneva, Dublin and Amsterdam will be drawn to the creative, media and global coordination talent of London. It is also fairly commonplace for both US businesses operating globally (e.g. Microsoft) and Asian businesses looking to access global markets (e.g. Huawei) to use London rather than the home market as the hub of global activities. This has a significant effect on the UK advertising industry, which continues to see international talent and international communications work as a central part of the UK media scene.

On a slightly smaller scale, London is also one of several cities that acts as a hub for the 'cluster' model favoured by many international organisations looking to create some simplicity in the management of Europe as a market. This is particularly relevant to some of the big global packaged goods businesses, such as P&G, Unilever, J&J, Beiesdorf, Coca-Cola and Reckitt Benckiser, all of which operate some kind of cluster system. It is most common to see a substantial proportion of northwest Europe aligned within a cluster that is usually driven from the UK. This cluster usually includes the UK, Ireland and the Nordic nations and sometimes extends further afield.

Marketing globalisation – what next?

For most international businesses, the roles and responsibilities of global, regional, cluster and markets are constantly being reviewed for their ability to deliver marketing efficiency, effectiveness, and creative and cultural relevance, and there are no easy answers. Most international businesses will demand efficiencies across markets, which lead to the consolidation of marketing, of creative development, of agency choice and of marketing approaches, and businesses see significant effectiveness and efficiency improvements in these areas. It can, of course, also lead to the commoditisation of the industry, and places pressure both on the ability of marketing to be culturally relevant, and on the business models of the partners and agencies involved. It is, however, difficult to see any likely reversal of the underlying trend of globalisation and therefore of the importance of the global market to the UK advertising industry.

The question that hangs in the air in the UK advertising industry is whether it can retain this strong role in the UK advertising business. In April 2016, the

Advertising Association launched a report called Advertising Pays 4, which showed a national industry more bullish than ever about its contribution to the global advertising business. This report attempted to quantify the huge contribution of the UK's status in global advertising on the UK economy, quoting £4.1 billion in annual 'exports of advertising services', 35 per cent of revenue in the top 20 UK ad business deriving from overseas custom, and the UK consistently punching above its weight in industry recognition (coming, a consistent second to the USA in subjective assessments such as Cannes Awards). As a strong understanding of emerging markets becomes more and more important, particularly those in Asia and Africa, the UK remains an important source of international talent and coordination.

But there is little doubt that the UK industry will continue to look over its shoulder. The location of the world's largest companies is changing over time—the depth of internationally focused talent in markets such as the US and China continue to build at pace, and levels of creative and digital sophistication are progressively accelerating all over the world. In this context, the spectre of 'Brexit' from the European Union casts potential uncertainty over the UK advertising industry. Whilst it is the short-term impact on the UK and European economy and, in particular, adspend budgets that is preoccupying minds at the moment, it is the potential longer-term impacts of access to talent that could cast more of a pall over the UK's role in the global advertising economy. If the free movement of talent from across Europe into London becomes more difficult, and if more international businesses look for hubs in other markets with easier access to the single European market, then the internationalism that has underpinned the UK's success over the last couple of decades could be compromised.

Globalisation – impact on advertising practice

With scalability so central to the role of the UK in the global marketing economy, it is unsurprising that this dynamic is also having a direct impact on the kind of work that is prevalent within the contemporary advertising industry. Historically, the UK's 'house style' of advertising has been humorous, tightly culturally observed and self-aware – and built around a tradition of TV and print advertising. With the increased focus on scalability across markets and through a more complex advertising ecosystem, it is difficult not to see the classic creative edge of UK advertising as slightly blunted.

There are, of course, exceptions. Work such as adam&eveDDB's work for UK retailers Harvey Nicholls and John Lewis, and FCB's perception shifting 'This Girl Can' campaign for Sport England (see Figure 6.2) has continued the British advertising tradition of emotional connection and brilliant cultural observation, whilst making the most of the opportunities for digital amplification. There is also exciting work happening in the market to localise global brands in a way that connects more deeply with local cultures, particularly through digital and experiential platforms that are most meaningful to the new generation of digital native customers. Adidas initiatives with Carat such as BaseBrixton

(Figure 6.2) and ProjectX are connecting with audiences in a way that links global equity to local experience, with a more direct impact on consumer. This kind of smart localisation is on the rise and is a challenge to the 'big is better' approach to global advertising practice.

But the prevailing focus of recent years has arguably been on standardisation and optimisation rather than on cultural resonance. There are two dominant strains of thinking which have brought advertising practice to its current state, and as these streams of thought mature, we begin to see the emergence of a new kind of practice.

The first is Byron Sharp's seminal work 'How Brands Grow', which has made deep roots in most global marketing organisations, particularly in FMCG. This has brought with it an intense focus on maximising reach and penetration at the expense of niche communities and platforms. In many businesses this has led to the creation of a series of best practice rules that are deployed in a more or less standardised way across markets, with a decreased focus on the cultural and media dynamics of the markets themselves.

This strain of thinking is now being challenged and refined at the most senior level of some businesses. Whilst it has been valuable in focusing organisation on the most scaled opportunities, it has become too restrictive for some, and not focused enough on the specific needs of attracting new and diverse types of customer. In the digital economy landscape scale can be achieved in many different ways, and, whilst the principle of 'penetration first' is likely to sustain, the primacy of recency-based TV communication and standardised international toolkits will continue to be challenged.

The second is an increased focus by most global organisations on the better leverage of data as a strategic asset. In a digital landscape activity is much more immediately visible and measurable than ever before, and the opportunity to use media not only as a distribution platform but as a sensor for the business is increasingly valuable. This has brought with it many challenges around the management, fusion and application of complex data sets, and the relevant application of technology for targeting and sequencing purposes – but as these challenges of delivery and attribution are resolved, businesses see uplifts in activity performance that are drawing an ever greater share of effort and of investment.

Figure 6.2 'This Girl Can' and BaseBrixton campaigns.

The danger of this practice is perhaps that it can create an over-focus on opti-misation of historical performance, rather than growth. If performance marketing is the yardstick of advertising quality, this challenges the primacy of creativity and emotional connection, and thus leads businesses to focus on those who are ready to convert rather than those who are still yet to be convinced. This also creates a clear conflict between the penetration and optimisation mindsets, which in many organisations is as yet unresolved, and creates a schism between brand and performance marketing specialists.

The need for scalable impact, combined with the need for intelligent, data driven optimisation to maximise short- and long-term business performance, are not dynamics that will go away any time soon. In fact, an ever more global, more digitised marketing ecosystem will drive the need for these dynamics further and faster as time continues. However, the nature of both disciplines is maturing rapidly, and a much-needed more balanced practice is emerging.

A new emerging practice – scaled and personal

There is a new emerging practice in advertising, focused on reconciling the potential conflict between scale and personalisation. It recognises the need for a clear unifying equity for a business, expressed in a recognisable and distinctive way over time, but in a way that is more driven by the fundamental purpose, values and proposition of a business, rather than by a neatly observed 'advert-ising layer' that acts as a proxy for brand equity. It also recognises the need to consistently meet the customer on their terms in the channel and moment that is most relevant for them, creating a meaningful next step in their relationship with the business that connects how they engage with a business, how they are ser-viced and how they transact. It is therefore more closely linked to practice in the rest of the business, with advertising operating more as an extension of the overall business rather than as a proxy for it.

In a sense, this represents no more than a return to the simplicity of communi-cations approach that you would see in a small business or a start up. However, the practice of applying this for scaled domestic and international businesses is extremely challenging, and lays down tough challenges for both the marketing organisation and for the agency model. It demands of businesses that they connect the many data sources and KPIs in their business to create a single view of the cus-tomer and a single view of growth. It demands ways of working that bring data much closer to decision-making, with areas such as visualisation and agility of marketing process thus extremely hot topics. And it also requires a reduction in the distance between creativity and technology, between long-term and short-term business planning, which generally requires some extremely aggressive silo-breaking within both client business structures and agency team structures.

We see an extremely dynamic moment in the marketing industry, where the status quo is being challenged on all sides, and this may be sharply accelerated by the pressures of a probable economic slowdown. In the short term, one effect is a wave of client-side restructures, and constant challenges to the agency model. To an extent, this is a transition, but more realistically this kind of less fixed agency–client relationship is probably the new normal – more reflective of the kind of practices one would see in the emerging start-up world than the established certainties of the traditional manufacturing-based advertising model.

As things stand, this more agile, innovative and data-centric approach is easier to deliver for smaller and more local organisations, meaning that scale is not the competitive advantage that it once was. In response, the world's major marketing organisations are looking to agencies to accelerate the pace of change, as well as to drive significant business efficiencies that support the cost of internal and external transformation. This is having a significant impact on the agency landscape.

Key players in the agency market – groups, networks and new challengers

Whilst it is the agency brands that continue to attract clients, talent and the attentions of journalists, agency groups increasingly represent the real competitive landscape of the UK advertising market for both global and domestic clients. Whilst waves of independents continue to challenge and disrupt in all the major agency sectors, the major holding companies (WPP, Dentsu Aegis Network, Publicis, Omnicom, IPG and Havas) dominate, and it is not only their brands and their commercial offerings but their combined capabilities and internal operating models that are in competition.

This is not in itself a new dynamic. The UK media marketplace has traditionally strongly advantaged scale, and group trading has been a fact of life for some time, a trend that has historically benefitted WPP's Group M brands, which some time ago secured a very large share of the UK market. Unlike in some other markets, the strong heritage of media independence in this market means that integrated creative and media models are relatively rare, and often driven by commercial rather than marketing considerations, meaning that some of the new models created are short-lived. However, the role of the agency group is now changing in response to the need for an ever-extending set of deep specialisms in data modelling, digital performance, social, mobile, content and ecommerce. Clients are demanding more dynamic agency models, and therefore there is stiff competition in the market to assemble the best specialist capabilities within one single client service model.

All holding companies are therefore looking to rapidly and dramatically extend their scope of capabilities. This is manifested in both internal diversification of services and products, particularly in the digital space, and also in a highly competitive acquisition market where the groups look to acquire in particular digital and data startups to round out their offerings. WPP and Dentsu have exhibited the most aggressive growth ambitions in the digital space and have been the most acquisitive. It is also notable that other players are looking to acquire UK-based agencies, with the arrival in the acquisition market of the major global consultancy firms particularly notable.

As well as the creation and acquisition of new capabilities, the major advertising groups are also competing on their ability to bring these capabilities together, and this is resulting in progressive change in leadership structures, P&L models and brand portfolios. There is no clear consensus on the best model, and this is one of the clearest differentiators between the different groups. The most clearly defined models are the 'client agency', built on horizontal capabilities drawn from across the group (most championed by WPP, and evidenced in the 'Team Red' construct for Vodafone), and the group 'single P&L model', where all agencies report into a single CEO and strategy per market (most fully realised by Dentsu Aegis Network.) Other groups, most visibly Publicis, continue to search for the most effective model to bring their resources together for their clients and to create the most fluid internal culture.

In an agency environment that is increasingly globalised and fluid at a group level, it is some of the big agencies with the proudest records that are finding the market most challenging, both culturally and in terms of the new economic model of advertising. Recent times have seen some of the most famous names, in UK advertising such as Saatchi and BBH suffer, while more recent names such as adam&eve and VCCP, have adapted more quickly to the changed landscape. They duly gained a reputation for effective collaboration and contemporary creative excellence, and thus thrived. As well as these fast-growing 'semi-independent' agencies, the UK continues to see success for new players who offer an alternative to the highly consolidated agency market, such as 7stars in media and Lucky Generals in creative.

However, over time it is likely that with the scale and complexity of the demands of the large global advertisers, the consolidation trend will continue. These businesses require the fusion of media, creative, data and digital specialist capabilities into one ecosystem and one solution, with the most simplicity possible. Thus the continuing battle to create hyper-consolidated advertising groups with fully rounded capabilities and integrated operating models will continue and accelerate, and as an international hub and an important talent centre for global businesses the UK will continue to be at the heart of the battleground.

The health of the global–local ecosystem – key tensions

The growth and vibrancy of the UK advertising market has been heavily informed by its intense connectivity to the global market. However, as in many markets around the world, there are tensions in the global–local ecosystem to which the industry will need to find solutions over the next few years.

One area of challenge is in the content creation business. The UK broadcast business remains fairly buoyant, with both Sky and ITV benefitting from diversified businesses, the strength of video in both the advertising and the content market, and, in Sky's case, the increasing potential of the convergent home. Of course, revenue growth in the market is almost entirely digital, with social, mobile and programmatic driving the fastest change, but across all media channels, media companies are taking up the gauntlet of media transformation and to different degrees of success are readapting their business models to future-proof themselves. However, of all the UK's media institutions, it is probably newspaper publishers that are the most iconic, but also the most pressurised by the simultaneous digitisation and globalisation of the media landscape.

A very large proportion of advertising growth in the last few years has understandably been concentrated within social, mobile and digital video platforms, and in this the greatest beneficiaries by far have been the major global media businesses, Google, Facebook, AOL, Microsoft and Twitter. These players offer huge perceived benefits to all advertisers in terms of access to attentive audiences and useful data to drive performance. They are particularly appealing to major global advertisers, as they offer the prospect of international standardisation and excellence, and are creating relationships with both advertisers and agencies that go beyond inventory and embrace data, customised solutions and capability development.

On the back of these platforms, new content businesses both international and local such as Buzzfeed, Vice and LadBible are growing in audience and revenue rapidly. But this growth in investment experience by platforms and new-era publishers has to come at someone's expense, and in the UK it is the traditional publishing businesses, particularly those focused on quality journalism, that are particularly hurting. The *Guardian* has recently announced huge operating losses and the pressure is on (as with other legacy content creation businesses) to find a redefined role and business model in response to a more globalised advertising economy.

The rise of globalisation is also creating in the UK increasing pressures and new challenges for parts of the agency value system. The services delivered by agencies have never been more obviously important in the delivery of business outcomes for businesses and indeed for their own internal transformation, but the emerging business model is far from clear. More globalised operation tends to bring with it more demand for global cost efficiency, but also for clearly defined and consistent measures of value and more transparent business practices. With the degree of complexity involved in some of the new disciplines this is not an easy feat, but needs to be resolved for agencies to continue to be successful drivers or growth and transformation. The resolution is most likely in more clearly outcome-dependent remuneration models, but progress on this front remains fairly slow.

Conclusion

This chapter has been written in the shadow of a referendum to leave Europe and the start of a 'Brexit' process that could last anything between three and 20 years. The jarring effect of this vote on British culture can hardly be overestimated, and the uncertainty of the potential future effect of Brexit on the British economy and on its relationships with the international community is being constantly scrutinised.

However, the UK and, in particular, its advertising industry are deeply and fundamentally entwined with the effects of globalisation. The UK is one of the most important hubs of an increasingly globalised marketing, creative, digital and media economy. The list of key advertisers in the market will become more dominated by global businesses over time, and they will continue to seek simplicity through different centralised structures in which the UK will continue to play a key role. Global businesses will continue to search for communications models that achieve both great scale and are also adaptive to the national and personal needs of their customers, and this will deeply affect the next phase of change for agencies, driven by access to data capabilities and organisational models. And the rise of the global media and technology players will continue – indigenous media will have to adapt at speed to the changing context.

Globalisation is a major disruption to deep-rooted local practices and cultures in advertising, as it is in other areas of business and society. Thus far, the UK has successfully adapted at the speed of the market and this supports an advertising industry that is as strong as any in the world. Its ability to continue to adapt will have a significant impact on its future.

7   Advertising in Western Europe

The influence of digital media and sustainability

Isidoro Arroyo-Almaraz and Lilia Ivana Mamic

Introduction

This chapter offers an overview of advertising practice in Western Europe, with a particular focus on southern European countries. It highlights two elements that have influenced and shaped recent advertising in the region as well as its near future: the financial crisis and digital media. The global financial crisis has had a significant in southern Europe, forcing countries in the region to adapt quickly and to embrace digital media fully. Specifically, this chapter addresses the case of Spain as the European country with the largest growth in ad spending – in 2015 Spanish advertisers increased their budgets by 21 per cent to advertise their brands on digital channels. In addition, the 48 awards obtained in the 2015 edition of the Cannes Lions International Festival and the 118 awards gained in the latest edition of the Ibero-American Advertising Festival El Sol demonstrate the effort and professionalism of Spanish advertising campaigns (Adforum, 2015a).

European industry and its role in the global market

The European Union (EU) occupies a major position in the world trade market, being one of the main global exchanges for goods and services, along with China and the United States. The EU represents the largest and most integrated free trade area in the world and its economic liberalization has had numerous beneficial impacts on member states. For instance, trade has been a major source of employment. According to the EU, 31 million jobs in Europe depend, directly or indirectly, on trade. Last year, the EU gross domestic product (GDP) was €18.46 billion (World Bank, 2016). Competitiveness and an operational banking union provide a stronger foundation for cross-boarding capital flows, which have transformed Europe into a more attractive place for business and foreign investors.

The EU has been able to maintain a strong position in the trade of goods while also reinforcing its leadership in the services trade market. EU members' trade accounts for approximately 20 per cent of imports and exports with the rest of the world. According to Eurostat, the EU exported a total of €1,702.9 billion in goods and €734.8 billion in services in 2014. The principal commodities that the EU exported outside its region were machinery and transport equipment, while the major export of services was related to business services. Imports reflect a similar situation.

When looking at EU partners, the main clients are the United States, which acquired 18.3 per cent of EU share in goods exports, and China, which absorbed 9.7 per cent. On the other hand, China is the principal goods supplier to the EU, followed by the United States (with 18 per cent and 12.2 per cent respectively). Leading services clients are also the United States (26.4 per cent of shares in EU exports) and Switzerland (14.1 per cent of shares) while the same relationships applied for imports, such that the leading supplier position is occupied by the United States (31.2 per cent of EU services), followed by Switzerland which supplied 11.3 per cent of imported EU services in 2014 (EUROSTAT, 2015).[1]

Despite the growing importance of emerging economies, the EU remains one of the largest investors in and recipients of foreign direct investment (FDI). Despite the financial crisis still hitting economies around the globe, the EU offers foreign-owned firms the guarantees they need to develop their businesses, which are also ensured by an open and competitive market. Furthermore, technological progress, particularly in transport and information and communication technologies, increasingly allows firms to reorganise their production processes given the expansion of global value chains, locating different parts of their activities around the world. In the context of an increasingly globalised and interdependent world economy, investments to and from the rest of the world ensure that the EU is well positioned in world markets and able to profit from worldwide technology flows.

How is the aforementioned reality reflected in the advertising industry? The rapid development of digital communications has brought together new opportunities for brands, ensuring global growth in advertising expenditure notwithstanding the financial recession and the volatility of some emerging markets like Russia and China. According to the Carat agency (Carat Report, 2016), global advertising spending will grow by 4 per cent in 2015 to US$529 billion in response to a positive global and regional outlook and solid growth, mostly in digital and mobile spending. Carat's report confirmed the ongoing positive momentum for the advertising industry around the world for the following years.

Western Europe continued its positive growth with a predicted rise in advertising spending of 2.6 per cent in 2015 and 2.9 per cent in 2016, mainly due to solid spending figures in the UK and Spain (+6.4 per cent and +6.9 per cent respectively). Spain occupies one of the principal positions on the global ranking of advertising spending, being above hegemonic countries such as the United Kingdom, Germany, the United States, Canada or China. Spain showed the highest growth in the region, reaching €4.8 billion in 2015 (Carat Report, 2016). Zenith Optimedia agency likewise reveals that the Spanish advertising market has increased by 6.4 per cent over the same period last year (January to August) (Optimedia Agency, 2015).

Overall, consumer demand has been growing in Spain, reactivating the economy. Consequently, advertisers have been returning to the market or increasing their advertising budgets. Undoubtedly, the market moves fast and is full of opportunities. Positive trends are predicted also for developing economies such as India (+11 per cent in 2015 and 12 per cent in 2016) and Latin America (12.7 per cent in 2015 and an expected growth of 13.6 per cent in 2016) that will experience an accelerated advertising spending growth in the near future (Carat Report, 2016).

Key changes in advertising industry

Tensions among media

The twenty-first century demands new ways to resolve the tensions between the old off-line and the new online media (which is generating the end of the traditional media supremacy). Enhanced measurability has placed the focus on results, while other aspects, such as talent, not to mention the talent appearing in advertisements, has become less important. Advertising has thus moved from being a type of art to becoming closer to a scientific discipline, thus new professional specialisation is needed.

In this scenario, new digital media gains prominence. Its novelty and diversity often sees it preceding the creative idea in the advertising process. Consequently, a good idea that is not in a digital format generates less noise than a mediocre idea developed for a digital media. Appropriate channels for a message might therefore increase the advertiser share. Burger King, for example, often uses traditional media such as TV ads and billboards for their commercial communications. However, it is also making use of a mobile device app, which promotes the company's weekly promotions directly to the consumer.

Increased measurability has also opened up other innovations. Advertisers can engage in retargeting (which sees the relaunching of an advertisement to a user who has visited the page while he or she is browsing in other sites). They can similarly enhance the optimisation of an online campaign by programmatic auction mechanisms or Real Time Bidding (also called programmatic buying), depending on the results. This situation has seen companies such as Mercadona, the leading Spanish food distribution company, invest millions (€120 million to be precise) in data centres over commercial communications (Torrejón, 2014, p. 83). Advertising communication increasingly calls for new professions that integrate creativity and technology with specialisation in data analysis metrics, user experience, and new contents such as branded content and gamification.

On the other hand, audiences are highly fragmented by the diversity of channels and possible targets. Facebook, for example, is perfect for branding fashion products, travel, video games and movies, as audiences can be segmented by different interests; while Adwords is perfect for accurate searches (64 per cent of the internet searches are for brand names, whereas the remaining 36 per cent are distributed among celebrities' names, distribution and retail chains, and words related with services, among others) (Marketing Directo, 2016). In addition, digital media creativity is more easily adapted to the consumers' tastes and needs and can be quickly modified because its effectiveness is tested in real time through Key Performance Indicators (such as Cost Per Click or C-P-C, Cost Per Acquisition or C-P-A, Share of Voice or S-O-V reports) and social media reach and engagement.

These metrics reports integrate a lot of metadata that may cause privacy to disappear, as everything done online leaves a trace (Pereira, 2015). Although this scenario may still seem distant for Europe, recent research reveals that is actually happening. A study conducted by the Massachusetts Institute of Technology (MIT), Rutgers (USA) and Aarhus (Denmark) universities found that, in a sample of 1.1 million 'anonymous' credit card users, 90 per cent could be re-identified using an algorithm and just a few pieces of information (De Montjoye *et al.*, 2015).

Tensions between the strategic and the tactical

Digitisation has made it possible to introduce changes in the communication strategy easily and efficiently. It has also resulted in changes in the decision-making of the advertiser as well. Increased levels of data allow the allocation of sales levels to a particular piece of communication as well as the constant rethinking of media plans, along with the rotation of the ads thanks to new digital media (YouTube, Facebook, Instagram, Twitter, etc.). Such immediacy and detail has directly affected the nature of advertising campaigns. BBDO Paris, for example, developed an advertising campaign for Foot Locker Company ('Trending in NYC') with original content filmed in the heart of Manhattan for each day of February 2015, which let them present their new sneakers (150 models) through 28 different online videos (Adforum, 2015b).

Tensions between seduction and connectivity

Interactive thinking is leading to some changes in creative thinking which are based on new knowledge in digital metrics, return on investment (ROI), and neuroscience. However, data must be incorporated to achieve a more efficient management and to avoid failure – the importance of the latter is underscored by the fact that 76 per cent of 60,000 analysed consumer introductions for 2014 failed to make it to the end of their first year on the shelf in Europe (Hood and Sjöstrang, 2014). Hence, different measures have to be used depending on the campaign (AdWords, cost per click; ROI, cost per lead, etc.). Moreover, new knowledge about decision-making from neuroscience is very important. Studies have shown that 90 per cent of the decisions that individuals make are taken at deeper layers of the brain (where the most basic emotions are managed); afterwards, the individual performs a rational reading to interpret those decisions, a reading which occurs in the prefrontal cortex of the brain. Thus, advertising is taking this knowledge in a fractional way, endorsing emotional ads to the detriment of rational messages, which leads us to the present hedonistic consumer way of life. Therefore, new business models will need to give a greater role to their environmental–social sustainability policies, which in turn will give greater prominence to the social and institutional advertising campaigns, as no company will risk its reputation on an unethical advertising message.

The nature and scope of advertising in Spain

Recent advertising in Spain, and in the rest of the southern European countries, is mainly influenced by three factors:

- the financial crisis, which has led to less investment in advertising and, consequently, greater fragmentation of marketing communication agencies;
- the rise of digital media, which has led to greater complexity in advertising creativity on account of the appearance of multiple digital media platforms; and
- the changes in the relationship between consumers and brands. Consumers are no longer passive receivers of information; they now produce media content, as prosumers, and distribute it to a worldwide audience through the new media and new advertising forms of branded content and viral marketing. In communicating through social media platforms, these consumers have also developed new expectations and demands concerning social responsibility of corporations and their products.

The financial crisis

Between 2008 and 2013 there was a drop in advertising investment in Spain. In 2009, there were 21,048 advertising agencies and 107,000 related jobs (Torrejón, 2014, p. 76). Advertising investment at this time represented 2 per cent of Spanish GDP (today, less than 1 per cent). However, in 2014 there was a 5.9 per cent increase in ad spending compared with 2013 – a fact which suggests that advertising is an indicator of economic recovery (Carat Report, 2015).

Currently, people in advertising agencies work in small teams. Only 16 per cent of them work in agencies of more than 20 employees. The vast majority, 72 per cent, work in agencies with fewer than ten people. Such independent agencies include Arroba, Irismedia, Comunica + A, Doubleyou, Territorio Creativo, Btob, Shackleton, Grupo Ontwice, d6 or la Despensa. The remaining 12 per cent work alone. This phenomenon has led to some changes in agency structures and functions. The highest percentage of advertising agency employees (46 per cent) work in traditional agencies (integrated or advertising agencies). There are also a large number of employees that work in design firms (13 per cent) while the remainder (41 per cent) work in other types of agencies, studios and production companies such as social media agencies, branding agencies and digital marketing agencies (Europages, 2016).

The digital gap between senior (digital settlers) and junior (digital natives) professionals

According to the online survey 'Creativos en España' conducted in June 2014, the Spanish advertising employee profile can be described as young (most are between 25 and 35 years), male (63 per cent), and educated (88 per cent have a degree in advertising, graphic design or arts). Respondents' positions varied between the creative direction (21 per cent), copy (18 per cent), art (18 per cent) and graphic design (15 per cent) (Creativos en España, 2016). The digital divide between digital settlers and digital natives has generated greater job possibilities for those junior professionals who fundamentally understand technology and can manage it.

This new agency model offers all the services needed by the advertiser, particularly in digital communications and for market expansion, especially in Latin America. Some examples of this type of agency and brands working together include: SCPF, which works for Ikea in Spain; Sra. Rushmore, which works for Coca-Cola worldwide (and helped create the 'Octogenario' campaign which was launched in eight Latin American countries); Atlético Internacional, which leads the global account of Seat; Tiempo BBDO, the first Spanish agency to create a spot for the American Superbowl (for Pepsi); Vitruvio Leo Burnett, which services Lancia in several European markets; and Lola, which developed advertising campaigns for various brands of the Unilever Group for Spain and Latin America. Movistar's campaigns for the Latin American market are similarly developed in Madrid by agencies such as Young & Rubicam or Publicis network (Moreno, 2007).

Changes in the consumers' relationship

According to Pereira (2015), conversations are not only Business to Consumer but also Brand to Community. The agencies (and brands) that achieve success will be those that connect with the consumer in a multichannelled way. They will also engage in a relevant conversations with the audience, people and communities who usually reject advertising, while seeking, consuming, and sharing information and entertainment. Shrum (2004) states that the lines between entertainment and persuasion are becoming increasingly blurred, mainly in social media due to the mixture of entertainment, interactivity and persuasion found in these platforms.

In light of the growing technologically empowered world of communicators, companies have to develop a bidirectional communication strategy for a multimedia and multi-screen connected consumer. The brand identity is now created and cultivated hand in hand with (or comment to comment with) social media users. In fact, empirical studies suggest users place more emphasis on social validation than on traditional expert sources when assessing online information (Hargittai *et al.*, 2010; Knobloch-Westerwick *et al.*, 2005). Although Spanish corporations maintain an active online presence and post frequent messages, they have a long way to go in the microblogging sphere in deploying and capitalising on the interactivity features that these sites offered (Mamic and Arroyo, 2013).

In recent years, consumers have not only sought to satisfy their own needs, they have increasingly engaged with brands that share their concerns and values, and conduct their business in a more socially and environmentally responsible way. Such engagement is partially accountable for the worldwide increase in the number of firms adopting a more environmentally friendly approach in their sourcing, operating, and marketing activities (Gurau and Ranchhod, 2005; Kilbourne, 2004; Menon and Menon, 1997; Polonsky and Rosenberger, 2001). As a consequence, marketing communications will need to do more to present themselves as good corporate citizens. This means that advertising will play a key role in communicating the pro-environmental credentials of corporate products, services and business. Moreover, it might also contribute to harnessing an eco-friendly consciousness among consumers and other organizations (Grillo *et al.*, 2008; Iyer and Banerjee, 1993). Green advertising could therefore contribute to behavioural changes in people's daily lives to create a low-carbon future for our planet and economy.

EU and sustainability

The EU, along with the United Nations (UN), is taking a leading role in reducing the impact of climate change and limiting global warming. One of the EU's ambitious targets is that by 2020 all EU members will have committed to reducing greenhouse gas emissions by 20 per cent from 1990 levels. Some of the measures include placing a limit on emissions from power production and manufacturing industries, and cutting home food greenhouse gas emissions by 40 per cent below 1990 levels by 2030. To reach these ambitious goals, the EU plans to devote 20 per cent of its budget (€180 billion for 2014–20) to climate-related actions in areas such as agriculture, research, transportation energy and energy-efficient buildings. In addition, the EU will provide €14 billion of public climate financing to partners outside Europe (European Commission, 2015). This scenario demands a prompt response from industry as well as public and private organisations. Although society as a whole will need to transform, there are some industry sectors that will need to develop faster, such as sustainable construction, green transport, energy-efficient products and renewable energy.

It is evident that western European states play a leading role in the transition towards a low-carbon economy and in mitigating climate change. A move back to an organic way of life, away from industrialisation and capitalism, is rising. Although Western countries are pushing forward legislation and public campaigns to tackle the degradation of the environment, it seems that this is not enough. Hence, they are now calling on developing countries to join their efforts to exchange industrialisation and the ruthless drive of capitalism for a more environmentally aware model that mitigates the negative consequences for the planet. This call tries to unify forces and treat climate change as an urgent international problem that should override national interests, and that seeks to achieve a new international agreement on the climate, applicable to all countries, with the aim of keeping global warming below 2°C (European Commission, 2015, 2013).

Europe and the globalisation of green culture

By definition, the culture of an era or social group emerges from the mixture of lifestyles and customs, knowledge and level of artistic, scientific and industrial development (Real Academia Española Dictionary, 2014) of the people that create it. It is undeniable that in the present time, western Europe is characterised by a postmodern ethos, where society is guided by a strong hedonistic desire: a desire that is satisfied by the constant consumption of goods and services, and the conquest of the self in the aspiration of being 'other'. Indeed, it is this society of consumption and the absorption in the present moment, without thinking beyond, which took us to where we are now, fighting to save our planet and ourselves as well. Therefore, a reaction against the post-war ethos based on the idea that accelerated consumption was a necessary part of development (Durning, 1991) was needed. Consequently, and in response to emerging environmental problems such as air pollution, climate change and increasing fuel costs, public concern for the environment is higher than ever (Bush, 2008; Chitra, 2007; Xue and Muralidharan, 2015). Development is now understood in terms of innovation and efficiency, and, more importantly, sustainability.

Past studies have found a positive relationship between level of education and environmental attitudes (Anderson *et al.*, 1974; Granzin and Olsen, 1991; Roberts, 1996; Zimmer *et al.*, 1994). In addition, Chan (2000), based on past academic studies, summarised the profiles of green consumers from different regions, finding that those from North America, Europe and Asia were better educated, had higher income and occupation status, and higher socioeconomic status. In certain western European countries green consumerism has had an important impact on purchasing trends, even forcing manufacturers to change the way they do things (e.g. moves away from testing cosmetics on animals in the UK) (Spear, 1993, p. 119). Individuals with higher educational levels, who consequently enjoy access to more information, are expected to be more predisposed to display a pro-environmental behaviour, just as those with higher income can more easily bear the marginal increase in the costs associated with supporting green causes and purchasing green products. In advertising, there has been a parallel growth of green message strategies (Segev *et al.*, 2016).

Western Europe is home to a large group of consumers with high proenvironmental values. Consequently, more environmentally responsible habits are being embedded in the culture. These include the use of energy-efficient light bulbs, the purchase of recycled products and less wasteful packaging, and the use of carbon-free forms of transportation (OECD, 1998). Social values occupy a great role in the organisation and self-discipline of people's social behaviour (Arroyo and Mamic, 2009). In this sense, adopting an ecological lifestyle allows people to accommodate their own hierarchical scheme of values to conduct themselves as environmentally responsible citizens. However, when it comes to advertising these products and values, consumers remain sceptical about them (Ulusoy *et al.*, 2016).

Some of the societal values that are identified by EU citizens as being distinctly European include: peace (61 per cent), respect for nature and the environment (50 per cent), social equality and solidarity (37 per cent), tolerance and openness to others (37 per cent), and freedom of opinion (37 per cent) (European Commission, 2007). Another qualitative study shared some of these findings, particularly when most respondents considered that Europe is relatively advanced in its environmental sensitivity[2] compared to the rest of the world. As we will see, these societal values are mirrored in the advertising that appears throughout Europe.

As governmental, social and cultural forces advocate greater environmental awareness, marketing communications will need to engage directly with these issues. Evidence has shown that in the past two decades, environmental advertising has grown exponentially (Futerra, 2008). It is anticipated that this trend will continue. Although advertising can play a key role in communicating this pro-environmental image of corporate products, services and business, it can also contribute to harnessing an eco-friendly consciousness among consumers and other organisations (Grillo *et al.*, 2008; Iyer and Banerjee, 1993).

Campaigns

Green campaign: 'ni un grado más' (not one degree more) for WWF Spain

When looking towards the next big United Nations event on climate change that will be celebrated in Paris (COP21), WWF in 2014 launched a campaign centered on the impact and solutions of climate change: 'Ni un grado más' (not one degree more) was created for WWF Spain. The far-reaching campaign included national advertising with a strong Internet presence (mainly through the micro-site www.niungradomas.org and with the hash tag #niungradomas to generate interest and engagement in social media) and direct public audience outreach. It sought to mobilise people to engage in the cause and to take action by motivating people to sign their online petition to put a stop to climate change.

On their micro-site 'niungradomas.org', WWF sought to generate awareness of climate issues through different infographics that depicted important facts concerning environmental challenges. These infographics provided information and important data on issues, while the foreground was occupied with an arresting photograph of a landscape depicting the theme that was being addressed: the loss of forests, rivers, species, beaches, crops, jobs, etc. Underscoring these themes, WWF's YouTube channel (YouTube, 2016) similarly alerted audiences to these environmental problems through a similar set of photographs and infographics. Additionally, street activities were undertaken in major public spaces of big cities such as Valencia and Madrid. These saw WWF representatives conducting various high impact performances, from using frozen penguin figures (which naturally melted due to the high temperatures) to reproducing a crime scene (where a WWF patrol 'investigated' the death of Arctic seals caused by environmental destruction) (El Boletin, 2015).

The informative component of the website was of great importance, too. The campaign used catchphrases around the idea of time to people to take action. When audiences entered the micro-site, the first thing they saw was a chronometer that marked the remaining time until the next Paris COP21 Summit. The infographics again presented valuable information about climate change implications and consequences (Cop21 Paris, 2015). In addition to the concise and clear information depicted in them, the campaign's micro-site featured a timeline of the last 20 years of negotiations about climate change (Cop21 Paris, 2015).

Global campaign: connecting with food and technology

Food is an integral part of European identities. To this end, the slow food movement, which started out in Italy, has played an integral role in maintaining traditional European cuisine whilst resisting the impact of fast food and culinary homogenisation (Slow Food, 2016). In Spain, food and technology have facilitated new ways of connecting with one another and, indeed, the world.

Starting out in the United States in 2011, *Kinfolk* (Kinfolk, 2016) is an independent magazine about the slow lifestyle that promotes values such as the simplification of life, the cultivation of communities and the importance of spending time with friends and family. *Kinfolk* focuses on one of the great pleasures in life: good food enjoyed in good company. In Spain, *Kinfolk* has become very popular, perhaps because of the similarities with the traditions of the Mediterranean lifestyle that charms so many people. At the beginning of 2015, Spain ranked fourth in the number of visits to the magazine's website (behind the USA, Indonesia and England) (González, 2015). Its followers share the magazine's taste for good food in good company in addition to its affinity for digital media, which they manifest mainly by sharing their experiences in social media networks (particularly in Instagram where the magazine has one million followers) (Instagram, 2016). Awareness of the brand has been also spread through a number of workshops on relevant subjects developed by the Arce sisters (Arce, 2016).

The Spanish Advertising Association's campaign of the year for 2015 was awarded to the rice producer La Fallera, for its campaign to persuade Unicode to include an emoji featuring Spain's national dish, paella. The campaign also sought to recast traditional La Fallera as a modern brand. As Spanish consumers are major users of WhatsApp, the campaign was launched on that platform. It then engaged Spanish comedian Eugeni Alemany to travel to San Franciso to lobby Unicode to create a paella emoji (Jones, 2015). His efforts were filmed and broadcast live over social media networks. Audiences were then directed to an 18-minute documentary of Alemany's efforts, which culminated in Unicode's explaining what it would take to get a formal endorsement of a paella emoji. A Twitter party was organised (#PaellaEmojiParty) to explain to the world the need for a paella emoji. The results were enormous – and instantaneous. It reached an audience of some 60 million and generated more than 30,000 tweets in 40 days in countries as diverse as Spain, Sweden, the USA, and Japan (Chicharro, 2016). The campaign was also covered by more than 150 newspapers across Spain and internationally (Jones, 2015). Other major brands (including Pepsi and Nescafé), organisations and politicians also joined the campaign.[3] The campaign was a success, with the paella emoji receiving official endorsement in 2016 (Jones, 2016). Such success will doubtlessly inspire other advertisers to pay closer attention to the marketing capacity of emojis. Moreover, Twitter's announcement that advertisers will be able to reach target advertising to consumers using emojis in their tweets points to emojis becoming a part of the future advertising landscape.

Glocal campaign: 'benditos bares' (blessed bars) for Coca-Cola

The Spanish agency Sra. Rushmore won first prize in the category Commercial Communications in the 'Premios a la Eficacia 2014', awarded by the Asociación Española de Anunciantes (AEA: Spanish Association of Advertisers) with the campaign 'Benditos Bares' (Blessed bars) for Coca-Cola (Reasonwhy, 2013) for developing the most effective and innovative strategy.

The campaign connects neatly with Spanish consumers by presenting the bar not only as a meeting place but as the key venue for Spanish social life (there are 350,000 bars in Spain, one bar for every 132 inhabitants) (Day, 2016). The campaign, with an approximate budget of €10 million, has achieved the difficult feat of adapting the professed values of global brand Coca-Cola – 'happiness, family, friends' – to Spanish pub culture.

For the campaign, Sra. Rushmore created the fictional series 'I+B. Go to bars more', the mini-series of 'Blessed Bars, Blessed Series', stand-up events and an official online account. They also created the San Bar-Tolo day, which they expect to celebrate annually on 29 June. In addition, they sought the support of some celebrities of the communication world in Spain and also used television, radio, press, digital and outdoor media to launch messages, while spreading the campaign in social networks with the hash tag #benditosbares. Coca-Cola's website recorded 110,000 visits in one week, and the 'Himno a los bares' became one of the most watched videos on YouTube in 2013 (Reasonwhy, 2015).

The effectiveness of the campaign has also had an impact on the hospitality industry, which represents today, according to the AEA, one of the main economic vectors in Spain. The campaign has helped to reverse the downward trend in bar sales (which between 2008 and 2012 had lost €13,000 million) and the closure of bars (some 72,000 bars closed during the economic crisis in Spain) (Anunciantes, 2016).

Conclusion

Western Europe's economic strength as well as its strong social values means that the region can play a key role in developing creative advertising which is socially aware and impactful. The region plays and will continue to play a leading role in the transition towards a low-carbon economy and in mitigating climate change. To this end, its embrace of environmentally inspired advertising principles will be instrumental in bringing about behavioural changes in people's daily lives to create a low-carbon future for our planet and economy. The region's wealth and infrastructure will see innovation in the digital media realm, too. As social media platforms allow for greater two-way interactive experiences between organisations and stakeholders, it appears that commercial firms will have greater access to means of monitoring consumer behaviour, but such access will be counterbalanced by the increasing need to actively listen to consumers and to address their concerns. To this end, advertising in western Europe also has an important role in maintaining local traditions and values as much as the region's broader values. Advertising in western Europe will therefore continue to be characterised by its efforts to strike a balance between local, regional, and global concerns.

Notes

1 For more information visit EU Trade in the World Index and the EU in the World reports online at: http://trade.ec.europa.eu/doclib.
2 The Europeans, Culture and Cultural Values, qualitative study.
3 See https://vimeo.com/125897188.

References

Adforum (2015a) 'Cannes Lions International Festival of Creativity 2015 winners archive 2015', *Adforum*, Available at: www.adforum.com/award-organization/6650183/show-case/2015/winners (accessed 13 November 2016).
Adforum (2015b) 'Foot Locker – Adidas Hard Court: Day 1', *Adforum*, Available at: www.adforum.com/creative-work/ad/player/34508594/adidas-hard-court-day-1/foot-locker (accessed 13 November 2016).
Anderson, Jr. W. T., Henion, I. I. and Cox, E. P. (1974) 'Socially vs. ecologically concerned consumers', *American Marketing Association Combined Conference Proceedings*, 36, pp. 304–11.
Anunciantes (2016) Spanish Association of Advertisers, Key Facts. Available at: www.anunciantes.com/ (accessed 13 November 2016).
Arce (2016) Homepage of the Arce sisters website. Available at: www.hermanasarce.com (accessed 13 November 2016).
Arroyo, I. and Mamic, L. I. (2009) 'Valores occidentales en el discurso publicitario audiovisual argentino', *Revista de Comunicación y Nuevas tecnologías, ICONO*, 14(13), pp. 8–23.
Bush, M. (2008) 'Sustainability and a smile', *Advertising Age*, 79(8), pp. 1–25.
Carat Report (2015) *Carat Ad Spent Report*. Spain: Carat Media Network.
Carat Report (2016) *Carat Ad Spent Report*. Spain: Carat Media Network.

Chan, K. (2000) 'Market segmentation of green consumers in Hong Kong', *Journal of International Consumer Marketing*, 12(2), pp. 7–24.

Chicharro, C. (2016) 'The Paella emoji is happening, thanks to a Spanish brand'. Available at: http://carlachich.com/paella-emoji/ (accessed 13 November 2016).

Chitra, K. (2007) 'In search of the green consumers: A perceptual study', *Journal of Services Research*, 7(1), pp. 173–91.

Cop21 Paris (2015) 'Sustainable Innovation Forum 2015'. Available at: www.cop21paris.org/knowledge-centre/infographics (accessed 13 November 2016).

Creativos en España (2016) 'Online omnibus survey'. Available at: http://ipmark.com/diez-mejores-creativos-publicitarios-espana/ (accessed 15 March 2017).

Day, J. (2016) 'Spain has more bars per inhabitant than any other country', *On the Pulse*. Available at: www.onthepulse.es/life-in-spain/spain-has-more-bars-inhabitant-any-other-country-160628 (accessed 13 November 2016).

De Montjoye, Y., Radaelli, L., Kumar Singh, V. and Pentland., A. (2015). 'Unique in the shopping mall: On the reidentifiability of credit card metadata', *Science*, 347(6221), pp. 536–9.

Durning, A. (1991) 'Asking how much is enough?' In: Brown, L. R. (ed.), *The State of the World*. New York: W. W. Norton.

El Boletin (2015) *Los pingüinos 'desaparecen' en Valencia por culpa del cambio climático*, Inos. Available at: www.elboletin.com/contraportada/122997/wwf-derrite-pinguinos-cambio-climatico.html (accessed 13 November 2016).

EuroPages (2016) *Advertising Agencies*. Available at: http://marketing-advertising-the-media.europages.co.uk/companies/Spain/Advertising%20agencies.html (accessed 13 November 2016).

European Commission (2007) *European Cultural Values*, Special Barometer 278/WAGE 67. TNS Opinion & social. Available at: http://ec.europa.eu/public_opinion/archives/eb_special_280_260_en.htm (accessed 15 February 2017).

Eurostat (2016) *The EU in the World: 2015 Edition*. Luxembourg: Eurostat.

Futerra (2008) 'The Greenwash guide', *Futerra*. Available at: www.futerra.co.uk (accessed 13 November 2016).

González, C. (2015) 'Slow magazines: comunidades para foodies y travelers', *Reasonwhy*. Available at: www.reasonwhy.es/reportaje/slow-magazines-comunidades-para-foodies-y-travellers (accessed 13 November 2016).

Granzin, K. and Olsen, J. (1991) 'Characterizing participants in activities protecting the environment: A focus on donating, recycling and conservation behaviours', *Journal of Public Policy & Marketing*, 10(2), pp. 1–27.

Grillo, N., Tokarczyk, J. and Hansen, E. (2008) 'Green advertising developments in the US forest sector: A follow up', *Forest Products Journal*, 58(5), pp. 40–46.

Gurau, C. and Ranchhod, A. (2005) 'International green marketing: A comparative study of British and Romanian firms', *International Marketing Review*, 22(5), pp. 547–61.

Hargittai, E., Fullerton, L., Menchen-Trevino, E. and Thomas, K. Y. (2010) 'Trust online: Young adults' evaluation of web content', *International Journal of Communication*, 4(1), pp. 468–94.

Hood, D. and Sjöstrang, J. (2014) *Nielsen breakthrough innovation report*. New York: The Nielsen Company.

Instagram (2016) Instagram Kinfolk. Available at: www.instagram.com/kinfolk/?hl=en (accessed 15 March 2017).

Iyer, E. and Banerjee, B. S. (1993) 'Anatomy of green advertising', *Advances in Consumer Research*, 20(1), pp. 494–501.

Jones, J. (2015) 'World gets taste of paella thanks to brilliant Spanish emoji campaign', *The Local*. Available at: www.thelocal.es/20151119/paella-emoji-campaign-one-of-the-years-most-successful-in-spain (accessed 13 November 2016).

Jones, J. (2016) 'Congratulations! Spain finally gets its very own paella emoji', *The Local*. Available at: www.thelocal.es/20160603/congratulations-spain-finally-gets-its-paella-emoji (accessed 13 November 2016).

Kilbourne, W. E. (2004) 'Sustainable communication and the dominant social paradigm: can they be integrated', *Marketing Theory*, 4(3), pp. 187–208.

Kinfolk (2016) Kinfolk website. Available at: https://kinfolk.com/info/about/ (accessed 13 November 2016).

Knobloch-Westerwick, S., Sharma, N., Hansen, D. L. and Alter, S. (2005) 'Impact of popularity indications on readers' selective exposure to online news', *Journal of Broadcasting & Electronic Media*, 49(3), pp. 296–313.

Mamic, L. and Arroyo, I. (2013) 'How the larger corporations engage with stakeholders through Twitter', *International Journal of Market Research*, 55(6), pp. 79–100.

Marketing Directo (2016) 'Cuáles son las búsquedas mas recomendadas por Google', *Marketing Directo 2016*. Available at: www.marketingdirecto.com/digital-general/digital/%C2%BFcuales-son-las-busquedas-mas-recomendadas-por-google (accessed 13 November 2016).

Menon, A. and Menon, A. (1997) 'Enviropreneurial marketing strategy: The emergence of corporate environmentalism as market strategy', *Journal of Marketing*, 61, pp. 51–67.

Moreno, D. (2007) 'La globalización publicitaria. La creatividad española traspasa fronteras', *ABC España*. Available at: www.abc.es/informacion/abcdariodelapublicidad/globalizacion.asp (accessed 13 November 2016).

OECD (1998) *Safety of Vulnerable Road Users*. Paris: Organisation de Coopération et de Développement Economiques.

Optimedia Agency (2015) *La inversión publicitaria crece el 6,4% en los 9 primeros meses de 2015*. Available at:www.optimedia.es/optimedia-intelligence/la-inversion-publicitaria-crece-el-64-en-los-9-primeros-meses-de-2015/ (accessed 13 November 2016).

Pereira, M. (2015) *Retos del futuro para las agencias digitales, El Publicista*. Available at: www.elpublicista.es/frontend/elpublicista/noticia.php?id_noticia=22745 (accessed 13 November 2016).

Polonsky, M. J. and Rosenberger, P. (2001) 'Reevaluating green marketing: A strategic approach', *Business Horizons*, 44(5), pp. 21–30.

Real Academia Española Dictionary (2014) *Diccionario de la Real Academia Española* (23rd edn), Madrid: Espasa.

Reasonwhy (2013) 'Coca-Cola quiere ser el departamento de marketing de todos los bares españoles'. Available at: www.reasonwhy.es/actualidad/audiovisual/coca-cola-quiere-ser-el-departamento-de-marketing-de-los-bares-espanoles (accessed 13 November 2016).

Reasonwhy (2015) 'Tres agencias de WWP crearán la próxima campaña global de Coca-Cola'. Available at: www.reasonwhy.es/actualidad/sector/tres-agencias-de-wpp-crearan-la-proxima-campana-global-de-coca-cola-2015-08-14 (accessed 13 November 2016).

Roberts, J. (1996) 'Green consumers in the 1990s: Profile and implications for advertising', *Journal of Business Research*, 36(3), pp. 217–32.

Segev, S., Fernandes, J. and Hong, J. (2016) 'Is your product really green? A content analysis to reassess green advertising', *Journal of Advertising*, 45(1), pp. 85–93.

Shrum, L. J. (2004) *The Psychology of Entertainment Media: Blurring the Lines Between Entertainment and Persuasion.* Mahwah, NJ: Lawrence Erlbaum.

Slow Food (2016) 'Our history'. Available at: www.slowfood.com/about-us/our-history/ (accessed 13 November 2016).

Spear, J. (1993) 'The environment agenda'. In: Rees, G. W. (ed.), *International Politics in Europe: The New Agenda.* London: Routledge.

Torrejón, D. (2014) *La creatividad publicitaria ante una triple encrucijada: La neurociencia, la reputación corporativa y el big data. Informe sobre el estado de la cultura en españa la salida digital.* Madrid: Lúa Ediciones 3.0.

Ulusoy, E. and Barretta, P. (2016) 'How green are you, really? Consumers' skepticism toward brands with green claims', *Journal of Global Responsibility*, 7(1), pp. 72–83.

World Bank (2016) *European Union.* Available at: www.worldbank.org/en/country/eu (accessed 13 November 2016).

Xue, F. and Muralidharan, S. (2015) 'A green picture is worth a thousand words? Effects of visual and textual environmental appeals in advertising and the moderating role of product involvement', *Journal of Promotion Management*, 21(1), pp. 82–106.

Youtube (2016) 'WWF's International'. Available at: www.youtube.com/user/WWF (accessed 13 November 2016).

Zimmer, M., Stafford, T. and Stafford, M. (1994) 'Green issues: Dimensions of environmental concern', *Journal of Business Research*, 30(1), pp. 63–74.

8 Advertising market in central and eastern Europe

Case study of advertising market in Poland

Tomasz Domański

Introduction

This chapter identifies distinguishing characteristics of the advertising market in central and eastern Europe and uses the example of Poland to examine in detail a representative local market. To gain a thorough understanding of the region, it is essential to first consider the region's unique economic, social and political history, as well as to clearly understand the difference between the emerging advertising markets in central and eastern European countries and those in Russia and other countries from the former Union of Soviet Socialist Republics (USSR).

The uniqueness of the advertising market in central Europe stems from the cultural diversity of the region, the development of independent media, the strong commitment to principles of free market economics, membership of the European Union (EU) and the confidence of global companies to invest in local markets over the past 25 years. Consumer behaviour is much closer to the model observed in western Europe, which often allows these companies to utilise global advertising campaigns. Central European countries are attractive to global companies as they are economically stable, have continuing growth in consumer income and have consumer populations that are typically receptive to global advertising and the 'universal consumer values' that underpin it. Young consumers are specifically susceptible to such advertising, as they identify themselves with the universal values promoted by global brands.

Central Europe comprises Poland, the Czech Republic, Slovakia and Hungary, with a population of around 70 million consumers. Although it is smaller than the neighbouring eastern European market, central Europe exhibits a great development potential. By comparison, eastern Europe, covering Russia, Ukraine, Kazakhstan, Belarus and other former countries of the USSR, contains about 220 million consumers.

This chapter profiles the advertising market of Poland. Poland was selected because of the scale of the market (some 40 million consumers), the presence in the market of active economic operators and global brands, and the number of highly professional global and domestically operating advertising agencies. There are more than 6,000 firms in Poland that operate with the involvement of foreign capital, many of which have been established by global companies. Total value of direct foreign investment in Poland has already exceeded €175 billion (US$191.97 billion). The growing importance of new forms of advertising in the Polish market, such as Internet and mobile app advertising, echo those in developed countries (MarketLine, 2015).

Overview of studies on advertising in Russia and in other countries of central and eastern Europe

Studies of advertising markets in the countries of central and eastern Europe often prioritise Russia. With a consumer population of some 127 million people, it is easily the biggest economy in the region. Such accounts analyse the impact of the previous political and social system on the form and content of advertising messages and consumer behaviour. More recently, Holak *et al.*'s (2007) study of the content of advertising messages and their nostalgia for the Soviet era provided a revealing account of the connections between the past and present. Other accounts also examined television commercials of certain product categories important to Russian consumers, such as alcohol. These analyses strongly refer to cultural differences and to their impact upon advertising strategies. One such example was beer. In 2005, beer was the second most advertised product on television after mobile phones (Morris, 2007). Studies of TV commercials for Baltika beer confirmed that the advertising message was adjusted to local circumstances. Despite the changes in brewery ownership following the fall of communism, when local Russian beer brands were taken over by global corporations, advertisements for these brands continued to refer to national and cultural values important to Russian consumers.

A second focus of research into advertising in Russia has examined Internet and television advertising (Fedotova, 2014). Among the post-Soviet states, Russian consumers have emerged as the most critical of commercial advertising as well as of advertising created by global companies. Due to low real income, more than half of Russian recipients of advertising are unable to acquire advertised products. Consequently, television advertising, particularly for global brands, has been a source of frustration for significant parts of the Russian market. At the present level of income, it is estimated that only 40 per cent of the Russian population can be considered to be realistic addressees of advertising (Saveleva, 2006).

An interesting element to explore in the context of globalisation is the use English in advertising to the Russian market. From 2000 onwards, the phenomenon was observed with electronic equipment, cars, body care products, washing powders and household products. Global companies use English language advertising slogans as they reinforce the coherence of their global marketing communication. For Russian firms, English words and terms are also used to symbolise innovation, prestige and high quality of products (Ustinova, 2006). However, this trend may change following the recent Ukrainian conflict and negative political propaganda vis-à-vis Western countries, particularly the United States and its NATO allies. To this end, a study exploring the impact of geopolitical factors upon global advertising strategies and the positioning of Western brands in the Russian market might yield revealing insights.

Various studies of the advertising market in Russia and eastern Europe have sought to estimate the distance between these countries and the nations of the West in terms of alignment of marketing communication narratives (Endaltseva, 2015; Saleem *et al.*, 2015). However, we need to be equally mindful of similar divisions between Russia and other countries of the former USSR and central Europe, where alignment of marketing communication narratives is also problematic. Earlier comparative studies conducted in Russia on groups of students demonstrated that 'Russians are more critical and suspicious of the practice of advertising and this negativism is even greater when other than advertising/business students are surveyed' (Wells *et al.*, 2007, p. 13). They also identified limitations of global advertising strategies conducted in Russia. Studies highlighted the need to take account of specific cultural circumstances affecting Russian consumer attitudes and behaviours when planning advertising.

Culture-wise, there are huge differences between the recipients of advertising in Russia and those in central European countries, such as Poland, where consumer behaviour rests on more universal foundations. From a Western perspective, the countries of central and eastern Europe, which had been under Soviet control during the Cold War, have all too often been assumed to be homogeneous. Such assumptions not only ignore the sizeable political, historical and cultural differences among them, but also fail to recognise more recent differences, including their respective rates of economic, political and cultural transformation. The accession of Poland and other countries in the region to the EU in 2004 also resulted in the building of national brands based on local identity and key cultural values (Kubacki and Skinner, 2006).

Consumer attitudes to advertising in central and eastern Europe have attracted significant scholarship. As the region shifted from communism to capitalism in the 1990s, scholars undertook various studies of consumer attitudes to advertising. Andrews *et al.*'s (1994) study, for example, was a small pilot study comprising small samples of university business students ($n=148$ in the United States and $n=64$ in Russia). That this survey was limited to students of business posed an immediate limitation upon the conclusions (Andrews *et al.*, 1994). Nevertheless, research on Russia and in central European countries found that it was generally believed that '[a]dvertising is the engine of trade', a view that had also been evident in earlier communist times (Wells, 1991). This was considered to be a universal rule in any well-performing economy. Hence, consumers understood advertising as a very positive symptom of the openness of the post-communist economy to global free market. Finding that 'Russian consumers held a more positive overall attitude toward advertising than US consumers (5.92 versus 5.36, on a seven point scale)' (Andrews *et al.*, 1994, p. 82) and that Russian business students perceived advertising as both 'an opportunity to help improve their economy' (Andrews *et al.*, p. 81) and 'a necessary part of their change to a market-driven economy' (Andrews *et al.*, p. 81), Andrews *et al.* generally found a more positive attitude to advertising in Russia than in the United States.

However, such attitudes were not fixed. By 2005, Russian consumers were adopting a more critical attitude to advertising, with a 'mean 3.9, on the seven point bad-good scale' (Wells *et al.*, 2007). This negative shift suggested that consumers were increasingly rationalising their behaviour and standing up to advertising pressure. As the markets in both Russia and central Europe matured, consumer attitudes to advertising generally adopted a more sceptical and critical view of advertising. Such shifts reflect the combination of excessive advertising activities as well as the emergence of a more demanding attitude to advertisers in respect to the content and format of advertising messages. A 2010 study on Czech consumer attitudes to advertising further illustrates this trend. The study found that almost 25 per cent of Czechs were happy with the presence of advertising, approximately 66 per cent were ambiguous and the final 10 per cent had negative views of advertising. Participants also expressed the view that advertising should place greater stress on 'product information, truth and ethical standards' (Millan and Mittal, 2010, p. 81) and that it should also provide 'additional true values' to consumers (Millan and Mittal, 2010, p. 94). Czech consumers thus demanded more objective information from advertising, albeit delivered in an attractive way (Millan and Mittal, 2010, p. 93). More recently, central European perceptions of advertising have been informed by the rise of new media. The maturation of new generations of consumers brought up in the market economy similarly poses a new challenge to the advertising industry. In light of the emergence of a new generation of consumers who use new media and expect other, often global forms of advertising, conclusions from pre-2010 studies may need to be revisited.

Characteristics of the European advertising market: the latest trends

Advertising markets across Europe, including central and eastern Europe, have been increasingly improving their monitoring capabilities through the establishment of specialised analytical centres. Consequently, more data can be accrued, facilitating more informed insights about these markets, and the ways that the Internet, social media and television channels can be used to reach them (M2Press Wire, 2014). The value of the European advertising market reached US$26.17 billion at the end of 2014 with a growth rate of 2.3 per cent over 2010–14. Looking to 2019, its value is estimated to increase by 22.2 per cent to almost US$32 billion (on average by 4.1 per cent annually).

Food, beverage and personal healthcare products are the biggest segments of the European advertising market, representing almost one-fifth of its total value (18.9 per cent). Media and telecommunications rank second (13.1 per cent). Retail networks are third (13.0 per cent), followed by the automotive industry (10.1 per cent) and financial services (8.2 per cent) (Marketline, 2015).

The largest European advertising markets are those of the United Kingdom, Germany and France, which account for approximately 40 per cent of the total European advertising spend (Marketline, 2015). The European market is dominated by global advertising agencies, such as WPP plc (US$18.14 billion),

Omnicom Group (US$15.3 billion of revenue in 2014), Publicis SA (US$9.62 billion) and Havas SA (US$2.35 billion) (Marketline, 2015).

In 2014, the European advertising market was dominated by TV advertising (39.6 per cent) followed by online advertising (23.8 per cent) and advertising in newspapers and magazines (15.2 per cent). Compared to 2007, online advertising has increased threefold, which is due to the increased use of both the Internet and the number of users of mobile devices (tablets, smartphones, and mobile phones).

Advertising market development in central and eastern Europe

Economics and geopolitics affected the advertising market in eastern Europe, particularly in Russia and Ukraine. Ukraine's conflict with Russia has seen the Ukrainian advertising market collapse, dropping by over 32 per cent in 2014. At the same time, sanctions imposed on Russia by the European Union and the resulting decrease in foreign investment have significantly slowed growth of the Russian advertising market. It grew by a mere 1.9 per cent in 2014, a far cry from the double-digit annual growth that it had previously enjoyed. Such figures were also well below the global advertising growth rate which, in 2014, was close to 5.3 per cent (ZenithOptimedia, 2014).

Advertising market in Poland: development trends

New technologies as development guidelines for Polish advertising market

The Polish advertising market, like the global market, is being transformed by the increasing and wider use of new technologies. In practice, this has seen a consistent increase in online advertising expenditure, which in 2014 exceeded advertising expenditure for printed media. According to the ZenithOptimedia Group, the value of the Polish advertising market at the end of 2014 reached approximately US$1.65 billion and has exhibited a steady growth (by almost 1.8 per cent annually) (ZenithOptimedia, 2014). Advertising expenditure growth in Poland was significantly higher than in the Eurozone (0.9 per cent), which is also reflected by differences in the GDP dynamics. Home to 23 million Internet users aged over 15 years, and who have access to broadband Internet, Poland presents an important market for online advertising.

The dynamic development trends in online advertising in the Polish market are consistent with trends in the global market. Currently, television stands as the major advertising medium globally, although ZenithOptimedia predicts that online media will replace it by 2017 (Kolenda, 2015). Online has already become the major medium in Austria, Denmark, the Netherlands, Norway, Sweden and the United Kingdom. Within the digital realm, it is likely that the greatest changes will be dictated by mobile channels. To this end, ZenithOptimedia predicts that in 2014–17 the share of advertising budgets directed to mobile Internet platforms will increase from 5.1 per cent to 12.9 per cent in the global market. Mobile channels will thus become a driving engine of the advertising market (Stysiak, 2014). The growth of online advertising has similarly encouraged programmatic media buying, which has optimised end results and further improved efficiency. Television still outperforms online as the major advertising medium in Poland. However, this gap is gradually decreasing with online media attracting around 28 per cent of the total Polish adspend (Stysiak, 2014). The scale of deployment of online advertising will be largely dependent on the terms and costs of streaming video content.

Online media in Poland over 2014 and 2015 accounted for approximately 12 per cent of advertising expenditure. This is more or less consistent with global trends which anticipate that, by 2017, online advertising expenditure will exceed adspend for radio, magazines and outdoor media. Mobile app advertising outlays for tablets and Smartphones have also been increasing rapidly – almost six times faster than those offered on fixed line devices, such as desktops. As demand for and usage of mobile devices increase, there will inevitably be a matching increase in the ways that these media are used for advertising. Mobile app advertising expenditure may even increase by 50 per cent annually. Such trends are in line with global patterns and predictions. ZenithOptimedia has claimed that mobile advertising outlays in 2016 will reach US$50 billion and will account for almost 8.6 per cent of all advertising expenditure and 30.4 per cent of all online adspend.

Young consumers hold the key to online media's future. Over 90 per cent of potential customers in Poland are seeking new products and services online and almost 11.5 million Poles are using the Internet to search for products online before actually buying them. A Millward Brown study found that most Polish consumers are willing to tolerate advertising on mobile Internet websites (68 per cent) and in mobile apps (65 per cent), provided they are free of charge. The tolerance for online ads is 36 per cent; for print ads, it is 47 per cent; and for TV commercials the figure is 51 per cent (Wójcicki, 2013). Further studies reveal an increasing irritation among Polish Internet users with the intensification of online advertising (6.5, on a 10-point scale) (Wirtualnemedia, 2012).

According to the 2012 World Internet Project study, 64 per cent of Poles used the Internet for an average of 15.5 hours per week. The time spent online has since increased by an average of almost two hours a week per annum, with Internet users progressively spending less time watching TV or reading newspapers. Online advertising budgets will further increase as Internet coverage and access speeds now expand across the country (Wójcicki, 2013).

The upsurge in online marketing can in part be attributed to the measurability of its effects, which enables advertising agencies and marketing specialists to calculate ROI coefficients more quickly and accurately than ever before. The ability for data to be analysed is further understood by the fact that 90 per cent of Polish traffic on Internet websites occurs through Google browsers (Małecki, 2008). The AdEx 2009 ranking, based on financial data from 23 European markets, listed Poland among the top three states with the highest increase of online advertising expenditure. In 2015, the value of the online advertising market was estimated at around US$300 million. On average, advertisers allocate approximately 17 per cent of their marketing budgets for online media and it is estimated that by 2019 it will reach 20 per cent (Newseria, 2015).

The largest online advertisers in Poland are the automotive industry (19 per cent), financial industries (11 per cent), and real estate and retail industries (11 per cent). Significant increases have also been identified for the beverages and liquor and media, books, CD and DVD product categories (IAB Polska, 2015). The Polish online advertising market is dominated by display advertising (46.6 per cent) and Internet search engine marketing (35.6 per cent). These two platforms alone represent over 82 per cent of the total value of the online advertising market.

The future outlook for online advertising will be largely informed by online shopping patterns. E-commerce in 2014 accounted for only 4.5 per cent of all transactions. In the United States, e-commerce represents almost 11.5 per cent of all trade transactions while, in the United Kingdom, this figure grows to 13.5 per cent. To this end, the relatively low Polish figure suggests significant potential, particularly as development dynamics of online trade in Poland are very high (22.6 per cent in 2014). It might also be noted that the share of m-commerce (mobile-commerce) in the total of e-commerce in Poland is still relatively low. In 2014, Poland's share of m-commerce amounted to 5 per cent of its e-commerce compared to the United States (20 per cent) and the United Kingdom (18 per cent). Development dynamics in all of these three markets exceeds 60 per cent and is highest in Poland where it amounts to 67 per cent, which reflects its lower starting point (Kolenda, 2015). M-commerce development dynamics will thus be crucial for the development of online advertising in mobile media.

As browsers are the main source of information about Internet users, effective online advertising requires a well-planned search engine marketing (SEM) strategy tailored to a particular business. It calls for search engine optimisation (SEO) services and the development of paid SEM campaigns for search results and a contextual network. Both SEM and SEO reinforce each other and support online sales (Kolenda, 2015). Currently, the key challenge is to build synergies between online and offline marketing with the help of analytical support using increasingly advanced tools to measure the overall effectiveness of online advertising. Greater use must be made of e-mail marketing, which provides greater reach to targeted groups. However, the Polish market displays some distinct attributes. Where the Western model of digital advertising is dominated by search engine marketing, the Polish model is dominated by display advertising. Display advertising is therefore the main source of funding for Polish online media (Kolenda, 2015).

It is anticipated that the future Polish advertising market will see greater focus on developing online advertising initiatives that will help to deliver specific market segments of strategic importance to the advertiser, otherwise known as 'audiences on demand'.

TV advertising in the Polish advertising market

Television advertising in Poland still accounts for approximately 50 per cent of the total advertising market. Poland's large television audiences are composed mostly of elderly consumers and the working population. Nevertheless, the size of the Polish television viewing audience has seen a continuous increase in television advertising budgets (*c.*7 per cent annually). Moreover, Polish audiences are spending more time watching television. While average daily TV viewing times in the United Kingdom and Germany have decreased, Polish figures are moving in the opposite direction with Poles currently spending an average of four hours and seven minutes watching television daily. Dominated by commercials for non-prescription drugs, healthcare products, insurance firms and financial services, Polish television advertising reflects its audience's demographics. In contrast, young Poles view television for just one hour 54 minutes daily, a figure that is significantly less than the Polish average and, indeed, international averages. Young Polish consumers are also more likely to use 'smart' TV options, requiring advertisers to consider different strategies to reach this elusive yet important market.

The strength of television advertising in Poland also results from the dynamic development of the network of TV broadcasters. In 2014, 13 new television stations entered the market. The buoyancy of the market was reflected by the fact that advertising space was fully consumed. Polish audiences can currently choose from among some 230 Polish-language TV channels. This increase has also seen the emergence of special interest channels, which provide advertisers with an opportunity to reach different market segments.

The state of the Polish media markets are clearly outlined in the *Media in Poland* industry profile by Marketline (2015). In addition to the advertising sector, the report covers the production of TV programmes as well as live shows, films and publishing activities. The value of Polish media market in 2013 was estimated to be approximately US$7.8 billion, which represents 2 per cent of the European media market (Marketline, 2015). Landline and cable TV account for over 50 per cent of this market, while advertising represents 12.9 per cent of the media market, publishing 29.7 per cent and production of films and entertainment shows 7.2 per cent. The Polish media market is almost three times that of the Czech Republic or Hungary, but it is roughly half the size of the Russian market (Marketline, 2015). The Polish TV advertising market is dominated by a small number of advertisers. In 2014, 130 leading advertisers (*c.*7 per cent of all operators who use TV advertising) controlled almost 75 per cent of the TV advertising market.

The main actors in the media market are Agora SA (total 2013 revenue US$380 million), Cyfrowy Polsat SA (US$608 million), regional giants Publicis Groupe SA (US$9.2 billion) and the Finnish group Sanoma Oyj, which operates mainly in Europe (US$2.94 billion). These media agencies also operate in other media.

Other distinctive aspects of the Polish TV advertising market were highlighted in the 2015 KPMG report for International Advertising Association,

Polska. As noted, Polish TV advertising market accounts for more than 50 per cent of the overall advertising market. However, the report also reveals that, despite a 35 per cent growth rate in 2008–14, the advertising market value during that time dropped by 16 per cent. This was a paradoxical result as the dynamics of economic growth usually stimulate advertising expenditure. The report suggests that this reduction in advertising expenditure can be attributed to general cuts in advertising budgets of global companies after the global financial crisis of 2008. Despite Poland's solid economic performance, global economic instability saw advertisers reduce their expenditure in Poland and, indeed, other markets. The advertising market in Poland is also affected by foreign exchange rate differences, as marketing budgets of global corporations are calculated in their home headquarters in foreign currencies (dollars, pounds, euro), which may fluctuate in relation to the Polish currency (*złoty*).

Polish TV and online advertising market: sectoral approach

Between 2010 and 2014, the key advertisers on Polish television were the retail sector (which devoted over 95 per cent of advertising expenditure to television), non-prescription drugs (32 per cent) and the financial sector (26 per cent). Sectors which saw the greatest reduction in television advertising expenditure included telecommunications (which dropped by 38 per cent), food processing (29 per cent) and personal healthcare products (23 per cent).

It is estimated that advertisers from the prescription and non-prescription drugs sector account for almost a fifth of television adspend in Poland (Aflofarm, USP Zdrowie, Polpharma). This reflects the dynamic growth of the Polish non-prescription drug market as well as the expansion of competing products and brands. Moreover, television audience demographics tie in strongly with this market. The level of advertising in this category in Poland is also a reflection of the relatively poor performance of the public healthcare system and its shifting of the costs of self-therapy to consumers (Woźniak-Holecka *et al.*, 2013).

The financial and telecommunications sectors are also significant advertisers. Their adspend reflects their status as high innovation sectors, which regularly bring new products to the market and which are also engaged in intense competition with other brands. In contrast, the advertising budgets for food producers and personal healthcare products have recently fallen. In the case of the food sector, such cuts can be explained by the relative stability of the sector as well as its lower innovation profile compared to other competing sectors, which have seen fewer new products and brands entering the market. Such shifts signal an important change, as the food processing sector had been the undisputed leader in television advertising over 2009–11.

Coca-Cola has been an active advertiser in the Polish market for almost 25 years, operating three production plants and 13 logistics centres across Poland. As the red and white colours of the Coca-Cola brand are the same as the national colours of the Polish flag, global advertising messages can be imbued with national references. This symbolism was used in both the online and social media activities surrounding Coca-Cola's recent global campaign 'Taste the Feeling' during the 2016 Union of European Football Associations (UEFA) European Championship in France. The campaign featured Robert Lewandowski, captain of the Polish national team, as the brand ambassador. Coca-Cola Poland's Instagram account was similarly dominated by Poland's national colours. But Coca-Cola's presence in Poland has not been limited to the sporting arena. The brand has sponsored the popular television programme *The Voice of Poland*, the campaign for which included an advertising series that centred on the programme's casting process. In both cases, the national context reveals itself in the selection of advertising content and the selection of advertising channels such as social media. Global advertising campaigns also contain significant opportunities for local interactivity. In addition to traditional advertising formats, Coca-Cola in Poland promotes an active lifestyle. Global advertising strategies are therefore accompanied by activities that mobilise local communities through social media. Such 'glocalised' activities often include sponsorship of mass events aimed at children and youngsters, such as the Coca-Cola Cup football tournament and the Woodstock Festival Poland, a large music festival that attracts thousands (Coca-Cola Journey, 2016).

Fluctuations in advertising expenditure of big retailers

Big international retail chains, which dominated large format retail sector over the period 1993–2015, remain powerful players in the Polish television advertising market. In comparison to other countries, Poland's discount stores are major advertisers that regularly increase their advertising budgets. National discount retail trade is dominated by international chains managed by the Portuguese group Jerónimo Martins and German-owned Lidl. The intensity of advertising campaigns for both chains results from their high market share and their dynamic growth across the country. Unlike other modern forms of retail, discount retailers typically have a more developed store base, which justifies constant growth of TV advertising. Adspend for discount chains in 2014 thus exceeded the previous year. While largely focused on television, these retailers' fiercely contested advertising campaigns also appear in other media outlets. Such intensity has been further fuelled by the challenges posed by other retail formats, notably hypermarket and supermarket chains as well as the so-called 'convenience stores'.

Lidl is one of the leaders of the format in Europe (Lidl, 2016). It trades across 30 European countries and also operates in the United States. Although it is not yet a global brand, it has clear international credentials. Lidl's advertising strategy for the Polish market strongly stresses the firm's relations with Poland. A recent television campaign featured various Polish TV personalities to highlight the pleasures of cooking products purchased from Lidl. The strategy was a response to the campaign by Lidl's main competitor, Jerónimo Martins, which emphasised its links with Polish food suppliers (Biedronka, 2016). By underscoring their close connections with the Polish market, both campaigns can be deemed 'glocal' insofar as they accentuate the international brand's proximity to the local environment. As discount chains operate across diverse markets with different consumption patterns and retail structures, 'glocalisation' has become an essential marketing strategy.

In contrast to the discount retail chains, sports brand Nike largely conducts its Polish advertising campaigns over the Internet. A de facto version of the global website, Nike's Polish website promotes the brand's current range of products and provides access to its online selling network in Polish. However, Nike's corporate presence links to the brand's global website and appears in English. To this end, 'glocalisation' is restricted to informing local audiences about the firm's range of products and online distribution channels, along with providing access to them. However, the ability to tailor individual user accounts to highlight specific sports activity models combines of global strategy with a highly individualised approach (Nike, 2016).

Conclusions

The most significant differences between eastern and central European advertising markets reflect cultural, social and political differences among Russia and former Soviet republics on the one hand, and Poland, the Czech Republic, Slovakia and Hungary on the other. These differences became more pronounced with the accession of central European countries to the European Union in 2004, which resulted in a significant inflow of foreign investment by global companies. This was also assisted by the presence of global advertising agencies which, in turn, had an impact on the region's advertising practices.

Currently, the main challenge facing international brands is the task of connecting global advertising messages with local markets. New communication channels, such as social media, the Internet and mobile technologies provide new opportunities to connect the global with the local. The Polish experience illustrates how global brands are increasingly utilising the Internet and mobile apps in their advertising strategies at the expense of traditional advertising media. Polish trends also illustrate the ways in which global firms are developing universal values for their brands by synchronising their strategies to meet the emerging behaviours and purchasing patterns of young consumers.

With respect to the character of advertising content produced by global and foreign brands for the Polish market, there is a discernible embrace of national values and symbols to complement the universal message. To this end, the Polish experience indicates that global advertisers will increasingly look toward a hybrid model where 'glocalised' approaches will be used to convey a global message to a local market.

References

Andrews, J. C., Durvasula, S. and Netemeyer, R. G. (1994) 'Testing the cross-national applicability of U.S. and Russian advertising belief and attitude measures', *Journal of Advertising*, 23(1), pp. 71–82.

Biedronka (2016) Website home page. Available at: www.biedronka.pl/ (accessed 14 November 2016).

Coca-Cola Journey (2016) 'Taste the Feeling. Nowa, globalna kampania dla wszystkich marek Coca-Cola'. Available at: www.cocacola.com.pl/historie/taste-the-feeling-nowa-globalna-kampania-dla-wszystkich-marek-coca-cola (accessed 22 February 2017).

Endaltseva, A. (2015) 'The present state of integrated communication in Russia', *Public Relations Review*, 41(4), pp. 533–40.

Fedotova, L. N. (2014) 'Twenty years of advertising in today's Russia', *Sociological Research*, 53(5), pp. 49–60.

Holak, S., Matveev, A. V. and Havlena, W. (2007) 'Nostalgia in post-socialist Russia: Exploring applications to advertising strategy', *Journal of Business Research*, vol. 60(6), pp. 649–55.

IAB Polska (2015) *IAB/PwC AdEx: reklama cyfrowa wciąż na fali wzrostowej*. Available at: http://iab.org.pl/badania-i-publikacje/iabpwc-adex-reklama-cyfrowa-wciaz-na-fali-wzrostowej-2/ (accessed 14 November 2016).

Kolenda, P. (2015) *Customer Journey Online: Perspektywy branżowe*. Available at: http://iab.org.pl/wp-content/uploads/2015/11/Raport_Customer-Journey-Online_2015.pdf (accessed 14 November 2016).

Kubacki, K. and Skinner, H. (2006), 'Poland: Exploring the relationship between national brand and national culture', *Brand Management*, 13(4/5), pp. 284–99.

Lidl (2016) Tradycyjnie czy nowocześnie. Available at: www.lidl.pl/pl/index.htm (accessed 14 November 2016).

M2Press Wire (2014) Press release distribution service. Available at: www.m2.com/m2/web/publication.php/m2presswire (accessed 15 March 2017).

Małecki, B. (2008) *Marketing i reklama w Internecie*. Available at: www.web.gov.pl/g2/big/2009_03/3570a391605a8575fa475bad543eb2fd.pdf (accessed 14 November 2016).

Marketline (2015) 'Advertising in Europe: March 2015', *MarketLine*. Available at: www.marketline.com (accessed 14 November 2016).

Millan, E. S. and Mittal, B. (2010) 'Advertising's new audiences. Consumer response in the new free market economies of central and eastern Europe: The case of the Czech Republic', *Journal of Advertising*, 39(3), pp. 81–98.

Morris, J. (2007) 'Drinking to the nation: Russian television advertising and cultural differentiation', *Europe–Asia Studies*, 59(8), pp. 1,387–403.

Newseria (2015) *Rynek reklamy internetowej w Polsce jest wart 1,2 mld zł*. Available at: www.wprost.pl/ar/489146/Rynek-reklamy-internetowej-w-Polsce-jest-wart-12-mld-zl/ (accessed 14 November 2016).

Nike (2016) *Nike Poland*. Available at: www.nike.com/pl/pl_pl (accessed 14 November 2016).

Saleem, S., Larimo, J. A., Umnik, K. and Kuusik, A. (2015) 'Cultural and paradoxical values in advertising in eastern Europe', *Baltic Journal of Management*, 10(3), pp. 313–30.

Saveleva, O. O. (2006) 'Advertising in Russia and Russian politics: Generator of social conflict or socially meaningful information', *Russian Politics and Law*, 44(5), pp. 71–84.

Stysiak, M. (2014) *Polski rynek reklamowy wzrośnie o ponad 3 proc. w 2015 r., 09.12.2014.* Available at: http://wyborcza.biz/biznes/1,101558,17104133,Polski_rynek_reklamowy_wzrosnie_o_ponad_3_proc__w.html (accessed 14 November 2016).

Ustinova, I. P. (2006) 'English and emerging advertising in Russia', *World Englishes*, 25(2), pp. 267–77.

Wells, L. G. (1991) 'The socioeconomic culture and the advertising process in the Soviet Union'. In Hofman, R. (ed.) *Proceedings of the 1991 Conference of American Academy of Advertising*. New York: D'Arcy Masius Benton & Bowles, pp. 203–12.

Wells, L. G., Van Auken, S. and Ritchie, W. J. (2007) 'Russian advertising attitudes: Reassessing the two-factor model', *Journal of International Consumer Marketing*, 20(2), p. 13.

Wirtualnemedia (2012) *Polacy w internecie rekordowo mocno zirytowani reklamami, 2012–12–05.* Available at: www.wirtualnemedia.pl/artykul/polacy-w-internecie-rekordowo-mocno-zirytowani-reklamami (accessed 14 November 2016).

Woźniak-Holecka, J., Grajek, M., Sobczyk, K., Mazgaj Krzak, K. and Holecki, T. (2013) 'Ekonomiczno-społeczne konsekwencje reklamy w segmencie leków OTC' (Marketing of OTC Medicines in Poland on the Example of television Advertising). *Prace Naukowe Uniwersytetu Ekonomicznego we Wrocławiu*, 305, pp. 853–60.

Wójcicki, P. (2013) *Reklama w internecie: wydatki rosną, skuteczność spada, 2013–01–10.* Available at: www.wirtualnemedia.pl/artykul/reklama-w-internecie-wydatki-rosna-skutecznosc-spada (accessed 14 November 2016).

ZenithOptimedia (2016) *Polski rynek reklamy będzie rósł.* Available at: www.brief.pl/artykul,2269,polski_rynek_reklamy_bedzie_rosl.html (accessed 14 November 2016).

9 Advertising cultures and global influences in sub-Saharan Africa

Nigerian, South African and Kenyan models

Rotimi Williams Olatunji[1]

Introduction

Civilisations are products of culture. The advertising institution is a significant part of the global civilisation, economy and culture. Sub-Saharan Africa (SSA) is selected for analysis in this chapter because of its rich mineral deposits, primary agricultural products and huge population size that have opened up the enclave to global influences and domination, including the activities of global advertisers and advertising agencies (Hatch *et al.*, 2011; *African Development*, 2015; Davies and Penanguer, 2016). The first section of this chapter clarifies concepts such as advertising, globalisation and consumers characteristics in sub-Saharan Africa. The origins and contemporary practices of global advertising institutions in Africa are then discussed, along with influences of advertisers, advertising agencies, media and consumers on advertising practices in sub-Saharan Africa in a globalising culture, using South Africa, Nigeria and Kenya as exemplars.

Conceptual clarifications

Advertising promotes commercial free speech and competition in the economy; it also creates awareness and persuades audiences to patronise available goods, services and ideas. Within this context, advertising is conceived as both economic and cultural institution that 'drives globalisation towards efficiency, cheapness of goods and services, and instant provision of selling messages', (Olatunji, 2005, p. 13). Advertising as a business venture has active players, such as advertisers, advertising agencies, media, consumers and regulatory agencies. Advertising equally reflects extinct and extant cultures, while also functioning as an agent of socialisation through provision of information, education, entertainment and escape. Hence, de Mooij (2004, p. 107) says 'advertising is not (only) made of words, but of culture', which means that advertising messages are culture-laden. McAllister and Mazzarrella (2000, p. 347) also posit that 'Culturally, advertising is a major symbol system in its own right, exposing us to thousands of promotional messages each week'. Thus the advertising institution exerts tremendous influences on peoples' changing habits, modes of living, consumption patterns, attitudes and belief systems.

> Every aspect of advertising represents cultural expression.... Word usage also acquires meanings within cultural contexts. Advertising visuals and dressing patterns of models are important aspects of culture, not to mention the products, services, or ideas being advertised, along with the brand manifestations.... Culture, or some aspects of it, can either be universal or localized. Hence, it is legitimate to talk about the global or the local (advertising) culture.
>
> (Olatunji and Thanny, 2011, p. 17)

Equally, advertising promotes social change and sustainable development, according to the European Association of Communications Agencies and the World Federation of Advertisers (EACA and WFA, 2002, p. 7). Advertising improves the quality of life globally by disseminating messages that are directed at diverse audiences (often paid for by identified sponsors) about products, services, business organisations and governments (or non-governmental organisations) through available media. Moreover, advertising contributes significantly to the three pillars of development identified by EACA and WFA (2002, p. 7), which are 'economic development, environmental protection and social responsibility'. As an inescapable part of the human contemporary existence, advertising promotes sales of goods and services, innovations, and sustainability; it also enhances political, social and environmental well being of nations.

Maynard (2003, pp. 57–8) argues that, although globalisation may suggest 'a monolithic sameness', it is better understood as 'cultural homogenization and cultural heterogenization, universalization and particularism, modernization and postmodernization'. Hence, those who subscribe to this notion associate globalisation with 'homogenisation' 'standardisation', 'Americanisation', 'Westernisation', 'McDonaldisation', 'Disneyfication', 'Walmarting', 'Coca-Colanisation' or Hollywoodisation' (Conversi, 2010); or capitalism (Olurode, 2003). As a consequence, Conversi (2010, pp. 41, 43) maintains that globalisation represents 'unfettered preponderance of American items of mass consumption ... to the virtual erasure of millions of (other) cultural producers'.

Against this backdrop, globalisation promotes standardisation of advertising, which tends to consider an advertisement as 'a universal commodity, product or brand that must offer "one sight, one sound, and one sell"' across cultures and markets (Olatunji, 2013, p. 104). Advertising standardisation promotes consistency in brand image; sameness in advertising campaigns across different markets; and uniformity in advertising production, illustrative materials and media buying. This rarely happens because factors such as consumer differences across cultures and differences in language, marketing environments, media channels, legislation and policies across nations often militate against the adoption of a centralised or standardised approach to advertising.

As an alternative, advertising campaigns can be glocalised, another term for adaptation or hybridisation of advertising. This occurs when global advertising messages and campaigns are modified to suit regional or sub-regional markets. It allows subsidiary advertising agencies to adapt a global advertising campaign, modified to suit market peculiarities. The slogan often associated with glocalisation is 'think global, act local'. Glocalisation is justified because people, places and brands differ. 'There may be global products, but there are no global people; there may be global brands, but there are no global motivations for buying these brands' (de Mooij, 1998, p. 3).

Glocalisation allows for separate messages to reach buyers in different markets by fitting the message to each particular market and accommodating differences in cultural, economic, legal, media and product features between and within countries. Cultural globalisation is rare since cultures are not uniform but frequently undergo hybridisation or remixing (Pieterse, 1994). The American culture, for instance, is not entirely American, but an amalgam of sub-groups, races and classes drawn from within and outside extinct and extant American society. Knobel and Lankshear (2008, p. 23) noted that 'No remix, no culture', which means that there are no monolithic, or stand-alone cultures. Therefore, hybridisation of advertising seems a more attractive paradigm because it allows sub-Saharan Africa to adapt its rich and diverse cultures to global influences.

The northern part of Africa (except Sudan) is classified as Maghreb; south from there is sub-Saharan Africa, comprising Central Africa; East Africa; West Africa; and Southern Africa (Countries of the World, 2016). Over 3,000 indigenous languages are spoken in Africa (Hatch *et al.*, 2011). The largest concentration of African population resides in sub-Saharan Africa (856 million out of the over one billion African populations) (National Geographic Society, 2016). Africa is largely economically dependent on advanced economies owing to its status as a producer of primary agricultural products and mineral resources, in addition to being a huge consumer of finished products of industrialised nations of the world. Africa is the fastest growing telecommunications market globally (Nyirenda-Jere and Biru, 2015). This, along with the Internet revolution, strengthens the integration of Africa with the global community. This chapter examines the dimension, depth and influences of globalisation on advertising in sub-Saharan Africa, with many examples drawn from Nigeria, South Africa and Kenya.

The African market, globalisation and advertising cultures

The partition of Africa at the Berlin Conference of 1884 and subsequent colonisation was largely to create the platform for the exploitation of Africa's economy:

> In 1886, the largest gold deposits in the world were discovered on the Rand in South Africa and there were rumours of Katanga copper. Few nations felt they could sit idly by and see undiscovered riches fall to their rivals. Even if a nation had no immediate need for African products and markets, it was believed to be both good business sense and insurance to take as large a slice as possible for future use.
>
> (Webster and Boahen, 1967, p. 234)

Today, Africa remains the 'bride of foreign investors' (*AdNews*, 2013a, p. 24); the competition for Africa's resources is intense and unabated.

In 2008, African countries received a total of US$72 billion foreign direct investments (FDI), five times more than was attracted in 2000; it exceeded the amount received by Brazil (US$45.1 billion). Consumer expenditure in Africa in 2010 was US$600 billion; US$1 trillion is predicted by 2020 (Hatch *et al.*, 2011, p. 3). Africa's equity market is on the increase: the Nigerian and Kenyan markets have risen more than 50 per cent since 2012. 'Over the past decade, Africa supplied six of the world's ten economies with the fastest growth', (*AdNews*, 2013a, p. 24). Moreover, there is a significant decrease in poverty levels in Africa along with rapid urbanisation on the continent (Hatch *et al.*, 2011, p. 11).

Nigeria's economy, the largest on the continent, climbed from 6.2 per cent in 2012 to 6.8 per cent in 2013; agriculture, services, construction and solid mineral sectors were the main drivers, in addition to crude oil. South Africa is very attractive to global investors because of its energy production and distribution, finance, real estate sector and business services, which rose by 3.9 per cent (*African Development*, 2015, p. 5).[2] The Kenyan economy is very prominent in the areas of services, tourism, manufacturing, construction and mining, although tourism suffered as a result of series of terrorism attacks on major targets in the country. It is important to note that the economic development in North Africa is stunted since the commencement of the Arab Spring and the series of political upheavals in Libya, Egypt, Tunisia and Algeria. Combinations of these factors leave sub-Saharan Africa with greater prospects for economic development and global attention (*African Development*, 2015 p. 5).

Leading economies in sub-Saharan Africa are Nigeria (West Africa), South Africa (Southern Africa) and Kenya (East Africa). South Africa and Nigeria account for more than 50 per cent of total consumer spending in sub-Saharan Africa: 'The new African consumer is a force to contend with and represents an opportunity no company can afford to ignore'; average income in Africa is growing, with a rising middle class (see Table 9.1) (Hatch *et al.*, 2011).

Based on 2010 population estimates, consumers in Africa are heavily concentrated in Nigeria (151 million), Ethiopia (83 million) and South Africa (49 million), with higher purchasing power in South Africa than elsewhere (US$215 billion); Nigeria (US$115 billion); and Kenya (US$23 billion). These three countries have a combined consumer spend of US$353 billion, which is 81 per cent of the total US$437 billion consumer expenditure in sub-Saharan Africa.

There are five basic categories of consumers in Africa:

- basic survivors;
- working families;
- rising strivers;
- cosmopolitan professionals; and
- the affluent (Hatch *et al.*, 2011).

Table 9.1 Economic focal points in sub-Saharan Africa

Sub-Region	Country	Population (2009)	2010 Spend (US$)	2020 Est. Spend (US$)
East Africa	Kenya	40 million	$23 billion	$37 billion
	Ethiopia	83 million	$20 billion	$43 billion
	Uganda	33 million	$15 billion	$30 billion
West Africa	Nigeria	151 million	$115 billion	$167 billion
	Ghana	24 million	$15 billion	$29 billion
	Senegal	13 million	$10 billion	$16 billion
Southern Africa	South Africa	49 million	$215 billion	$315 billion
	Angola	19 million	$14 billion	$18 billion
	Zambia	13 million	$10 billion	$23 billion
Total		425 million	$437 billion	$678 billion

Source: Hatch *et al.*, 2011, p. 16

The largest group (in 2015) were basic survivors at 45 per cent, followed by rising strivers (16 per cent), cosmopolitan professionals (3.1 per cent) and the affluent (2.8 per cent). Even though cosmopolitan professionals and the affluent still constitute a relatively small position of the market, their spending power translates into significant opportunity for luxury products and services.

It is thus the growing size of the African market, especially middle-class consumers, that makes the market all the more attractive to global advertising influences.

Multinational corporations and indigenous companies in sub-Saharan Africa

There are several categories of advertisers in sub-Saharan Africa, including multinational corporations (MNCs), continental brands and sub-regional and national advertisers. Advertising spend on the continent is dictated by these advertisers. Global advertisers operating in Africa include brands such as Coca-Cola, Procter and Gamble (P&G); Nestlé; Apple; Pepsi Cola; Lufthansa, British Airways; Air France; UAC; Shell Petroleum Development Company, Total, Mobil Oil Producing and Chevron.

In addition, other strong brands abound. For example, around 40 per cent of Guinness Breweries sales are from sub-Saharan Africa, while Africa's third largest cellphone, Airtel had its revenue in Africa increased by over 16 per cent in recent years. Celtel, a mobile-phone company founded by a British-Sudanese entrepreneur, MO Ibrahim, was later sold to Zain, a Middle Eastern cellphone outfit, but now owned by Bharti Airtel of India. Walmart investment in Africa is also on the increase with its acquisition of Massmart (SA) and its recent agreement to build its chains of stores in Lagos, Nigeria (Adelakun, 2015, p. 64).

The growing dominance of Chinese firms in Africa is also noteworthy. Ogunlesi (2015, p. 25) observes that about 20 per cent of SA's Standard Bank shares are owned by the Industrial and Commercial Bank of China: 'the acquisition, in 2007, at the cost of US$5.5 billion is … China's biggest single foreign investment ever'. The Chinese firm (Sinoma) is a major builder of cement plants in Africa. Ogunlesi (2015, p. 25)[3] observes that:

> One of Africa's big tragedies is that so little of its trade is carried out among its countries. In fact, only about 12 per cent of all African trade takes place among African countries, the lowest in the world, compared to about 50 per cent for Asia and North America, and 70 per cent for Europe.

South Africa accounts for almost half the continent's entire manufacturing exports; it is the only African country in the G20, and its financial markets and infrastructure are ahead of the continent. 'For every Nigerian brand (Dangote, Globacom) making an inroads across Africa, there are several South African ones' (Shoprite, Pep, Mr. Price, Woolworths, MTN, Promasidor, Naspers, Tiger, and Nampack and SA's Standard Bank) (Ogunlesi, 2015, p. 25). Again, ECOBANK, a Togo-based bank raised US$250 million in 2012 from the South African state-employee Pension Fund, to purchase OCEANIC Bank, Nigeria (*AdNews*, 2013a, p. 24). Although Nigeria provides content through Nollywood, SA's Naspers GOTV and DSTV, and Kenya's Nation Media Group are dominant.

MTN makes much of its money from Nigeria rather than other parts of the continent, and is now listed among the top 100 most valuable global brands. 'MTN is rated No. 88 at US$9.2 billion and becomes the first African brand to enter the ranking, citing the 7th Annual BrandZ™ Top Most Valuable Global Brands in May 2012; it moved to the 79th position in 2013' (*AdNews*, 2012b, p. 7; 2013b, p. 10). MTN arrived in Nigeria as 'a little known GSM operator that has leveraged Nigeria's huge population to become the biggest telecoms operator in Africa with over 60 million subscribers in Nigeria alone' (Adelakun, 2015, p. 54).

Nigeria's position as an economically powerful nation is furthered by brands such as Nigeria's Dangote Group, which has cement plants in 15 African countries, including Kenya, Nigeria and Mali, with Nigeria's plant having the largest capacity of 29.3 million metric tonnes per annum and an additional plant scheduled for Nepal, Asia (Ihua-Maduenyi, 2015, p. 3). The Dangote Group (Nigeria) began in 1981 as an importer of cement, later sugar, flour, salt and fish, but has moved 'up the value chain from commodity trading to producing these commodities' (Davies and Penanguer, 2016, p. 10). Additionally, Nigerian Breweries PLC, half-owned by Diageo and prominent Nigerian investors, is listed in the Nairobi Stock Exchange, with a combined market of over 120 million in Kenya, Uganda and Tanzania, but smaller than the 167 million Nigerian market size (*AdNews*, 2013a, p. 24). United Bank for Africa, Zenith Bank, First Bank and ECOBANK are other continental brands. There are also Nigeria's Jumia (an e-commerce platform), and IROKO TV, which are contributing in the digital economies of the world.

Other examples of advertisers from Africa are Kenya's Safaricom and Bridge International Academies, Morocco's Saham Group, an insurance corporation with a solid presence in 12 African countries, along with BMCE, another Moroccan bank with a dominant presence in 17 other African countries, and Danone, a French dairy giant that acquired 41 per cent of West Africa's largest, Ghana-based frozen dairy producer, Fan Milk International. Eagles gather wherever carcasses are found! The growing concentration of global advertisers in Africa largely explains the huge concentration of global advertising agencies and media channels in Africa, since agencies follow advertisers wherever they go. Operations of multinational advertising agencies in sub-Saharan Africa are now discussed.

Multinational advertising agencies and their affiliates in sub-Saharan Africa

The advertising industry is an integral part of the global economic system. In addition, advertising agencies often trail corporations to nations that offer greater economic prospects. Remarkably, Western advertising agencies followed European corporations into Africa, the same way colonialism followed European trade and missionary activities. In the Nigerian case, the Royal Niger Company (RNC) (which later became the United African Company (UAC) and Lever Brothers International), incorporated the first advertising agency in Britain on 13 August 1928, called West African Publicity Limited, headquartered in Lagos, Nigeria (Molokwu, 2000). The agency was later called LINTAS (Lever International Advertising Services), the first global advertising agency to operate in West Africa, in 1928. Nigeria's LINTAS is a member of the SSC&B LINTAS Worldwide, the Interpublic Group and now AMMIRATI PURIS Worldwide, a group with offices in more than 80 countries globally (Olatunji, 2013, p. 34). Other foreign advertising agencies that made incursions into the Nigerian marketing environment during the colonial era were Ogilvy, Benson and Mather (OB&M), Graham and Gills (G&G), Advertising and Marketing Services (AMS) and Grant Advertising. For recent examples of foreign advertising agencies with Nigerian affiliates are, see Olatunji (2010, 2013) and Table 9.2 below.

The oldest advertising agency established in South Africa is J. Walter Thompson (JWT), established in 1927; it originated from the US over 150 years ago, and has over 200 offices globally, and a direct workforce of more than 10,000. JWT produced the first-ever television commercial in 1938 (J. Walter Thompson Johannesburg 2016, 2014). Global advertising conglomerates and subsidiaries operate in Africa, predominantly through affiliations and partnerships with local agencies. Selected examples from South Africa are presented in Table 9.2 (Marklives, 2016). Y&R pioneered integrated marketing communication in Kenya, and others include Ogilvy and Mather (EA), Ogilvy Kenya, Access Leo Burnett and TBWA East Africa, among others (Commonwealth Network, 2016).

Global advertising agencies operating in sub-Saharan Africa are concentrated in South Africa, Nigeria and Kenya, in that order. Havas, for instance, has its African

Table 9.2 Global advertising agencies and affiliates in selected sub-Saharan African countries

Nigeria	South Africa	Kenya
Worldwide Centerspread/FCB	FCB Johannesburg	Ogilvy and Mather (EA)
Prima Garnet/O&M	O&M Cape Town	Ogilvy Kenya
LTC/JWT Worldwide	JWT South Africa	
Sunrise/DMB&B Worldwide	Y&R Johannesburg	Ayton Y&R
CT&A/G&G	Havas SA/Havas Worldwide	Acasia Media Services
Insight/Grey	Volcano/Grey SA	ScanGroup Limited
STB/McCann	Aqua Group (SA)	Buzz Afrique
141 Worldwide/WPP Group		Medialinque International
Casers/DDB Worldwide	DDB SA	4 × 4 Kenya
LINTAS/Lagos/LINTAS WW	Network BBDO	
	140 BBDO	
Concept Unit/TBWA	TBWA/Hunt/Lascaris	TBWA East Africa
SO&U/Saatchi & Saatchi	M&C Saatchi	
Rosabel/Leo Burnett Worldwide	Leo Burnett Publicis Group	Access Leo Burnett
Zepol/Impulse Ad	Quirk Advertising (SA)	

Sources: Author's compilation.

headquarters in SA, its second largest office in Tunisia and smaller offices in Nigeria, Kenya, Ivory Coast, Cameroon and Senegal (Bender and Vranica, 2010). Notable examples of multinational advertising agencies in Senegal, a French-speaking country in West Africa are McCann Erickson and Ocean Ogilvy. Kofi Amoo-Gottfried, Chief Executive Officer of Publicis Worldwide in Ghana, West Africa, consequently explains that, 'Ad executives believe Africa is the next big market opportunity, after China, Latin America and India' (Bender and Vranica, 2010). He noted further that 'growth in emerging markets will offset other regions, such as Western Europe, where expenditure growth is slowing'. WPP generated about US$500 million in revenue yearly from the African continent with the hope of a 10 per cent increase from 2010; it purchased a 33 per cent stake in SA's Smollan Group; and another 27.5 per cent in Kenyan-based Scangroup Limited. The amount might be considered 'small', but the CEO says it represented the equivalent of what the group earned in India plus about half of its revenue from China and Brazil during the same period (Bender and Vranica, 2010).

A news release provided justification for a joint venture agreement between Dentsu and Media Fuse, a Media Independent firm in Nigeria, stating that 'Nigeria is the most populous country in Africa, and the flow of foreign capital into the country is increasing' (Dentsu, 2014). It claims further that Nigeria's GDP has been growing at a rate of 6–7 per cent over the past few years and by April 2014 the country's economy surpassed that of South Africa's thus becoming the largest on the African continent (Kannan, 2014).

The huge presence of MNCs, advertising agencies and media in sub-Saharan Africa represents the continuation of colonial domination, since most of the local partners merely serve as appendages of prominent global advertising agencies. However the acclaimed benefits of advertising agencies affiliation are the provision of professional training opportunities, the sharing of technical ideas and technology, and opportunities to partner on global creative briefs (Olatunji, 2010). On the other hand, the tendency towards the subordination of local advertising agencies to global affiliates in terms of the design of creative advertising concepts and capital flight through repatriation of profits by foreign agencies points towards the negative influences of globalisation on advertising practice in sub-Saharan Africa (Olatunji, 2005, 2010, 2013).

Moreover, there is growing dominance of South African-based advertising agencies in sub-Saharan Africa. 'Marketing in an inter-connected world tends to produce (global), continental, regional and sub-regional powers' (Olatunji, 2005, p. 15). Thus, while advertising agencies from Europe, North America and Asia exert overwhelming dominance on advertising agencies of African origin, advertising agencies originating from South Africa are dominant players in the entire sub-Saharan Africa. Nigeria's influence is equally pronounced in the West African sub-region, while the influence of Kenya in East Africa is glaring. The foregoing represents a 'pecking order' phenomenon in advertising agencies operation, where the more economically powerful agencies tend to dominate the weaker ones.

Advertising media stakeholders in sub-Saharan Africa

Advertising messages are often channelled to heterogeneous audiences through existing media vehicles. In addition to the traditional media (word of mouth, print, broadcast, outdoor), new/digital and social media are growing in importance. In Table 9.3, advertising expenditure based on media category in Egypt (North Africa) and South Africa (SSA) are presented.

Television, newspaper, magazine and radio are still very popular in SA and Egypt. On a comparative basis, SA spends more (US$1.215 million) on television advertising than Egypt (US$762 million). In 2010, there was a decline in media spending on TV in Egypt in 2011 (US$410 million) compared to SA (US$1.330 million). Digital media and Internet advertising spend is on the increase in SA, although data were not largely available for Egypt, due to 'continued political upheaval [that] has led to a major decline in advertising spends in Egypt' (Aegis Media, 2013, p. 154). Also, because of near-government dominance of broadcast media in Egypt, youths and other dissenting voices tend to migrate to using social media.

Similarly, media are active in Senegal, West Africa. Although with limited circulation figures, examples of popular print media are *Sud Quotidien, WalFadjri, Le Populaire, Il Est Midi* and *Nouvel Horizon*, to mention just a few. According to US FCS and DoS (2012) 'Radio advertising is very efficient.... Radio is the medium of choice for much of the population outside major cities because of easy accessibility'. There are some 75 radio stations in Senegal, four television stations and 21 newspapers. Satellite broadcast into Senegal comes mostly from the South African DSTV and France's CANAL; Internet access is very efficient, along with telecom-

Table 9.3 Advertising expenditure in Africa: Egypt and South Africa compared (in US$ million)

Media	2010		2011		2012		2013		2014f*	
	Egypt	S.A	Egypt	S.A	Egypt	S.A	Egypt	S.A	Egypt	S.A
Television	762	1,215	410	1,330	201	1,464	251	1,611	314	1,740
Newspaper	314	653	263	708	44	729	55	751	68	774
Magazine	14	266	10	274	1	254	2	241	2	229
Radio	36	355	30	434	5	502	7	562	8	630
Cinema	**	28	**	47	3	0	4	0	5	0
Outdoor	**	125	**	140	**	162	**	181	**	199
Digital	**	66	**	75	**	82	**	88	**	92
Display	**	42	**	57	**	41	**	44	**	46
Search	**	9	**	10	**	16	**	18	**	18
Mobile	**	13	**	17	**	20	**	22	**	23
Other	**	1	**	2	**	4	**	4	**	5
Total	1,126	2,707	712	3,007	255	3,193	318	3,434	398	3,664

Source: Aegis Media, 2013, pp. 156, 188

Notes
* 2014 Forecast.
** Not available.

munications infrastructure. There are about 9.6 million mobile phones, and 361,000 landlines for a country with nearly 14 million inhabitants. French is the most dominant language of the media/press, along with the indigenous language Wolof. France-based Outdoor Media, JCDecaux acquired a 70 per cent stake in Continental Outdoor Media, which, in 2015, was Africa's largest outdoor agency. Davies and Penanguer (2016, p. 9) explain that through the acquisition of Continental Outdoor Media JCDecaux Group became the largest outdoor advertising firm in Africa, where it owns over 36,000 advertising panels in 16 countries.

In Nigeria, the traditional media (print and broadcast) provide wider channels to advertising messages. Oso (2012, p. 11) reports that the 'Nigeria mass media system is market-driven'. There are a total of 82 television stations in Nigeria: 41 owned by the federal government, 29 state government-owned and 12 privately owned. There are also 121 radio stations: 43 owned by the federal government; 54 owned by state governments; and 24 privately owned. Broadcasting is 'not liberalized in eight sub-Saharan African (SSA) countries; they are partially liberalized in 15; and completely liberalized in 25 countries', including Nigeria, South Africa and Kenya (Balancing Act, 2014, p. 17). Liberalisation of the media led to multiplicity of broadcast media channels and increased audience fragmentation; advertising media planning is more challenging (Olatunji, 2007). With new signal carriers, 'all broadcasters will have access to a larger national footprint'; two signal carriers are already transmitting 50 new channels in Kenya, and a total of 19 countries in Africa are switching to digital broadcasting (Balancing Act, 2014, p. 19; Nyirenda-Jere and Biru, 2015).

Social media platforms are rising in importance in Africa: 'Over five years, Facebook has grown from practically no users in sub-Saharan Africa to become the most widely used social platform' (Balancing Act, 2014, p. 9). The heaviest users of social media and mobile communications in Africa are Nigeria (12 million), South Africa (10.2 million), Kenya (3.8 million), Ghana (2.4 million), Angola (1.3 million), Senegal (1.0 million), Uganda (1.18 million) and Tanzania (1.34 million). While traditional media will help advertisers 'reach out to the mass, social media will.... Engage them. Retain them. Keep them loyal to you' (Adedeji, 2015). The use of the Internet to get news and information on a daily basis is growing: Ethiopia (55 per cent), South Africa (62 per cent), Ghana (63 per cent), Kenya (68 per cent) and Nigeria (69 per cent). Online news blogging is rising in Nigeria, South Africa, Ethiopia, Kenya, Tanzania and Senegal: South Africa's *Metro FM* (301, 208 likes); *Daily Sun*, SA (275,850 likes); Information Nigeria (1.4m likes), followed by Naija.com (1.25m likes) (Balancing Act, 2014).

The telecommunications industry in Africa in 2014 contributed nearly US$102 billion to the continent's GDP. In addition, the industry created over two million jobs, with nearly 900 million connections, thereby serving 80 per cent of the African population:

> The rapid adoption of mobile technology is changing the continent's socio-economic and political circle.... From SMS and Voice services to surfing the Internet, mobile devices are becoming indispensable tools for many Africans, both old and young.
>
> (Elegbede, 2015, p. 15)

Advertisers were early adopters of the mobile phone as a medium for advertising in Kenya, Tunisia and Uganda. The Kenyan mobile service provider, M-Pisa introduced mobile money in 2007: 'Since its inception, the cumulative value of the money transferred via M-Pesa was over US$3.7 billion – almost 10 per cent of Kenya's annual GDP' (Aker and Mbiti, 2010, p. 221). Hollis (2013), Chief Global Analyst at Millward Brown, concludes that 'mobile communication is the next big opportunity for brands' in Africa; in Kenya alone, 96 per cent of subjects interviewed agree that their mobile phones help them become more efficient, '19 per cent higher than the global average' (Hollis, 2013, p. 23). About 367 million people were subscribed to mobile telecommunications in Africa by mid-2015. Additionally, there are about 160 million smartphones in Africa, which is expected to rise to 540 million by 2020 (Elegbede, 2015). This confirms the status of Africa as the fastest growing telecommunications market globally: 'Sub-Saharan Africa is the cockpit of change in terms of the global digital divide and changing media use' (Balancing Act, 2014, p. 5). Nyirenda-Jere and Biru (2015, p. 3) also reported that 'Africa has the highest growth in mobile subscriptions year-on-year since the turn of the century. Mobile revenues are about 3.7 per cent of GDP, three times as much as in developed countries'. The effectiveness of advertising media in Africa is hampered by infrastructural and human capital deficiencies, along with endemic poverty (Olatunji, 2013). Access to electricity is highest in Ghana (74 per cent), South Africa (34 per cent) and Senegal (33 per cent), but as low as 25 per cent (Nigeria), 23 per cent (Tanzania) and 16 per cent (Kenya) (Balancing Act, 2014. p. 20). The rural populace is largely under-served; access to electronic media and Internet penetration both tend to be low amongst the rural populace. This is not surprising considering the relative socio-economic status of rural versus urban populations.

Advertising language and culture in sub-Saharan Africa

Foreign languages are widely adopted as official languages in Africa, with few exceptions: English is the official language of Nigeria, Ghana, Kenya and Tanzania; French is officially spoken in Algeria, Cameroon, Senegal, Republic of Benin and Gabon. Advertising through mainstream media takes place mostly through the official languages. However, indigenous language use in media is growing: Swahili is the official language in Tanzania; Afrikaans is used in South Africa; WAZOBIA FM is broadcast in Pidgin English; the NIFAAJI FM Channel entirely broadcasts in Yoruba in Lagos, Nigeria; Kass TV is broadcast in Kalenjin, Kenya; Uganda has a Bukkede TV station that broadcasts in the Lugande language; and Wolof is used in Senegal. There are about 107 vernacular radio stations in Kenya, as of 2010, and these are popular amongst some 81 per cent of Kenyans aged 15 and over who communicate more in indigenous languages outside official settings.

Balancing Act (2014, p. 6) reports that, in a study based in Nigeria which involved the use of Pidgin and the English language to disseminate an SMS advertising campaign, the Pidgin version of the ad secured a higher level of response than the English language version of the ad. A similar study reports the effectiveness of the local languages in South Africa, which led Balancing Act (2014, p. 6) to conclude that, although English, French, Portuguese or any other foreign language 'may be [the] most effective language to reach already educated people (in Africa), ... one or more vernacular languages may be needed to reach those who have received less education'. This implies that advertising in Africa will not only be increasingly glocalised, but also localised. 'Sub-Saharan Africa has developed a rich vernacular language media' (Balancing Act, 2014 p. 28). The potentials of vernacular language needs to be harnessed to promote the development of advertising in Africa.

Multinational advertising agencies and creative advertising campaigns in Africa

The reputation of an advertising agency lies in its ability to produce creative selling messages. There are close rivalries and competitiveness among existing advertising agencies in Africa in the sphere of creative campaign executions. In South Africa the rivalry was once between Grey Philips and BBDO (in the 1980s), followed by Grey and Ogilvy, Ogilvy and TBWA Hunt Lascaris; and later between Hunt Lascaris and Jupiter, and Drawing and Network BBDO.

Jupiter and TBWA Hunt Lascaris were named joint winners in 2010, but there-after Ogilvy Johannesburg was named agency of the year. 'Now the process has gone full cycle as Ogilvy Cape Town has become the biggest and most creative agency in the country' (Koenderman, 2014, p. 5). In terms of brands, Ndirangu (2014) says 'Kenya's Top Ten TV Ads', were those of brands that adopted a glocalised approach: Unilever's OMO 'Stain removal', 'KCB Home Loan' campaign, Saraficom's 'Chattitude Bundle', the Crown Paint's 'Colour Your World' and Johnny Walker's 'Walk with Giants', to mention a few; while Coca-Cola (which adopted a global approach) was reported at the bottom ten in terms of creative execution.

The Association of Advertising Agencies of Nigeria (AAAN), since its maiden edition in 2006, organises the Lagos Advertising and Ideas Awards (LAIF) annually to honour advertising agencies and brands adjudged to be most creative. In the 2009 edition, DDB Lagos (with its MTN advertisement) emerged as the most creative advertising agency; Lowe Lintas was the most creative agency in 2011, winning 'the only grand prix at the event with its Star TV commercial' (*AdNews*, 2012b, p. 4). In 2012 and 2013, Insight Communications emerged as the most creative advertising agency, a position that went to DDB Lagos in 2014.[4]

While these are the most creative campaigns in Nigeria, a past President of the AAAN emphasised the need for 'increased localized advertising in Nigeria; a lot of South African ads are strictly South African'. He concludes that Nigerian advertising needs to find its place 'in the global advertising sphere' by emphasising Nigeria's rich and diverse cultures (*AdNews*, 2012b, p. 4). EACA and WFA (2012, p. 18) say the current trend is not towards the creation of global campaigns: 'what worked for one market did not necessarily work for another ... brands do not cross cultures easily'. Thus glocalised and localised advertising campaigns by advertising agencies in sub-Saharan Africa will potentially promote more culturally relevant advertising campaigns than the globalised variant, as the case study below shows.

Case study: ETISALAT's press advertisement – 'we have roots across 9ja'

The purpose of this case study is to demonstrate the effectiveness of Pidgin English in Nigeria in the design and dissemination of culturally sensitive advertising campaigns in sub-Saharan Africa.[5] In the campaign, the copy platform presents Etisalat as a telecommunications brand that enjoys national coverage and responds to the nation's diverse cultures. The campaign theme: 'We have roots across 9ja' means 'We have roots across Nigeria'. Olorunnisola (2009) refers to words such as '9ja' as 'Click', 'Net Lingo' or 'GSM Lingo' language. Visuals in the advertising campaign include local models, attired in local costumes of selected multi-ethnic groups and languages in Nigeria. Local historical landmarks and nature-related tourist sites are also featured. For example, a young couple dressed in Yoruba attire are displayed on Olumo Rock in

Abeokuta, South-West. There are local variations of this in Benin, (South-South), Imo (South-East), Plateau State (North-Central), and other northern states of Nigeria. The historical landmarks are 'Mapo Hall' (a colonial heritage), in Ibadan, the National Theatre, Lagos, the famous Onitsha Bridge (South-East) and the ancient Palace of Emir of Zaria, described as 'the traditional Hausa design', which surrounds 'the 500 year old palace of the Emir of one of the original seven Hausa city states'. Body copy reads: 'a quality network connecting over 10 million people, our roots are firmly entrenched in all 36 states across 9ja'. The campaign emphasises Nigeria's diversities, a country with more than '250 living languages … more languages than any other African country'. It calls for 'Unity in diversity', among Nigerians who should 'Keep speaking the language of unity and togetherness'. Thus the campaign is more than brand advertising: it represents a social responsibility advertising that promotes national integration, peace and development.

Conclusion

Globalisation produces increasing foreign direct investment in Africa, including increasing presence of global and affiliate advertising agencies. For advertising institutions, agencies and stakeholders to remain relevant in a globalising context, there is a need for increasing sensitivity to Africa's diverse languages, values and cultures, along with the changing media landscape, highly segmented and increasingly sophisticated audiences. Thus, in the era of globalisation, there is an urgent need for cultural remixes, hybridisation and adaptation in the advertising industry so as to enhance the sustainable growth and development of the African continent.

Notes

1 Acknowledgement: Dr Lekan Fadolapo, Executive Secretary of the Association of Advertising Agencies of Nigeria (AAAN), for providing data on creative awards won by advertising agencies in Nigeria (2013–14).
2 With the rapid decline in crude oil prices in the first half of 2016, Nigeria's economy, like most other oil producing countries in Africa, has continued to shrink.
3 Ogunlesi (2015) is the review of a recent title by McNamee, T., Pearson, M. and Boer, W. (2015) (eds). *Africans Investing in Africa: Understanding Business and Trade Sector by Sector.* London: Palgrave Macmillan.
4 Data were provided by the Executive Secretary of the AAAN, organizers of LAIF.
5 The campaign was launched by 141 Worldwide and exposed in *The Punch*, 17 November 2011, pp. 28–41).

References

Adali, E., Diaz, A., Page, P., Shanadi, G, Woo, Z. M. and Zabal, H. (2000) 'Global best practices'. Paper presented at the American Academy of Advertising, 14 April, Newport Marriot, Newport.
Adedeji, B. (2015) 'Advertising can kill your business', *The Punch*, 11 June, p. 15.

Adelakun, A. (2015) 'As Ambode lusts after Walmart', *The Punch*, 13 August.

AdNews (2012a) 'MTN joins top most valuable brands', *AdNews*, May, p. 7.

AdNews (2012b) 'Nigeria's most creative agencies, according to LAIF 2012', *AdNews*, December, pp. 4–5.

AdNews (2013a) 'Africa as a bride of foreign investors … foreign ad agencies want to upstage Nigerian counterparts', *AdNews*, February, pp. 18–24.

AdNews (2013b) 'MTN moves up in BRANDZTM Top 100 most valuable global brands: Apple remains number one', *AdNews*, June, p. 10.

Aegis Media (2013) *Aegis Global Advertising Expenditure Report*. London: Aegis Media.

African Development (2015) 'Global growth and Africa's economic trends editorial', *African Development*, 2(2), pp. 4–5.

Aker, J. C. and Mbit, I. M. (2010) 'Mobile phones and economic development in Africa', *Journal of Economic Perspectives*, 224(3), pp. 207–32.

Balancing Act (2014) *The sub-Saharan Media Landscape: Then, Now and in the Future*. Available at: www.telecoms.internetandbroacastinginafrica (accessed 14 November 2016).

Barta, R., Myers, J. G. and Aaker, D. A. (1996) *Advertising Management*. New Delhi: Prentice-Hall of India.

Bender, R. and Vranica, S. (2010) 'Global ad agencies flocking to Africa', *The Wall Street Journal*. Available at: www.wsj.com/articles/SB10001424052702304741404575 564193783950352 (accessed 14 November 2016).

Commonwealth Network (2016), *Sectors in Kenya*. Available at: www.commonwealthof-nations.org/sectors-kenya/business/advertisingmarketingandpr/ (accessed 14 November 2016).

Conversi, D. (2010) 'The limits of cultural globalisation', *Journal of Critical Globalisation Studies*, 3, pp. 36–59.

Countries of the World (2016) *List of Countries in Africa*. Available at: www.countries-ofthe-world.com/countries-of-africa.html (accessed 14 November 2016).

Davies, M. and Penanguer, A. (2016) *Becoming an African Champion: Ingredients for Business Success*, Deloitte Tohmatsu Limited.

Dentsu (2014) 'Dentsu announces joint venture agreement with Nigerian media agency media fuse', News Release by Dentsu Inc., Yokyo, Japan, released on 5 August. Available at: www.dentsu.com (accessed 14 November 2016).

EACA and WFA (2012). *Industry as a Partner for Sustainable Development*. London: European Association of Communications Agencies and World Federation of Advertisers.

Elegbede, T. (2015). 'The worth of Africa's mobile industry', *The Punch*, Thursday, 15 October, p. 5.

Hatch, G., Becker, P. and van Zyl, M. (2011) *The Dynamic African Consumer Market: Exploring Growth Opportunities in sub-Saharan Africa*. South Africa: Accenture.

Hollis, N. (2013) 'Mobile is the big opportunity in Africa', *AdNews*, March, p. 23.

Ihua-Maduenyi, M. (2015) 'Dangote builds plant in Nepal', *The Punch*, 27 August 27, p. 3.

J. Walter Thompson Johannesburg (2014) *JWT wins 17 Accolades including Grand Prix and 4 Gold at African Cristals*. Available at: www.jwt.com/en/jwtkenya/news/jwt-wins-17-awards-including-grand-prix-4-gold-at-african-cristals/ (accessed 14 November 2016).

J. Walter Thompson Johannesburg (2016) Home page. Available at: www.jwt.com/en/jwtjohannesburg/ (accessed 14 November 2016).

Kannan, S. (2014) *Dentsu Announces Joint Venture Agreement with Nigerian Media Agency Media Fuse*. Available at: www.dentsu.com (accessed 14 November 2016).

Knobel, M. and Lankshear, C. (2008) 'Remix: The art and craft of endless hybridization', *Journal of Adolescent & Adult Literacy*, 52(1), pp. 23–33.

Koenderman, T. (2014) 'Ad Agency of the Year Awards: Ogilvy Cape Town: Full circle', *AdNews*, February, p. 5.

McAllister, M. P. and Mazzarrella, S. R. (2000) 'Advertising and consumer culture', *Mass Communication & Society*, 3(4), pp. 347–50.

Marklives (2016) *Ranking South African Ad Agencies by Revenue*. Available at: www.marklives.com/ranking-south-african-ad-agencies-by-revenue/ (accessed 14 November 2016).

Maynard, M. L. (2003) 'From global to glocal: How Gillette's Sensor Excel accommodates to Japan', *Keio Communication Review*, 25, pp. 57–73.

Molokwu, B. (2000) *Principles of Advertising*. Lagos: Advertising Practitioners' Council of Nigeria.

de Mooij, M. (1998) *Global Marketing and Advertising: Understanding Cultural Paradoxes*. Thousand Oaks, CA: Sage.

de Mooij, M. (2004) 'Translating advertising: Painting the tip of the iceberg', *The Translator*, 10(2), pp. 179–98.

National Geographic Society (2016) 'Africa: Physical geography', *National Geographic Society*. Available at: http://nationalgeographic.org/encyclopedia/africa-physical-geography/ (accessed 14 November 2016).

Ndirangu, M. (2014) 'Revealed: Kenya's Top Ten TV Ads', Press release, *AdTrack*.

Nyirenda-Jere, T. and Biru, T. (2015) 'Internet development and internet governance in Africa', Geneva: Internet Society, Available at: www.internetsociety.org (accessed 14 November 2016).

Ogunlesi, T. (2015) 'For Africa by Africa', *The Punch*, 17 August, p. 25.

Olatunji, R. W. (2005) 'Marketing communication in an inter-connected world opportunities and challenges in the advertising industry in Nigeria', In: Demoranville, C. (ed.). *Marketing in an Inter-Connected World: Opportunities and Challenges VOL. XII.* Miami, FL: Academy of marketing Science, pp. 13–17.

Olatunji, R. W. (2007) 'Advertising media planning, buying and selling in an open economy'. In: Kaynak, E. and Harcar, T. D. (eds) *Beyond Borders: New Global Management Development Challenges and Opportunities.* Hummelstown, PA: International Management Development Association (USA), pp. 767–73.

Olatunji, R. W. (2010) *Advertising, Economy and Societies in Africa: The Nigerian Perspective.* Saarbrucken: VDM Verlag Dr. Muller Aktiengesellschaft & Co. KG.

Olatunji, R. W. (2013) 'Advertising in a globalising culture: The Nigerian experience'. In: Olatunji, R. W. and Laninhun, B. A (eds), *Dimensions of Advertising Theory and Practice in Africa*. Dakar: Amalion Publishing, pp. 100–110.

Olatunji, R. W. and Thanny, N. T. (2011) 'Youth culture and new media: A study of telecommunications advertisements in Nigeria', *Journal of Development Communication*, 22(2), pp. 14–28.

Olorunnisola, A. A. (2009) 'GSM telephone in Nigeria's political, socio-economic and geo-cultural landscapes'. In: Olorunnisola, A. A. (ed.). *Media and Communications Industries in Nigeria: Impact of Neoliberal Reforms Between 1999 and 2007.* Lewistown, NY: The Edwin Mellen Press, pp. 103–56.

Olurode, L. (2003) 'Gender, globalisation and marginalization in Africa', *African Development*, 23(3 & 4), pp. 67–88.

Oso, L. (2012) 'Press and politics in Nigeria: On whose side?', Lagos: Lagos State University Inaugural Lecture Series 47th Edition.

Pieterse, N. (1994) 'Globalization as hybridization', *International Sociology*, 9(2), pp. 658–68.

US Foreign Commercial Services and US Department of State (2012) *Doing Business in Senegal: 2012 Country Commercial Guide for U.S. Companies*. New York: US Foreign Commercial Services and US Department of State.

Webster, J. B. and Boahen, A. A. (1967) *The Growth of African Civilisation: The Revolutionary Years, West Africa since 1800*. London: Longman.

10 Advertising in the Middle East and Western Asia

Advertising culture and global influences

Reza Semnani Jazani

Introduction

With globalisation rapidly affecting the marketing, advertising and communications landscape, brands face diverse challenges in designing global strategies that effectively communicate with target audiences worldwide. The choice of whether to develop a global or regional campaign, or alternatively tailor communication to local markets, is an important question for brands operating in the Middle East, especially in the Arab Gulf countries.

Global advertising campaigns are an efficient way of delivering a consistent corporate image worldwide. This cost effective strategy, however, is not always feasible in the Middle East, where strong cultural and religious norms and values are embedded in the lives of the consumer base and recognised in government regulation, which varies country by country. Global brand success in the Middle East, therefore, often depends on glocalisation, a process whereby contentious global advertising elements are modified to strengthen the communication of messages locally, without compromising the integrity of a brand's global advertising strategy.

Despite cultural, religious and political constraints, rewards in the local market are numerous for global brands which can establish the right balance between their global strategy and the local realities of the Middle East, and some global brands are making significant headway in achieving this.

Globalisation has contributed greatly to exposing the region to Western and global brands. Regional taste for Western brands has similarly been incorporated into the societal fabric, but strict cultural and religious dominance has forced global brands to adapt to standards deemed appropriate. Furthermore, the Middle East is geographically strategic, being placed at the nexus of Europe, North Africa and Asia. The combination of this diversity with the many international vested interests makes this region a complex yet highly profitable one for global corporations.

As a result of the race between multinational corporations to mark territory in the region, advertising in the Middle East is being incrementally affected by global advertising principals and practices. Global brands are influencing the advertising landscape in terms of creativity, consumer insight mining and strategic planning. Technology is also heavily influencing advertising in the region. With a relatively well-off, young consumer base adopting new technology at a rapid pace, digital advertising is now a new and important frontier.

This chapter explores some of the apparent paradoxes of the Middle East with case studies of brands, campaigns and advertising agencies and the challenges they face in the region. Global corporations cannot afford to ignore opportunities in the Middle East, but the unique set of challenges posed by these countries forces global corporations to take a uniquely local approach to the region.

The Middle East

The Middle East is a diverse region, encompassing a range of different societies. Geographically, the region is made up of Bahrain, Iran, Iraq, Israel, Jordan, Kuwait, Lebanon, Oman, Palestinian Territories, Qatar, Saudi Arabia, Syria, United Arab Emirates and Yemen (Encyclopedia Britannica Online, 2016). Whilst some countries in the region have been subject to political instability in recent years, continued economic growth and rapid population increase present strong opportunities for global and local brands. Arab Gulf countries, also known as the Gulf Corporation Council (GCC) are globalising faster than other countries in the Middle East region due to the prosperity of the oil states, and the widespread uptake of new technology and social media by the majority youth population.

The region's ethnic majority is overwhelmingly Arabian, with 95 per cent of people Muslim and 5 per cent Christian and Jewish (CIA World Factbook, 2016). Despite this common thread, there are many variables at country and even regional levels within countries, such as wealth, social class, religion and education, and there is no single societal type (Keegan and Green, 2013).

Since the 1980s, GCC countries have been diversifying their economies to reduce reliance on oil and resource revenue. This shift has resulted in investment in importation, the opening borders for international investment and, consequently, the creation of opportunities for global companies to establish their brands in the region. In particular, the United Arab Emirates (UAE), as the region's central commercial hub, is a model economy for other countries in the region, with a GDP purchasing power parity (PPP) of US$66,000 per capita (CIA World Factbook, 2016). The UAE is not only a global marketing hub for the Middle Eastern region, but also a global logistics hub, strategically positioned at the centre of the South Silk Road between Asia, Europe and Africa, to provide a business gateway for trade between the world's most important regions. It is used by China as a hub for Africa, by India as a portal to the rest of the world, by Latin America as a portal to Asia, and by Western global companies as a portal to the Middle East. Furthermore, the UAE's political stability and strong economic growth provide optimum trading conditions, signifying the importance of the UAE in the global marketplace (Expo 2020 Dubai, 2016).

When considering the impact of globalisation on marketing and advertising in this region, the UAE becomes an important case study in this rapidly developing region. This chapter therefore focuses broadly on the Arab Gulf countries, with emphasis on the UAE, and the impact of globalisation throughout the region.

The majority of the UAE population is expatriate, compared with other GCC countries, which consist mainly of Arab nationals (CIA World Factbook,

2016). The UAE majority, consisting of mainly young educated consumers with large disposable incomes, shows similar consumer purchasing patterns to those found in Western markets. Equally, they have consumer expectations more in-line with European and North American consumers, thus providing the impetus for global brands' presence in the region. Of all GCC countries, the UAE is the most lucrative market for global brands due to a combination of prosperity, demographics and deregulation, and the most flexible for marketing and advertising execution.

In the recent past, women in Arab countries such as the UAE faced many restrictions and it was not acceptable for them to work or gain higher education. However, in the twenty-first century, women are experiencing more freedom. They are educated, entering the professional workforce and have a high level of disposable income and purchasing power. These factors make them a key and growing audience for purchasing goods and services.

The advertising industry has gone through significant change, alongside the commercial world. Until the 1980s, the GCC advertising industry was made up of a small network of local, independent agencies. In the 1990s, however, a sharp increase in investment from international agencies and enterprises seeking to capitalise on growing opportunities in the region changed this landscape (Melewar *et al.*, 2000).

While the Arab Gulf countries are globalising faster than other countries in the region, and the UAE is an international marketing hub, there are still entrenched cultural, religious and regulatory marketing constraints. Brands need to understand how these challenges may impact on them, and where risks lie, prior to entering the market.

Culture and religion

The socio-cultural influence of global advertising, which selectively reinforces particular social roles, language and values, can result in radical changes in lifestyle and social behaviour patterns, and encourage the adoption of new trends and models of consumption. Often, the symbols, values and mores that global advertising promotes are those of Western society, either in their Western origin or as a reflection of Western values. However, in Arab Gulf countries, where there is a strong emphasis on cultural and traditional norms, resistance to these persuasive and pervasive global advertising characteristics forces marketers and advertisers to rethink their global strategy in the region.

One of the major challenges local and global firms have to confront when designing marketing and advertising strategies for Middle Eastern markets, especially for GCC countries, is overcoming a complex set of religious and cultural obstacles. This is because religion and culture have a significant impact on consumer behaviour, and are powerful mediators of how advertising messages are decoded. Consumers apply a religious filter to advertising messages, and, if advertising is perceived as contentious and against religious beliefs, it reflects badly on the brand or advertiser.

People of the Muslim faith see Islam as more than just a religion: it is a complete way of life. Islam, with its doctrine derived from the *Quran*, influences Muslims' decision-making attitudes based on the principles within. Islam centres around the concepts of well-being and a virtuous life, emphasising the spirit of brotherhood and socioeconomic justice.

Advertising regulation is not exempt from the ubiquity of religious influence, and, consequently, regulation has been developed to guide local and global advertisers regarding appropriateness of content. This affects advertising in a myriad of ways. Despite this apparently difficult terrain, advertisers should not fight against these restrictions, but rather use them as a guiding light for how to engage the Muslim consumer base. For example, regulations surrounding the exposure of female or male bodies not only indicates to brands what they need to do to gain approval for public showing, but they also serve to illustrate how brands can comply with Islamic values of modesty in their advertising.

Another important element of Islamic society is racial and ethnic diversity, which is highly visible and more prominent in advertising in Muslim Arab countries than other parts of the world. This goes back to the origins of the Islamic religion, which emphasises the equality of all races and ethnic groups. In countries such as the UAE, where the majority of the population are Arab expatriates, brands are at pains to showcase a wide range of ethnic groups in their advertisements rather than just the local Arab Emirati population. In this way, they are demonstrating their respect for the equality of all people, and at the same time widening their target audience and engaging broadly.

Cultural and religious factors exclude some forms of advertising appeals in Arab Gulf countries, and brands and agencies must consider this reality when implementing advertising strategies. The cultural values embedded in advertisements must reflect respect for religion and tradition, and family values. In this regard, the cornerstones of successful Western advertising are at odds with an Islamic market. For instance, the use of emotional or sex appeal in the form of romantic or indecent language, attention-seeking displays of feminine beauty and nudity are unacceptable. Islamic wisdom must be interpreted and incorporated in Muslim audience advertising, hence the use of beautiful women, so successful in a traditional Western advertising context, flies in the face of the Islamic principle of not using feminine beauty for personal or corporate gain.

Sex appeal and the objectification of women in advertising is similarly opposed by contemporary Islamic feminism in the GCC. Following twentieth-century Western feminism, which saw suffragettes, financial independence and general freedoms, Islamic feminism takes the cause a step further by using the Islamic principle of not objectifying women's bodies but respecting women as people. Islamic feminists view their traditions, such as the use of the *hijab*, as empowering rather than restricting – women are seen for who they truly are and not as objects of the 'male gaze'.

Despite this, women in GCC countries lag behind in terms of personal freedom and independence even though the role of women in Arab Gulf countries is changing and growing as women gain more rights within society and the women's cause is becoming increasingly visible. Recently, in 2015, women obtained the right to vote and stand for election in Saudi Arabia. Albeit a small step in a highly patriarchal society, developments such as this reflect the inevitable development of Arab society to include women as decision-makers in public and private life. Further, more and more women are graduating from university and launching professional careers in GCC countries (Al Dabbagh, 2012). As a result, women are more and more visible in advertising, highlighting their important role in family and society, and so becoming a genuine target audience for advertising in a way that is respectful of Islamic principles, without resorting to common Western advertising tactics of sexualisation and objectification.

Religious values also have a major impact on tactics employed by advertisers. Whereas in the US, the Federal Trade Commission (Federal Trade Commission, 2016) actively encourages competition between corporations, in Islamic countries one of the highest values is justice and fairness, so Muslims may not harm other Muslims, even corporations. Therefore, negative publicity is frowned upon as it may cause harm to another Muslim, and because of this there are no overtly comparative advertisements in the GCC.

This reflects Hofstede's cultural dimensions theory regarding collectivist societies such as the Arab world versus individualist societies such as the US (Hofstede and Bond, 1988). Negative publicity campaigns between brands such as Coca-Cola versus Pepsi in the US, in which each brand has been trying to tear down the opponent for more than a century, would not be appropriate in the Arab world. Therefore, global advertisers must rely on other tactics to engage consumers. Collectivist societies also force advertising agencies to emphasise the norms and values of collectivism. For instance, collectivist societies such as GCC countries emphasise respect for and obedience to elders such as parents and authorities, and this includes group loyalty and customs. To communicate these standards to consumers, global advertisers intentionally use culturally appropriate language to highlight these values.

Religion is at the heart of Muslim traditional celebration, especially in the Arab Gulf countries. The two most significant religious celebrations affecting Muslim consumer behaviour are Eid-al-Adha and Eid-al Fitr. The importance of these key festivals is not lost on global and local brands: advertising campaigns are planned months in advance to ensure companies are associated with the celebrations.

Eid-Al-Adha is celebrated on day ten of the last month of the Islamic calendar. Mosques are decorated with strings of lights and other decorations. It is known as the Festival of Sacrifice, and an animal is sacrificed in the name of God. People celebrate this festival by shopping for themselves and their loved ones, distributing food to other families, friends and poor people, and preparing extravagant meals as gestures of generosity. Many marketing campaigns centre around this festival, taking advantage of the atmosphere of shopping, generosity and frivolity (Bley and Saad, 2010).

Eid-al-Fitr, 'Festival of Breaking the Fast,' is the most significant festival marking the end of fasting during Ramadan. The Islamic holy month of Ramadan is the most important spiritual event on the Muslim calendar, and, similarly to the Eid Al-Adha, it has strong emotional ties to Muslim tradition and culture. Ramadan occurs during the ninth month of the Islamic calendar and Muslims refrain from certain activities, including food and drink during daylight hours (Al-Hajieh *et al.*, 2011).

Just like Christmas, Ramadan in the twenty-first century has become a season for increased consumerism. With the growing correlation between Ramadan and consumer spending, many global and local brands for fast moving consumer goods (FMCG), car brands and clothing brands increase their advertising spend to capitalise on this. Consequently, some of the best creative commercials are launched during this season (Yalcin and Cimendag, 2012).

However, advertisers must understand how to effectively leverage this season whilst avoiding Ramadan marketing mistakes. Creating catchy ads that go too far run the risk of offending values and norms. To hedge against these common pitfalls, it is important for ads to be reviewed by local experts within the agency or client-side to prevent misunderstanding and damage to brand identity.

To convey the spiritual nature of the month, global and local brands often use traditional Ramadan symbols and messaging in their advertisements. One of the most iconic symbols, not just for Ramadan but for the Muslim faith in general, is the crescent moon, signifying the start of the month. The crescent moon is a clear visual cue referencing the Muslim faith. Other important symbols seen in Ramadan campaign materials include dates – the traditional way for Muslims to break their fast in the evening – and lanterns, referencing the late hours people keep in this period.

Brands and agencies also use religious terminology or Quranic injunctions and words during the month of Ramadan to elevate the spiritual mood of advertisements, making them more appealing to Muslim consumers in the region. Commonly used phrases include 'Ramadan kareem' (Ramadan is generous) 'Ramadan Mubarak' (Blessed month of Ramadan) and, in more Westernised countries such as the UAE, 'Happy Ramadan', all of which encapsulate the spirit of giving, sharing and generosity. Advertisers intertwine this consumer need with their own campaign goals, and seek to convey the message that consumers should be generous to themselves with the purchase of a new car, clothes or other consumer goods, and generous to others, through sharing, giving and helping. Brands also seek to position themselves as corporately responsible by forming joint campaigns with non-government organisations such as Red Crescent during this month.

The month of fasting culminates in the festival of Eid-al-Fitr, literally the 'Festival of Breaking the Fast'. At Eid al-Fitr, people dress in their best attire, adorn their homes with lights and decorations, give treats to children and visit loved ones. Towards the end of the month, ads appear with the refrain 'Eid Mubarak', literally 'blessed festival' or 'happy Eid', signifying the end of the holy month. It is important for brands to be part of the celebration of this spiritual month and demonstrate their inclusion.

Interestingly, although Muslims fast during the day, the sale of food rises during Ramadan, in particular delicacies and meats, due to the season being characterised as a time to break bread with family and loved ones. Food supply companies increase their advertising budget during this month to take advantage of the increased household grocery spend. Similarly, global fast food chains, including McDonald's and Burger King, also capitalise on these celebrations by increasing advertising expenditure to target families that spend their evenings out of the home or prefer not to cook.

For advertisers to leverage the season, as with Christmas in other parts of the world, it is necessary to plan ahead as many advertising outlets book out well in advance due to the popularity of the month. Furthermore, when the Ramadan month hits, brands can expect reduced working hours and slower response times from businesses and government departments, and this should be taken into account during planning stages. To maximise media planning, many agencies and brands schedule media towards the end of the day, when people have broken their fast. After *Iftar* (when the fast is broken) it is common for families to get together and watch a TV series at home. As a result, ad space is competitive in this time slot.

Given the tendency to stay up late at night during Ramadan, Muslims spend an increased amount of time on social media into the late evening. Consequently, many advertisers focus Ramadan campaigns around digital media in order to reach a wider target audience. In fact, many campaigns are strictly digital in nature, such as Renault's 2011 and 2012 Ramadan digital campaigns, developed by Publicis Graphics Dubai.

With the increasing expansion of global brands into all global markets, advertising agencies need to establish an extensive network of offices to consolidate client service delivery. For example, most Nestlé regional accounts remain with the global agency Publicis, including the Nestlé accounts in GCC countries. Agencies expand their networks parallel to global clients by taking over wholly owned subsidiary agencies, or establishing formal relationships with local advertising agencies. As a result, global agencies with smaller global networks are at risk of losing new clients to competitors, and struggle to keep existing clients looking to expand globally.

Many global agencies have found that entering the Arab Gulf countries without local expertise can hamper their campaigns' best efforts to engage the local population. They overcome this by partnering with local marketing and advertising firms or set up their own in-house resources by recruiting local experts. These arrangements allow global agencies to delegate the responsibilities of identifying appropriate target segmentation, creative execution and media strategy to local partners. However, budget decisions remain with the head office.

Publicis Group, a French global agency, entered the Middle East in 1999 by acquiring the Middle Eastern networks of a local agency based in Dubai, buying a majority share in the local company and renaming it Publicis Graphics. In 2013, the Publicis Group completed the acquisition by buying out the remaining shares and incorporating the local subsidiary under its Publicis Worldwide umbrella. This development enabled Publicis Worldwide to familiarise itself with the Middle Eastern market through their local partner and handle global accounts such as Nestlé, Renault, Procter & Gamble, and Chrysler, at the local level without encountering any client dissatisfaction due to cross-cultural differences.

Global brands already engaged in the region also prefer to partner with agencies that have local expertise and hold other major global accounts. This strategy helps global brands maintain high standards in their marketing and advertising strategies, both regionally and worldwide. Therefore, it is a good opportunity for well-known agencies to manage global accounts in the GCC. Most global agencies have headquarters in Dubai as it is the business epicentre of the region, and from their Dubai offices they manage operations throughout the region. Top ranking global agencies such as Y&R, Impact BBDO, Ogilvy and Publicis hold the most important global accounts, which include Ford, Land Rover, Coca-Cola, Mercedes Benz, Emirates Airline, P&G, HP, Dove, Etihad Airways, Ikea, Gillette, Nissan, Renault, Nestlé, Nescafé, Maggi, Nestlé nutrition, Chrysler Jeep, Dodge, Duracell, McDonald's and Heinz.

In conjunction with this, well-known local brands such as Emaar, *Gulf News*, Dubai Shopping Festival (DSF), RAK Bank and Dubai Duty Free benefit from the presence of global agencies in the region, and hire them for advertising strategy development and promotional activities, so global agencies influence the standard of local advertising. As a consequence, the traditional, outdated creative approach has been replaced by professional international agency standards. Global agencies, by taking on local accounts, are able to maximise their operation in the region, and have the opportunity of familiarising themselves with regional cultural and regulatory variables.

A further example of a successful joint working relationship is American cable TV network MTV, which in 2007 entered the Arab region through a strategic decision to launch MTV Arabia under a licensing agreement with local media company Arab Media Group (AMG). Despite AMG's lack of experience in television, their remarkable regional consumer insight knowledge made them an excellent choice for MTV (WARC, 2010)

MTV is a media corporation well known for its controversial content and penchant for breaking social convention. Although it may seem unlikely that such a corporation could be successful in a region renowned for its religious conservatism, MTV Arabia had no problem entering the Arab market because it reflected and respected local cultural values. With two-thirds of the population under the age of 30, educated and tech-savvy, and having no major competitors broadcasting mainly Western music content, MTV provided the missing link between Arab youth and the global music scene. The combination of 'Arabised' music and content and international music gave the MTV Arabia audience relatable content and connection to the global music scene, for which MTV is famous.

Despite global convergence of technology, media and financial systems, consumer thinking and behaviour have not resulted in a similar convergence. This is most evident in Arab countries, particularly the GCC countries, where cultural and religious sensitivities have to stay at the forefront of brand and agency considerations, as they are ever present. Offence can spark a consumer backlash. In extreme cases, offence can result in brand boycotts, which directly or indirectly can be influenced by politics. For example, a perceived religious slight by a Danish cartoonist in 2006 resulted in a region-wide boycott of Danish products from consumers, and also from suppliers themselves such as Carrefour super-market. In spite of the favourable conditions for advertisers and marketers, brand strategy must keep the propensity for cross-cultural instability in mind when operating in this region (Keegan and Green, 2013)

Another cultural dilemma for global agencies entering the region is dealing with linguistic issues. Given that the communication of any message or content into Arabic or the local dialect for each Gulf country requires a complete understanding of the region's local culture, the presence of native Arabic speakers as copywriters or creative directors is essential. This extends to a firm's account management team to minimise the risk of message miscommunication.

The presence of native Arabic speakers in international agencies enables global brands to communicate messages in Arabic without the risk of *back translation*, the literal translation of messages into words that do not convey the intended meaning. Due to their extensive knowledge of the local culture and traditions, native local Arabs are able to improve the message in Arabic through *transcreation*, whereby an understanding of the message behind the words enables copywriting teams to come up with an appropriate equivalent in the target language. This applies equally to Arabic text, as dialects differ across GCC countries. Dialects are not so different so as to be misunderstood, but losing local flavour in a message can produce a subtle inference that the content is meant for another market, alienating the consumer from the product.

Yahoo side-stepped language and cultural barriers in 2009 when it acquired Arab Internet portal Maktoob, the Arab world's first free Arabic email service provider, operating since 1990 and reaching 16.5 million people (Kincaid, 2009). Yahoo's home page, email application and Instant Messaging components were translated into Arabic, but Maktoob's local flavour and content was kept largely intact. This resulted in significant new ad revenue for Yahoo.

Regulations and guidelines

GCC countries have some of the strictest advertising regulations in the world, which all advertising and marketing firms operating in the region must adhere to, possibly at the expense of efficiency and/or profitability. Government regulations in Arab countries are based on adherence to cultural and Islamic religious guidelines, with great emphasis on family values.

The basic advertising rules and regulations are similar across GCC countries. However, being based on a tradition of modesty in dress and behaviour derived from Sharia law, interpretation is contentious and attitudes vary across a spectrum of observance. Some Gulf States, guided by religious scholars, observe a stricter interpretation than others. For instance, Saudi Arabia and Kuwait have the strictest set of limitations regarding women in advertising. In Saudi Arabia, women's heads must be covered by a *hijab*, and are only allowed to bare their face and hands in line with Sharia Law. Customary clothing to conform with these standards is the *abaya*, a long robe-like dress. Conversely, in Qatar and UAE, there are fewer overt regulations punishable by law, but basic modesty standards remain and must be adhered to. Alongside religiously endorsed interpretations of gender roles for advertising, there is a spectrum of public acceptance which ranges from highly conservative, or Islam-dominant, to less conservative moderates, and this spectrum of religiosity is used to draw up segments for advertising purposes. Highly Islam-dominant segments are a challenging group to engage and advertisers aiming to reach this segment of the population require carefully designed advertising strategies.

In addition to overt factors such as exposure of women's bodies, subtle inferences are also subject to interpretation, such as the positioning of men and women together in ads. Because in many GCC countries it is either unlawful or at least socially inappropriate for unrelated men and women to be together, advertisements tend to place men and women in the context of a legal relationship in order to avoid public objection.

An example of advertiser self-regulation is female clothing brand H&M, a youthful, 'fast fashion' brand with global popularity. In their 2007 Dubai campaign launch, with supermodel Giselle Bundchen, advertisers digitally altered ads to fit Dubai modesty standards. They achieved this by adding a t-shirt or vest under the clothes to cover arms and a hint of cleavage.

Food advertising regulation, determined by culture and religion, demands that global and local food chains certify food products as *halal*, or 'acceptable' for Muslim consumption. *Halal* refers to the slaughtering of animals in the Islamic way, and food that is free of forbidden products including alcohol and pork. Food chains add this assurance to health messaging in advertising but it is still one of the biggest obstacles global food chains such as McDonald's and TGI Friday face in the Middle East, as opposed to their European and North American operations. To combat international competition, local food suppliers such as Al Islami Co. base advertising campaigns around the premise that their food is 'real *halal*' or 'guaranteed *halal*' and prepared according to Islamic rule.

Non-*halal* commodities such as alcohol and pork are forbidden in Islam and are not allowed to be advertised. Equally, the display of drinking paraphernalia such as wine glasses is banned, as it can be perceived as an endorsement for drinking alcohol. Sharia law thus influences most aspects of Middle Eastern society.

Standardisation and adaptation

In general, when brands expand globally, standardisation and/or adaptation is a central element of marketing and advertising strategy. In the Middle East, global brands entering the marketplace face the challenge of having to factor in the limitations of cultural and religious values, corresponding government regulation and consumer diversity across GCC countries. Although there is a considerable diversity of consumers in GCC countries, there are still enough similarities in terms of culture and beliefs for global companies to implement a successful regional marketing and advertising strategy.

Global company Renault is a good example of successful regional standardisation: it has established a consistent regional corporate image with the flow-on cost saving benefits. Renault's Middle Eastern operation is based in Dubai, from where it delegates adaptation decision-making power to satellite offices in GCC countries. Publicis, a global agency with a regional base in Dubai, manages and coordinates Renault's major regional advertising campaigns. Coordination requires liaising with Renault satellite offices, obtaining approval for creative execution elements such as casting, headline, sub headline, body text, slogans and terms and conditions. This ensures relevant elements are culturally appropriate and conform to local government regulation.

A good example of global campaign execution in the GCC is the 2012 Renault Duster 'Shockingly affordable' campaign. Renault launched the new Duster SUV globally in South America, South Africa, India, Europe, the United Kingdom and the Middle East, using affordable off-road capability as the main draw-card. The catchphrase 'our apologies to anyone who bought an SUV yesterday' showed SUV buyers crying after seeing the Duster. The campaign effectively engaged a worldwide audience through a 360° outreach featuring below-the-line (BTL), above-the-line (ATL) and digital platforms, the headline-grabbing price central to the campaign. Globally, the Renault Duster campaign idea remained the same, showing a male SUV buyer crying after seeing the Duster, but GCC country advertising rules and regulations meant campaign materials had to be modified for regional consumption. The TV commercial required considerable attention. The song used in the global campaign, 'Boys don't cry' by Reel Big Fish, was replaced with a generic instrumental jingle. Certain scenes were deleted, including those containing partly dressed men and unfamiliar settings. These were replaced with readily identifiable Arab actors and more familiar backgrounds (see Figure 10.1). Although Renault GCC followed the global campaign theme for the whole GCC region, for other below-the-line (BTL) and above-the-line (ATL) materials, such as lamp post, bridge banner and press ads, Renault adapted certain elements of the campaign for each GCC country separately. Therefore, the main creative elements such as car pack shot, headline and background were maintained for the same reasons of consistency, but the cast and attire for the photo shoots were chosen based on each GCC country's tradition, using different images of men crying, each

Figure 10.1 Renault Duster 'shockingly affordable' UAE campaign lamp post 2012.

Source: developed by Publicis Graphics Dubai.

dressed in easily identifiable national dress (see Figure 10.2). This created a highly targeted campaign for each country the Duster was launched in.

It is common for global brands to adapt campaigns to a local context using local celebrity endorsement. Consumers identify more readily with local, as opposed to international, celebrities as they see themselves, their culture and their experiences reflected in local celebrities. Furthermore, local celebrities provide essential endorsement as gatekeepers to local culture and society.

In 2011, Coca-Cola launched a region-wide campaign across the Middle East called 'Brr' featuring a collection of local celebrities, including Egyptian actor Omar Sharif, Saudi footballer Yasser Qahtani and Lebanese-born Canadian musician Carl Wolf (Campaign Middle East, 2011). Regional creative was produced by the global agency FP7 Dubai. The campaign idea reflects the 'icy' feeling one has when drinking a Coke, with celebrities dressed in snow-going attire. This 360° campaign included media touch points such as TV spots on local networks MBC and Rotana, outdoor, in-store execution, joint partnership with Ski Dubai, and ice rinks in Qatar, sampling drive and online activity via Facebook and YouTube. This regional standardised approach worked by incorporating thought leaders from many parts of the region, creating an all-inclusive 'Arabised' campaign.

Future of advertising in the Middle East

Compared to Europe, Australia and North America, the Middle East still relies heavily on the traditional advertising mediums of print, outdoor and TV commercials. Yet there is a huge shift towards online advertising, which is growing rapidly. Although still behind Europe in terms of digital advertising, the impact of new technology such as smartphones is influencing the advertising methods available to advertisers.

The Arab Gulf states have been experiencing an increasing shift towards digital media consumption in the twenty-first century, in common with the rest of the world. Compared with the rest of the Middle East, Arab Gulf countries have the most active online populations, in terms of social media use, active blogging and

Figure 10.2 Renault Duster 'shockingly affordable' campaign bridge banner 2012.

Source: developed by Publicis Graphics Dubai.

related digital communication tools. Media consumption trends are an indicator of advertising trends, and spending on online advertising increased 64.6 per cent in the 2007–12 period, and is expected to continue (Ken Research, 2014).

Factors driving the rapid uptake of new media in Arab countries include a growing number of Internet users, innovation in communications technology, and smartphone ownership. In fact, economic prosperity in the region allows people to own more than one smartphone and have access to simultaneous multi-screen usage, providing more and more consumer touch points. The growing trend is further buoyed by a surge in the proportion of young people in the Gulf countries, with 50 per cent of the population under the age of 25, a demographic that adopts new technology easily and stays abreast of media communication advances (PR Newswire, 2014).

With more international companies establishing themselves in the region, Arab countries are unable to avoid being influenced by Western values and practices. However, this shift does not apply to religious and cultural traditions, which remain steadfast and require careful consideration. Inevitably, an increasingly digital media landscape and the impact of globalisation, particularly the purchasing of goods and services, will become further entwined with traditional cultural and religious values, and it is important for advertisers to achieve an appropriate balance of these factors in order to be effectual in the Arab Gulf countries.

Conclusion

The Middle East, and in particular the GCC countries, remains a lucrative market for global brands. The majority youthful Muslim population have made it clear with their purchasing habits that they want 'Western' products and brands, as evidenced by the large number of multinational companies established in the region. However, these wants and needs centre around the desire to modernise, not Westernise. Furthermore, Muslims want their participation in the global marketplace to be in line with Islamic law, and this consumer insight is highly relevant to brands and agencies operating in the region. Even though consumer preferences are becoming more Westernised, culture and religion are not convergent with this, and remain a distinct part of national and religious identity throughout the region.

Advertising in the Middle East is a landscape fraught with cultural and religious sensitivities, and advertisers need to be cautious not to fall foul of this. International–local partnerships reflect the prioritisation of a culturally acceptable approach that respects Muslim religious and cultural norms and values and corresponding government regulation, and acknowledges regional and linguistic variables. These many overlapping considerations affect the extent to which advertisers can standardise campaigns, alongside more costly modified tailor-made regional solutions. To a large extent, brands and advertising agencies operating in the Middle East are self-regulatory, such is the risk associated with consumer or regulatory backlash. Those that do get the balance right are recognised as trustworthy and reliable by consumers, and this coveted status continues to reward advertisers and brands operating in a region that is offering more and more opportunity.

References

Al Dabbagh, M. (2012) *The Impact of Globalisation on Women in the GCC*, Dubai School of Government. Available at: http://gulfresearchmeeting.net/index.php?pgid=Njk=&wid=MzA=&yr=2012 (accessed 14 November 2016).

Al-Hajieh, H., Redhead, K. and Rodgers, T. (2011) 'Investor sentiment and calendar anomaly effects: A case study of the impact of Ramadan on Islamic Middle Eastern markets', *International Business and Finance*, 25(3), pp. 345–56.

Bley, J. and Saad, M. (2010) 'Cross-cultural differences in seasonality', *International Review of Financial Analysis*, 19(4), pp. 306–12.

Campaign Middle East (2011) *Coca-Cola signs up celebrity trio*, Available at: http://campaignme.com/2011/05/22/11986/coca-cola-signs-up-celebrity-trio/ (accessed 14 November 2016).

CIA World Factbook (2016) Available at: www.cia.gov/library/publications/the-world-factbook/geos/ae.html (accessed 14 November 2016).

Encyclopedia Britannica Online (2016) *Middle East*. Available at: www.britannica.com/place/Middle-East (accessed 14 November 2016).

Expo 2020 Dubai (2016) *A Global Hub*. Available at: http://expo2020dubai.ae/en/the_uae/a_global_hub (accessed 14 November 2016).

Federal Trade Commission (2016) *About the FTC*. Available at: www.ftc.gov/about-ftc (accessed 14 November 2016).

Hofstede, G. and Bond, M. R. (1988) 'The Confucius connection: From cultural roots to economic growth', *Organisational Dynamics*, 16(4), pp. 4–12.

Keegan, J. W. and Green, C. M. (2013) *Global Marketing: Global Edition* (7th edn). Harlow: Pearson Education.

Ken Research (2014) *Middle East Online Advertising Market Outlook to 2017: Rapid Broadband Penetration to Foster the Growth*. Available at: www.kenresearch.com/it-enabled-services/e-commerce-industry/middle-east-online-advertising-market-research-report/460-105.html?src=whatech (accessed 14 November 2016).

Kincaid, J. (2009) *Confirmed: Yahoo Acquires Arab Internet Portal Maktoob*. Available at: http://techcrunch.com/2009/08/25/confirmed-yahoo-acquires-arab-internet-portal-maktoob (accessed 16 February 2017).

Melewar, T. C., Turnbull, S. and Balabanis, G. (2000) 'International advertising strategies of multinational enterprises in the Middle East', *International Journal of Advertising*, 19, pp. 547–9.

PR Newswire (2014) *Middle East Online Advertising Market Outlook to 2017: Rapid Broadband Penetration to Foster the Growth*. Available at: www.prnewswire.com/news-releases/middle-east-online-advertising-market-outlook-to-2017-rapid-broadband-penetration-to-foster-the-growth-253235641.html (accessed 14 November 2016).

WARC (2010) *Media Giants Target Middle East*. Available at: www.warc.com/Latest News/News/Media_giants_target_Middle_East.news?ID=27674 (accessed 14 November 2016).

Yalcin, E. and Cimendag, I. (2012) *Global Marketing Advertising with Cultural Differences: How Can Global Companies Better Address Cultural Differences in Marketing Advertising in the Middle East?* Jönköping: Jönköping International Business School.

11 Indian advertising in the context of globalisation

Hari Sreekumar and Rohit Varman

India is the second largest populated country in the world with 1.21 billion persons according to the latest census (Business Standard, 2015). In recent years, the country has been witnessing a spurt of economic growth, with a projected GDP growth rate of 7.6 per cent in the 2016/17 financial year, making it one of the fastest growing, if not the fastest growing, economy in the world (Economic Times, 2016). At the same time, India has high levels of poverty, with 37.2 per cent of consumers assessed as poor (Economic and Political Weekly, 2009). Despite widespread poverty, a large consumer market and the presence of a large number of Indian and multinational corporations have led to a thriving advertising industry. Globalisation has led to the rise of consumerism and myriad social changes. In this chapter, we highlight some of the ramifications of globalisation on Indian advertising. We also examine the ways in which advertising itself shapes the consumer experience of globalisation.

Indian advertising and consumer culture

The advertising industry in India is fairly large, and clocks up billions of dollars in advertising spending every year; for 2016 it is expected to be US$7.6 billion. TV and press advertising are expected to contribute to the majority of this share, followed by digital, outdoor, radio and cinema hall advertising (Advertising Age India, 2016). The Indian advertising market is projected to be the second fastest growing market in Asia, after China. Moreover, by 2018, advertising spend is expected to contribute to 0.45 per cent of the GDP (IBEF, 2016). The top advertising agencies in India are Ogilvy & Mather Ltd., GWT Hindustan Thompson Associates and Rediffusion DY&R (Kumar, 2016). Almost all the agencies are collaborative ventures between Indian agencies and multinational advertising agencies. Not surprisingly, companies that target end consumers are the top advertisers. Unilever India, Mondelez, Procter & Gamble and Reckitt Benckiser India are among the top spenders on advertising (Adbrands, 2016).

Since the 1980s, and in a more pronounced way from the 1990s, India shifted from centralised economic planning to a neoliberal economy. This process of liberalisation and the increasing pursuit of neoliberal policies coincided with the birth of national television (Rajagopal, 1998). Neoliberal policies have contributed to high growth rates and a substantial reduction in poverty, albeit accompanied by a rise in inequity in the country (Patnaik, 2007; Weisskopf, 2011). Several marketing institutions, such as organised retail, retail credit and e-commerce, have developed and attained strength over the past few decades. There is a proliferation of consumer goods, with an entrenchment of consumer culture (see Varman and Belk, 2012; Venkatesh and Swamy, 1994). Some scholars (e.g. Sheth, 2004) have pointed out the positive sides of an open economy, arguing that India can capitalise on globalisation by focusing on the right skills, industries and sectors. On the other hand, neoliberalism has also been criticised for contributing to environmental degradation and the neglect of poorer consumers (Shrivastava and Kothari, 2012). In describing the proliferation of consumer culture and rising standards of living of some sections of Indian society, accompanied by persistent poverty and rising inequality for others, Dreze and Sen (2013) have commented that India faces an 'uncertain glory'. Advertising remains largely insulated from these inequalities and fundamental economic problems. This is understandable, since the broader marketing discipline, of which advertising is a part, has a predominant concern with managerialism and corporate interests (see Varman and Sreekumar, 2015). Marginalised citizens, when targeted by marketing and advertising, become subsumed under over-arching frameworks such as the 'Base of the Pyramid' (Prahalad, 2013). Such frameworks recast them as potential consumers with scarce resources, who can be the targets of marketers selling low-priced products and services. In sum, our brief review of contemporary consumer culture in India reveals proliferation of goods and services, and a sizeable and growing middle class that is open to consumption along with a considerable segment of the population struggling to meet basic needs. Indian advertising operates contingently in such a diverse and unsettled environment.

Indian advertising: a brief history

A historical account of how Indian advertising reached its current state will help us in understanding the field better. Such an account also contextualises the influences of globalisation on advertising in the country. While reading through this history, it has to be kept in mind that the 'India' referred to in the pre-1947 period (1947 was the year of Indian Independence from British rule) includes present-day Pakistan, Bangladesh and Sri Lanka, all of which were under the British Crown. However, this distinction is relevant to us only for purposes of tracing the historical trajectory of Indian advertising and identifying the origins of the field. In subsequent parts of the chapter, in our discussions on the relationship between globalisation and advertising, we focus on the present-day country of India.

While there is an increasing economic and academic focus on contemporary globalisation, the phenomenon itself is not new, and can even be traced back to prehistoric times. Arguably, the visibility and pace of globalisation increased in the nineteenth century and during the colonial encounter. We have accounts of international trade occurring during early periods, but little is known about the usage of these traded products by ordinary consumers. It is quite likely that the average consumer participated little in such global flows of goods. This changed with the colonial encounter, and foreign goods and ways of living became entrenched in the lives of ordinary Indian consumers (see Venkatachalapathy, 2002, for a fascinating history of coffee drinking in southern India). The economic liberalisation of the Indian economy in the 1990s has arguably accelerated the pace of globalisation, and heralded a new wave of consumerism in India (see Varman and Belk, 2008; Venkatesh and Swamy, 1994).

While there are records of temple inscriptions and some early forms of advertising by merchants in the BCE period, advertising as we know it began in India in the second half of the eighteenth century. In January 1780, James Augustus Hicky started publishing *Hicky's Bengal Gazette* in Calcutta. This was the first newspaper to be published in India, and was also known as the *Calcutta General Advertiser*. Interestingly, the name of the newspaper itself indicates that it was a medium for advertising. The *Madras Courier* was launched in 1785, and, in 1790, the *Bombay Courier*, which still exists as *The Times of India*, the leading English language newspaper in the country. The presidencies of Bombay, Madras and Calcutta were administered then by the British East India Company. These early newspapers predominantly published advertisements and tenders put up by the government of the time. For example, an advertisement by the government from 1793 announced to the public that war had been declared by France against Great Britain and Holland. Another advertisement from the same year declares that the authorities have given permission to any individual to make bricks, tiles or *chunam* (lime-based cement or plaster used in India). Both these advertisements were comprised entirely of text. Advertisements with illustrations started appearing towards the end of the eighteenth century. Advertisements were also repeated in order to aid in memory and recall of the readers. The key feature of almost all advertisements of the period was that they were addressed to the British in India. Indians had no role to play as consumers, and were rarely targeted by these advertisements. These early advertisements gradually gave way to ads for consumer products such as toothpaste, soap and apparel. Such ads carried illustrations, and became common by the early twentieth century (Chaudhuri, 2007).

The first Indian advertising agency to be set up was B. Dattaram & Co., which was established in 1905 (Shah, 2014). The agency claims to have created India's first ever press ad, for a client named West End watches, in 1907 (Dattaram, 2016). The agency is still in operation, and celebrates its heritage. Subsequently many other agencies were set up to exclusively service multinational corporations such as General Motors, Levers and some other American firms. In 1934, the first full-service advertising agency named Sista Advertising and Publicity Services was set up (Shah, 2014). Clarion, one of the largest post-independence ad agencies was founded in 1956 with the Indian takeover of the British agency D. J. Keymer, which had decided to wind up its operations in the country (Sanyal, 2012).

After Indian independence in 1947, advertisements became increasingly 'Indianised' and targeted towards Indian consumers, since much of the British population had left the country. Advertisements in the 1950s were predominantly in black and white. The few colour ads published appeared in limited shades, since printers found it difficult to reproduce rich colours on newspaper and magazine paper at that time. An early ad for Brylcreem from the 1950s features Tenzing Norgay (Figure 11.1), who, with Edmund Hillary, was one of the first to climb Mt Everest (see Chaudhuri, 2014). This was one of the earliest examples of a celebrity endorsement in the Indian context. Hindustan Lever Limited, the Indian subsidiary of Lever, was the first company to use marketing research (Chaudhuri, 2014). In fact, an early HLL ad shows a happy family with the ad copy touting the virtues of marketing research and communicating to consumers that the company used its in-house marketing research department to understand changing consumer preferences (Chaudhuri, 2014). The 1960s saw advertising becoming increasingly sophisticated with advances in technology. Ads in colour were still rare, but photographs started becoming common. The Lifebuoy (toilet soap brand of Lever) campaign in 1964 and the Amul moppet (a prominent brand of butter) launched in 1967 were noteworthy campaigns (Shah, 2014). Interestingly, while there have been some changes in its positioning, Lifebuoy still uses good health as an important selling point. Amul continues with the moppet, and its campaign based on topical humour is the longest running ad campaign in the world (Chaudhuri, 2014). Ads in colour started becoming common during the 1970s, and photographs were widely used. In 1977, ad agencies became involved in political advertising for the first time (Sanyal, 2012). The 1980s saw the advent of mass television in India, and ad films were produced in large numbers. Advertising was no longer just about communicating product features, but also about positioning and branding.

Early Indian advertising was predominantly in print, or shown in movie halls and hoardings. While it was arguably effective, it is doubtful as to whether advertisers could reach a truly national market with such ads. Advertising remained constrained by the available technology. That changed with the advent of television in India, in the 1980s. For the first time, advertising could reach large numbers of consumers, many of them with low levels of literacy. In this early phase of television, there were no cable and satellite television channels. Doordarshan was the only TV station available, with two channels: one 'national', predominantly Hindi, with a little English; the other 'regional', which broadcasted in the language of the respective state (India's multiple states have their regional languages, such as Tamil, Bengali and Telugu, each with millions of speakers). This resulted in limited choice for advertisers in television advertising. Advertisers usually produced one version of a TV commercial, usually in Hindi or English. Hindi versions were then dubbed in regional languages when broadcast on the regional TV channels.

In sum, our brief historical review shows how Indian advertising had its origins in the British-controlled press, selling British products to British subjects in India, and has evolved gradually, with changes in the political environment

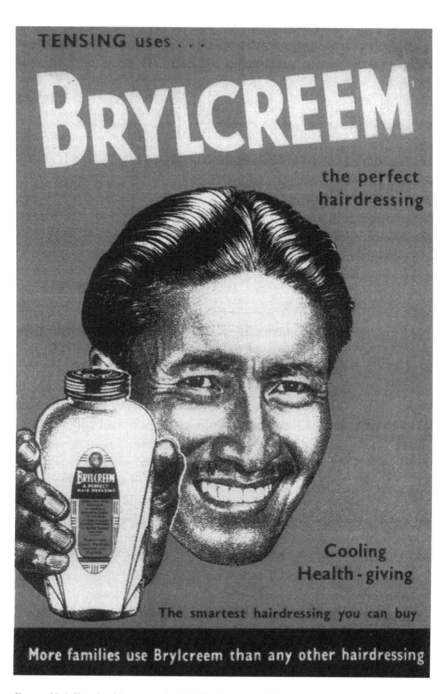

Figure 11.1 Tenzing Norgay endorsing Brylcreem (ad from the 1950s).

Source: reproduced from Chaudhuri, 2014, with kind permission of Niyogi Books, New Delhi.

and technology, to become the creative enterprise that it is today. Our review also shows that globalisation in a certain sense impacted on Indian advertising as early as the eighteenth century. In subsequent sections we will unpack the complex relationship between advertising and globalisation through an examination of contemporary Indian advertising.

Globalisation and advertising in India

Appadurai's (1996) influential work on globalisation describes different dimensions of global cultural flows. Among these dimensions, two in particular – the notion of mediascapes and ideoscapes – are relevant to advertising. By mediascapes, Appadurai refers to the electronic capabilities and images produced by various interests around the world that circulate globally, and help consumers in imagining and desiring Other ways of consuming and living. Ideoscapes also comprise images, but these are more explicitly political, and reflect state power or movements that counter it. Moreover, these ideoscapes encapsulate notions such as freedom, democracy and welfare (Appadurai, 1996). Despite these flows of ideas, globalisation leads to uneven development and production of diverse subject positions. Gupta (2000, p. 13) laments that, 'an analysis of contemporary India will reveal that while there has been a definite move from tradition, what we see around us is not modern'. Therefore, with India waiting to become 'modern', advertising depicts some of the tensions between the ideas of being Indian and being transnational. As Mazzarella (2003) suggests, advertising is a key point of mediation between the local and the global, and between capital and culture. Our examination of contemporary Indian advertising reveals the ways in which these mediations are performed.

Transnational aspirations

Given the position of India as a postcolonial society, and its history as a British colony, it is inevitable that there was a huge Western influence on the advertising profession. As our historical review has shown, early advertisements were targeted towards the British. After independence, advertising messages were aimed at the few Indian consumers with purchasing power, who were mostly a Westernised elite audience. Since TV was nonexistent and even radio was unheard of in large parts of the country, print was the most common form of advertising. These print advertisements by and large used English copy. Ads for aspirational products of the time such as shoes and cigarettes showed consumers dressed in Western attire. For example, an ad from the 1950s for Gold Flake cigarettes shows a man dressed in elegant evening wear, with a smug expression on his face, smoking and watching a Western performance featuring dancing women. The man is so immersed in enjoying the cigarette that he ignores the performers, much to their bewilderment. The women in most ads were shown in Indian attire, reflecting Chatterjee's (1993) point about women being the bearers of tradition in a patriarchal society. The exceptions were when women were shown in a specifically Western setting, as in the Gold Flake ad. Apart from women, marginalised consumers such as farmers and those carrying out other low-paid occupations were shown in Indian attire.

In an early article on advertising agencies, Banerjee (1968) commented that advertising ideas were conceived in English, and the copy too was written in the same language. He further suggested that commercial radio might force advertisers to write copy in Indian languages, and lamented the paucity of talent to carry out the same. Cayla and Elson (2012), in a study of the Hindi and English versions of a popular Indian magazine, argue that English is used as a prominent marker of cultural capital and upward mobility. The ability to use English becomes a prerequisite for engaging in sophisticated forms of work and pleasure, and the language denotes the ability to be the global Indian. They observe that brand managers express the worry that using vernacular languages to communicate to consumers could dilute or degrade the brand by compromising its association with the Westernised elite. Accordingly, globalisation in the Indian context has only furthered the reproduction of a cultural hierarchy borrowed from the West. Ladousa (2002) further comments on the language issues in the Indian context through a study of the north Indian city of Varanasi, and suggests that English communication is suggestive of centrality and access to global opportunities, whereas Hindi conveys locality and a peripheral situation.

While language is unquestionably a marker of cultural capital in these cases, it is also likely that advertisers struggle to find a commonly acceptable language in a country with more than 15 major languages, and could be employing English due to pragmatic considerations. It has also become common for advertisers to employ a mix of Hindi and English, popularly referred to as 'Hinglish' in their ads (see Padamsee, 1999, for a brief description of Hinglish). This mixing of languages enables marketers to use cultural markers that appeal to the large number of Hindi-speaking Indians, and at the same time maintain the Western, global aura around their products. Moreover, such use of language also ensures that the large number of non-Hindi speaking consumers, such as those in southern India, are not alienated. For example, Domino's, the popular brand of pizza, has a tagline which reads 'Hungry Kya', translated as 'Are you hungry?' Virgin Mobile's tagline is 'Think Hatke', roughly translatable to 'Think different'. This is akin to the English-mixing observed by Lee (2006) in South Korean commercials, wherein mixing English with Korean becomes a linguistic expression of modernity. Venkatesh and Swamy (1994) provide a different perspective on the language issue, and comment that knowledge of English has facilitated consumerism in India. While it is debatable as to whether mass consumerism is beneficial to the country, the key point is that in a multilingual market such as India, languages, even Indian languages, are constantly in a state of contestation.

The tendency to glamorise transnational and use global references to market aspirational products is widespread among advertising executives. White models, with presumed Western origins, convey aspirational product positioning. Whites are presumed to be superior also because they travel, indicating the lionisation of travel employed in discourses on cosmopolitanism, wherein travel becomes a means for the enlightened Westerner to encounter primitive cultures and expand his or her intellectual horizons (Thompson and Tambyah, 1999). The advertisements for Gillette razors provide an example of selectively using Western references. While the ad for Gillette Mach 3 (an expensive razor) uses an English narrative with a Westernised male model, the advertising for Gillette Presto, a lower-priced razor uses Hindi, and an explicitly Indian setting.

Assertive Indianness

As we have suggested in the previous section, Indian advertising, especially in the case of expensive and lifestyle products caters to the desire of sections of the middle class to be transnational (Derne, 2008). Given the political and cultural nature of globalisation, discourse of the transnational Indian is often fractured with its cultural anxieties. Any discussion of globalisation is accompanied by concerns of cultural displacement and neocolonialism (Varman and Belk, 2009). As a result, globalisation is sometimes resisted, feared and denigrated in different ways. The colonial experience has made the relationship of Indian consumers to transnational identity problematic, accompanied by admiration, suspicion and sometimes hostility. Advertisers constantly engage in a process of negotiation wherein they try to appropriate desired meanings from transnational images and cultural referents without setting off local anxieties over cultural invasion and homogenisation.

Zacharias (2003) suggests that the 1980s marked two important political developments in India – economic liberalisation, and the rise of neoconservative cultural nationalism. The launch of a soap named 'Ganga' in 1993 was a crucial marker of an explicit use of Indian, more specifically Hindu cultural referents in advertising a product. Ganga is the Indian name for the river Ganges, which is considered to be a holy river by Hindus. Rajagopal (1998) suggests that this campaign indicated an explicit search for local cultural symbols, and a move away from an elite Westernised advertising practice to one that could cater to a larger number of consumers, and a genuinely mass market. The campaign was clutter-breaking, and the soap initially did well. However, the brand had to be withdrawn from the market in early 2000, possibly indicating the limited attraction of such an explicitly framed cultural nationalism. Zacharias (2003) further points out that early national television set off tensions between consumption, modernisation of the family and traditional impulses in the form of constrained gender roles. This resulted in the constitution of a 'TV family', which could passively accept marketing messages promoting consumption without violating societally prescribed roles for its members. In national debates surrounding the screening of late night adult-oriented films on television, women were cast as the subjects of forbidden sexuality, and the living room with its television set became the site of national culture (Zacharias, 2003). The discourse against cultural Westernisation became transformed through these debates into a call for cultural surveillance by the state (Zacharias, 2003).

Moreover, Mazzarella (2003) observes that local advertising managers strategically create the idea of essentialised Indianness to countervail the power wielded by their multinational clients. This leads to the creation of auto-orientalist advertising in which cultural stereotypes of otherness are deployed by Indian advertisers to claim uniqueness and difference. According to Mazzarella (2003, p. 141):

> auto-orientalist advertising closed the circle. Consumers had already made the realisation of the universal community compatible with the particularity of embodied preference. Now, in an apparently paradoxical move ... the dynamics of globalisation were making the realisation of the universal community dependent upon the rearticulation of cultural identity.

As a result, advertisers sometimes negotiate the transnational through co-opting it or 'Indianising' it in their ads. Transnational brands are often advertised in an Indianised form, either to make them more acceptable to Indian consumers or to indicate a value proposition that could be better understood by Indian consumers. For example, McDonald's, the burger chain known for its meat-based burgers, has an extensive vegetarian menu in India. McDonald's had to localise to the extent of even having completely vegetarian outlets near religious places in India (Kannan, 2014; Newcomb, 2012). McDonald's is often touted as an example for the difficulties multinational corporations face in the Indian market, and the need to adapt. Alyque Padamsee, the famous Indian advertising film maker comments on the need for an Indian adaptation of Western advertising using the famous 'Lalitaji' campaign of Surf, a detergent powder brand of Lever. In the 1980s, Nirma, an Indian brand of detergent powder became popular among Indian consumers. Nirma was priced much lower than Hindustan Lever's Surf. To counter Nirma, Padamsee launched a campaign using the imagery of Lalitaji ('ji' is a respectful suffix attached to a name in north India), a hard-bargaining and shrewd housewife. Padamsee suggests that the rational appeal of Surf, that it cleaned better than Nirma, would not work with Indian consumers: they had to be convinced with the emotional appeal of a hard-bargaining, shrewd Indian woman (see Padamsee, 1999).

Advertisers also play on the rhetoric of *Swadeshi* to portray Indian-origin products as superior. *Swadeshi* literally means 'of one's own country', and is an ideology that was potently employed by Mohandas Gandhi during India's struggle for independence from the British (see Mazzarella, 2003). Post economic liberalisation, the term was reappropriated by various right-wing groups. Politicians belonging to the right wing often also had neoliberal economic beliefs which contradicted the *swadeshi* ideology. This led to the idea itself getting stretched to accommodate a neoliberal economic order (see ibid. for a discussion on this). Patanjali Ayurved, a new company founded by yoga guru and spiritual personality 'Baba' Ramdev ('Baba' is a prefix that can be roughly translated to 'holy man') is a company that employs this variant of *swadeshi* wedded to neo-liberal economics. Patanjali markets a range of products such as toothpaste, shampoo, hair oil, detergent powder, cornflakes and various other personal and home care products, and targeting revenues of Rs.10,000 crore (approximately US$1.4 billion), which is posing a significant threat to multinational corporations such as Unilever, Colgate-Palmolive and Procter & Gamble (Dutta, 2016). Gandhi's concept of *swadeshi* was opposed to industrialisation and big business (Chatterjee, 1999; Mazzarella 2003). However, Patanjali's interpretation of *swadeshi* suggests an Indian industrial resurgence and advocates reclaiming the country's past glory by overcoming MNCs in the business arena. A recent ad by Patanjali explicitly invokes the *swadeshi* movement of 1906, and suggests that foreign companies harm the country by pilfering its resources. Ramdev appears in the ad and claims that Patanjali's profits will be used for charitable purposes, unlike what the MNCs do. The advertisement further urges its viewers to free the country by consuming Patanjali's products (see www.youtube.com/watch?v=Lh2GLVba3CU). The ad uses the *swadeshi* ideology, and evokes the perfidious nature of foreign companies as opposed to an Indian company that ostensibly uses local knowledge to promote products for the country's benefit.

In sum, we see that transnationalism is an important cultural marker in Indian advertising, employed by creatives to denote aspirational value, and appeal to middle-class Indians. Transnational models and settings are frequently used for products that cater to the upper middle and upper classes. Advertisers and consumers use these international references in communication and consumption to denote the 'transnational' Indian.

Globalisation through an Indian prism – an example

The ads for Bajaj two-wheelers clearly show the complex relationship between Indian advertising, consumption and globalisation. Bajaj Auto is a large Indian corporation that had scooters as its main product until the 1990s, and then moved successfully to motorcycles. In 1989, the company launched a campaign stressing nationalistic themes, titled 'Hamara Bajaj' (our Bajaj) (see YouTube www.youtube.com/watch?v=scltYH13uEY). The hugely successful TV commercial showed the Bajaj scooter being used by a variety of middle-class Indians. The adline 'Buland Bharat Ki Buland Tasveer' (roughly translated as 'the great portrait of a great India') positioned the Bajaj scooter firmly in the lives of middle class Indians cutting across occupations and settings. The campaign is considered to be a creative and commercial success, due to its imaginative use of visual imagery, emotional appeal and clever positioning of the product. The next 'Hamara Bajaj' campaign was launched in 2001 (www.youtube.com/watch?v=zCDsbD4EHr4). Neoliberalism was well-entrenched, and Bajaj was now a successful manufacturer of motorcycles. The 2001 campaign opens with a jeans and jacket-clad young man riding a Bajaj cruiser motorcycle. As he races along the road, he spots a small Hindu shrine on the side of the road, and respectfully bows his head and utters a prayer. The ad then goes on to show a group of leather-clad bikers, a man and his girlfriend riding a motorcycle, a group of bikers carefully avoiding a *rangoli* (Indian art form created on the ground with colours having Hindu connotations) and numerous other visuals. The sound track in Hindi refers to Bajaj as 'Nayi Bharat ki Nayi Tasveer' (the new portrait of a new India). However, the soundtrack is creatively interspersed with the old 'Buland Bharat ki ...' line. The characters in the commercial behave in very Westernised ways, wearing leather jackets, jeans and doing stereotypically Western activities such as biking. However, they simultaneously pray to Hindu shrines, carry *sitars* (stringed Indian musical instrument) and behave in a very 'traditionally Indian' manner. The Bajaj campaign exemplifies the complex narrative of globalisation in India, trying to show a transnational 'outside' that is, however, accompanied by an incorruptible Indian 'inside' (Chatterjee, 1993).

Conclusion

Our analysis of Indian advertising from its origins in the eighteenth century to present day practice shows a complex relationship with globalisation. The global in advertising is refracted through transnational Indian as a cultural category. Transnational is an aspirational position that connotes higher status and material rewards. However, as our analysis shows, this relationship is riddled with contradictions and globalisation is also denigrated. This is not surprising given India's colonial past and the continuing fears of cultural imperialism. Advertisers modify transnational symbols and meanings to render them more accessible to Indian consumers. In the process, advertising creates and contributes to culture (Hall, 1980; Schroeder and Zwick, 2004). Given the enormous size, complexity and diversity of India, our review will be at best a partial uncovering of these broad trends. India is rapidly globalising, and there are also new movements emerging in the country, promising interesting times ahead for the study of Indian advertising.

References

Adbrands (2016) 'India advertisers'. Available at: www.adbrands.net/in/index.html (accessed 14 November 2016).

Advertising Age India (2016) 'TV advertising shrinks in H1 2016, says Madison midyear advertising report'. Available at: www.adageindia.in/advertising/tv-advertising-shrinks-in-h1-2016-says-madison-mid-year-advertising-report/articleshow/53666634.cms (accessed 14 November 2016).

Appadurai, A. (1996) *Modernity at Large: Cultural Dimensions of Globalization.* Minneapolis, MN: University of Minnesota Press.

Banerjee, S. (1968) 'The advertising agency: A new service,' *Economic and Political Weekly*, 3(21), pp. M-19 to M-23.

Business Standard (2015) *India's Population at 1.21 Billion.* Available at: www.business-standard.com/article/current-affairs/india-s-population-at-1-21-billion-hindus-79-8-muslims-14-2-115082600038_1.html (accessed 14 November 2016).

Cayla, J. and Elson, M. (2012) 'Indian consumer kaun hai? The class-based grammar of Indian advertising'. *Journal of Macromarketing*, 32(3), pp. 295–308.

Chatterjee, P. (1993) *The Nation and its Fragments: Colonial and Postcolonial Histories.* New Delhi: Oxford University Press.

Chatterjee, P. (1999) *Nationalist Thought and the Colonial World* In: Chatterjee, P., *The Partha Chatterjee Omnibus*, New Delhi: Oxford University Press.

Chaudhuri, A. (2007) *Indian Advertising: 1780 to 1950 A.D.* New Delhi: Tata McGraw-Hill.

Chaudhuri, A. (2014) *Indian Advertising Laughter and Tears*. New Delhi: Niyogi Books.

Dattaram (2016) 'One hundred years of being the first mover'. Available at: www.dattaram.com/inside.html (accessed 8 September 2016).

Derne, S. (2008) *Globalization on the Ground: Media and the Transformation of Culture, Class, and Gender in India.* New Delhi: Sage.

Dreze, J. and Sen, A. (2013) *An Uncertain Glory: India and its Contradictions.* Princeton, NJ: Princeton University Press.

Dutta, A. (2016) *Baba Ramdev's Patanjali Aims to Double its Revenue to Rs10,000 cr in 2016–17.* Available at: www.business-standard.com/article/companies/baba-ramdev-s-patanjali-aims-to-double-its-revenue-to-rs-10-000-cr-in-2016-17-116042700061_1.html (accessed 14 November 2016).

Economic and Political Weekly (2009) 'Recounting India's poor', *Economic and Political Weekly*, 44(51), pp. 5–6.

Economic Times (2016) *India's Growth at 7.6% in 2015–16 Fastest in Five Years.* Available at: http://economictimes.indiatimes.com/news/economy/indicators/indias-growth-at-7-6-in-2015-16-fastest-in-five-years/articleshow/52522153.cms (accessed 14 November 2016).

Gupta, D. (2000) *Mistaken Modernity: India Between Worlds.* New Delhi: HarperCollins.

Hall, S. (1980) 'Encoding/decoding'. In Hall, S., Hobson, D., Lowe, A. and Willis, P. (eds) *Culture, Media, Language.* London: Hutchison.

IBEF (2016) *Advertising and Marketing Industry in India.* Indian Brand Equity Foundation Available at: www.ibef.org/industry/advertising-marketing-india.aspx (accessed 14 November 2016).

Kannan, S. (2014) 'How McDonald's conquered India'. Available at: www.bbc.com/news/business-30115555 (accessed 14 November 2016).

Kumar, R. (2016) 'Top 10 best advertising agencies in India 2016'. Available at: http://scoophub.in/top-10-best-advertising-agencies-in-india/ (accessed 14 November 2016).

Ladousa, C. (2002) 'Advertising in the periphery: Language and schools in a North Indian city,' *Language in Society*, 31(2), pp. 213–42.

Lee, J. S. (2006) 'Linguistic constructions of modernity: English mixing in Korean television commercials', *Language in Society*, 35(1), pp. 59–91.

Mazzarella, W. (2003) *Shoveling Smoke: Advertising and Globalization in Contemporary India.* Durham, NC: Duke University Press.

Newcomb, T. (2012) 'McDonald's goes vegetarian in India'. Available at: http://newsfeed.time.com/2012/09/04/mcdonalds-goes-vegetarian-in-india/ (accessed 14 November 2016).

Padamsee, A. (1999) *A Double Life: My Exciting Years in Theatre and Advertising.* Gurgaon: Penguin.

Patnaik, U. (2007) *The Republic of Hunger and Other Essays*. Gurgaon: Three essay Collective.

Prahalad, C. K. (2013) *The Fortune at the Bottom of the Pyramid: Eradicating Poverty Through Profits.* New Delhi: Pearson.

Rajagopal, A. (1998) Advertising, politics and the sentimental education of the Indian consumer, *Visual Anthropology Review*, 14(2), pp. 14–31.

Sanyal, S. (2012) *Life in a Rectangle: The World Around 55 B Mirza Ghalib Street.* New Delhi: Fingerprint.

Schroeder, J. E. and Zwick, D. (2004) 'Mirrors of masculinity: Representation and identity in advertising images,' *Consumption, Markets and Culture*, 7(1), pp. 21–52.

Shah, K. (2014) *Advertising and Integrated Marketing Communications*. New Delhi:
McGraw-Hill Education.

Sheth, J. (2004) 'Making India globally competitive', *Vikalpa*, 29(4), pp. 1–9.

Shrivastava, A. and Kothari, A. (2012) *Churning the Earth: The Making of Global*. New
Delhi: Penguin.

Thompson, C. J. and Tambyah, S. K. (1999) 'Trying to be cosmopolitan,' *Journal of
Consumer Research*, 26, pp. 214–41.

Varman, R. and Belk, R. W. (2008) 'Weaving a web: Subaltern consumers, rising consumer culture and television', *Marketing Theory*, 8(3), pp. 227–52.

Varman, R. and Belk, R. W. (2009) 'Nationalism and ideology in an anti-consumption
movement' *Journal of Consumer Research*, 36(4), pp. 686–700.

Varman, R. and Belk, R. W. (2012) 'Consuming postcolonial shopping malls', *Journal of
Marketing Management*, 28(1–2), pp. 62–84.

Varman, R. and Sreekumar, H. (2015) 'Locating the past in its silence: History and marketing theory in India', *Journal of Historical Research in Marketing*, 7(2),
pp. 272–279.

Venkatachalapathy, A. R. (2002) 'In those days there was no coffee: Coffee-drinking and
middle-class culture in colonial Tamilnadu', *The Indian Economic and Social History
Review*, 39(2&3), pp. 301–16.

Venkatesh, A. and Swamy, S. (1994) 'India as an emerging consumer society: A cultural
analysis,' *Research in Consumer Behavior*, 7, pp. 193–223.

Weisskopf, T. E. (2011) 'Why worry about inequality in the booming Indian economy',
Economic and Political Weekly, 46(47), pp. 41–51.

Zacharias, U. (2003) 'The smile of Mona Lisa: Postcolonial desires, nationalist families,
and the birth of consumer television in India', *Critical Studies in Media Communication*, 20, pp. 388–406.

12 Advertising in Singapore

Regional hub, global model

Peter Ling

Introduction

Researching Singapore's advertising history is like being on an archaeological expedition. One discovery leads to another, often in unexpected sites. Further excavations uncover hidden treasures that reflect the rich advertising heritage in Singapore between the nineteenth century and the early twentieth century, an era that has attracted little attention in academic literature on advertising. Long before international advertising firms had started showing interest in the tiny country, colonial Singapore was home to an active and competitive advertising scene, particularly in the period spanning the 1900s to the 1930s.

This chapter therefore digs into the past before discussing the current advertising scenario. Specifically, it:

- provides a historical overview of Singapore;
- traces Singapore's advertising history from its establishment as a trading post of the British East India Company (BEIC);
- discusses key industry players in Singapore and their regional affiliations;
- reviews Singapore's consumer culture, creative approaches and popular campaigns;
- describes the uniqueness of the region, its attraction to global marketers and its varied media growth; and
- concludes that the traditional media sales agent role has taken on a more regional and global role in twenty-first-century advertising.

Historical overview of Singapore

Singapore has a rich cultural and political heritage covering five eras: Classical Emporium (1299–1599); Maritime Rivalry (1600–1818); Colonial Port City (1819–1945); Political Change (1946–1964); and Nation and Global City (1965–present) (eResources, 2016).

During the Classical Emporium era, Singapore was home to settlers and traders from China, the Riau Archipelago (now Indonesia), Siam (now Thailand)

and Portugal. The Maritime Rivalry era saw the Dutch East India Company disrupting Portugal's Asian empire, such as the naval battle near Changi (now more popularly known for Singapore's international airport) and the capture of Malacca, the Portuguese capital in southern Malaya.

For the 1819–1945 era, several developments changed Singapore's history. Sir Stamford Raffles established a trading post in Singapore for the British East India Company (BEIC) to weaken Dutch influence. The Dutch gave up Malacca and any interest in Singapore in exchange for British settlements in Sumatra. Singapore, Malacca and Penang became colonies of the British Crown known as the Straits Settlements. Singapore again became a hub that attracted Arabian, Chinese, European, Indian and Malay traders and companies. The British, who had a naval base in Singapore, surrendered to the invading Japanese. The country would be occupied from 1942 to 1945.

Singapore also endured hardships during the 1946–64 Political Change era. Singapore became a separate British colony but endured the subversive anti-colonial Malayan Communist Party, racial riots and separation from Malaysia. The Nation and Global City era saw Singapore become an independent nation in 1965 at the same time that it endured disruption by Indonesian saboteurs. Singapore also coped with the withdrawal of British troops in the 1970s and competitively transformed itself into an economic success, regionally and globally.

Singapore's history has also contributed to its current ethnic mix. The majority Chinese population are descendants of early migrants from China's southern provinces. The second largest ethnic group, the Malays, originated from Indonesian islands and the Malayan peninsula. Many of the third largest ethnic group, the Indians, have ancestry in southern India. The other smaller ethnic groups are the Eurasians, who have mixed European-Asian lineage, and the Peranakans, descendants of mixed marriages between Chinese or Indian men and Malay or Indonesian women (Singapore Tourism Board, 2016).

History of Singapore's advertising industry

The Singaporean advertising industry has always been linked to Britain, Australia, Asia and the United States of America (Anderson, 1984; Crawford, 2015; Frith, 1996). This section examines the early newspaper scene, the appearance of advertising agents, advertising agencies between the 1900s and 1930s, post-war advertising and the emergence of a new advertising era from the 1980s.

Newspaper scene

After Sir Stamford Raffles established Singapore as a British Settlement on 6 February 1819, the colonial authorities introduced the so-called 'Gagging Acts' in 1823 to ensure that there was no criticism of the BEIC and its policies. This involved the licensing of newspapers and content screening before publication (eResources, 2014). However, this did not deter the *Singapore Chronicle and Commercial Register* from commencing operations on 1 January 1824 as Singapore's first English-language newspaper, with advertising notices on government, shipping and trading activities (Tan, 1950).

The *Singapore Free Press and Mercantile Advertiser* (*TSFPMA*) emerged in 1835 as a rival newspaper to what had become known as the *Singapore Chronicle*. *TSFPMA* enjoyed strong financial backing from lawyers and private merchants. It was running classified advertisements for properties and display advertisements for Raffles Hotel, Adelphi Hotel, Sea View Hotel and Bigia Tea (TSFPMA, 1835). After the abolition of the Gagging Acts, the *Singapore Chronicle* sought to halve its advertising rates but it was still unable to compete with *TSFPMA*, and it eventually ceased publication on 30 September 1837 (Cornelius-Takahama, 2001; Thulaja, 2005). The *Straits Times* emerged as a rival competitor in 1845; the *TSFPMA* subsequently lost readership, and ceased then resumed publication twice before eventually becoming part of the *New Straits Times Press* in 1972 when the Straits Times Press Group split its operations across both Singapore and Malaysia (Thulaja, 2005).

Over the decades, many newspapers appeared and disappeared, including: *Daily Advertiser, Eastern Daily Mail and Straits Morning Advertiser, Singapore Weekly Herald, Straits Chinese Herald, Singapore Daily News, Straits Observer* (Singapore), *Straits Telegraph and Daily Advertiser, Straits Mail, Straits Advocate, Straits Eurasian Advocate, Weekly Sun, Singapore Monitor, New Nation, Sin Chew Jit Poh*, and *Nanyang Siang Pau* (eResources, 2015). Each newspaper promised to reach a specific demographic. Some sold themselves as the 'cheapest advertising medium' (*Straits Chinese Herald*, 1894) or 'the best advertising medium' for the ethnic Indian segment (EDMSMA, 1906) while the *Union Times* Chinese newspaper declared it would 'make your goods known to the Chinese' (*Weekly Sun*, 1913).

As the longest-running newspaper in Singapore, the *Straits Times* has also been 'home' to two heritage retail brands (Lijie and Fanf, 2015): John Little & Co, the oldest department store in the country established in 1842; and Robinson and Company, which started trading in 1858 and acquired John Little in 1955 (John Little, 2015).

Advertising agents

The world's first advertising agency, Volney Parlmer, started in 1843 in Philadelphia (AdAge, 1999). It was not long before the words 'advertising agent' were used in Singapore. On 8 January 1848, the *Straits Times* featured an advertisement for subscriptions to 'L'Observateur Francais: A French Journal', placed by 'William Thomas, British and Foreign Advertising Agent' (*Straits Times*, 1848). In 1876, the (now defunct) *Straits Observer* revealed an increase in the number of advertising agents in the colony when it announced its subscription-cum-advertising agents as 'Mr Andrew Wind, advertising and subscription agent, 133 Nassau Street, New York', Wind's Advertising Agency, and

Gordon & Gotch, Australian, Foreign and General Advertising Contractors (*Straits Observer*, 1876a, 1876b). By 1914, the term had gained greater currency. Under the heading 'The Advertising Agent', an American advertising agent offered to 'advertise the British Empire in the United States' (*Straits Times*, 1914). A complaint from a reader about agents and their role in the appearance of advertisements on the backs of rickshaws revealed a growing unease with the medium and its growing presence (*Observer*, 1914).

Agencies in 1900s–1930s

A search of digital records of the National Library Board (NLB, 2016) indicates that at least nine advertising firms were operating in Singapore between the 1900s and 1930s. These were: The Oriental Company Ltd; Anderson Advertising Agency; Tank Road Advertisement Writers; Progressive Publicity Company; Stanley Tann Advertising Company; Warin Studios; Advertising and Publicity Bureau; Millington Ltd; and Masters' Advertising. While most of these advertising agencies covered Singapore and the Malaya peninsula, Advertising and Publicity Bureau, Millington Ltd and Masters' Advertising were more regional in their operations, with Masters' leaving a legacy for Ogilvy & Mather.

Advertising and Publicity Bureau (APB)

The Advertising and Publicity Bureau (APB) was the first regional agency network in Singapore. Established in 1922 in Hong Kong, APB opened a Singapore branch in 1931 at Raffles Place to handle advertising for its American and British clients in the Far East (APB, 1931).

Born in 1902, APB's founder, Beatrice Thompson, was the daughter of a British railway worker. She grew up in Shanghai and studied in Shanghai and Kent before moving to Hong Kong in 1918 to work as a teacher. Her exposure to advertising occurred when she worked as a proofreader at the *Hong Kong Daily Press* to supplement her teaching income. Thompson went on to sell advertising space to clients in Colombo, Japan, Shanghai and Singapore. After marrying, she returned to England to raise twins but ended up working for Sir Charles Higham, a prominent advertising practitioner. Thompson returned to Hong Kong to be advertising manager of the *Hong Kong Daily Press* and later created APB (SCMP, 1979).

Following the death of her solicitor husband, Thompson became managing director of the Singapore branch of APB, where she was described as being 'well-known to the advertising profession in England, America and the East' (TSFPMA, 1932). The local press regularly reported on Thompson's and APB's activities. Reports reveal a wide range of activities, including their participation in the British Trade Fair, their promotion of the Advertising and Marketing Exhibition in England, and their marketing of the *Hong Kong Daily Press* publication *Directory and Chronicle*, which was aimed at advertisers interested in reaching commercial and industrial businesses in the Far East (*Straits Times*, 1933a, 1933b, 1934). By 1940, APB was thanking its reputable clients for making it the 'largest Advertising Agency in the Far East'. Its client list included A. Wander (proprietors of Ovaltine), Borneo Company, Bovril, Brands, Cold Storage Creameries, Diethelm, Fraser & Neave, H. J. Heinz, John Little, Malayan Breweries, Sime Darby and Sterling Products International (APB, 1940).

Thompson later married C. J. Church, who went on to become a director of APB. Unfortunately, the Japanese occupation of Singapore disrupted the APB business growth and APB. Together with her daughters, Thompson fled Singapore but her husband was imprisoned (SCMP, 1979). Church survived the war but suffered ill health and died in 1950 (*Straits Times*, 1950). The agency did not survive the Japanese occupation. By 1952, a news report referred to Thompson as 'a former Singapore business woman' (TSFP, 1952). A 1960 reference showed it as a defunct company (ROC, 1960). By 1969, Thompson had retired and sold her business. She died in 1979 (SCMP, 1979).

Millington Ltd

F. C. Millington started British billboard advertising in Shanghai in the 1920s as well as a radio station 'Millionton' in China in 1931. He opened a Singapore branch in 1937. Millington was credited with introducing Western advertising art to China through billboard advertising. The company was associated with British advertising agency London Press Exchange (TSFPMA, 1936; *Straits Times*, 1937). Only periodic reports about the agency's activities were published. These revealed that its staff were travelling through the region and beyond (*Straits Times*, 1949a, 1957a). The company had ceased operations in Singapore in 1957 (*Straits Times*, 1958).

Masters

Australian-born Ernest George Mozar from Progressive Publicity Company was reported to have started Masters Ltd in 1928 (TSFP, 1949). However, court reports indicate that Progressive Publicity had recruited him in 1929 and wrongly sacked him the same year while he was convalescing in hospital (*Straits Times*, 1931). A 1949 Masters advertisement nevertheless celebrated '21 years of advertising in Malaya' (*Straits Times*, 1949b).

By 1957, Mozar was thinking about the agency's long-term future advertising. He announced that Masters was employing specialists who could pass on skills to younger recruits and that a local studio manager had been sent abroad to learn from established companies such as S. H. Benson Advertising Agency (*Straits Times*, 1957b). In 1959, with British partners Bensons Overseas Marketing & Advertising Service and CPV International, Masters Ltd became 'Masters (1959) Ltd'. Mozar became chairman and D. G. Bell became managing director. The agency's media representation and outdoor services came under a new company, Publicity Services Ltd (*Straits Times*, 1959a). Mozar retired from

Masters (1959) in 1962 and continued as Chairman of Publicity Services until he died in 1965 (*Straits Times*, 1965a).

Under the leadership of new managing director Alec Jones, Masters (1959) established a full service office in Kuala Lumpur and a public relations-marketing division for clients with interest in Southeast Asia (*Straits Times*, 1960a, 1960b). By 1961, Masters (1959) became S. H. Benson (Singapore) Ltd while its Kuala Lumpur office was renamed S. H. Benson (Malaya) and the Hong Kong branch became S. H. Benson (Hong Kong). The managing directors of all three agencies reported to Chairman D. A. Bain (*Straits Times*, 1961). When S. H. Benson merged with Ogilvy & Mather in 1971 to become Ogilvy Benson & Mather (HAT, 2011), the Singapore office welcomed Michael Ball, who was Managing Director of Ogilvy, Benson and Mather UK, and later hosted Jock Elliott, the new Chairman of Ogilvy & Mather (*Straits Times*, 1971a, 1975). Hence, Masters was the first Singapore agency, albeit founded by an Australian, to have evolved into an international agency.

Post-war advertising

When the Association of Accredited Advertising Agents (4As) Malaya was established in 1948, its first three members were Masters Ltd, Millington Ltd and C. F. Young Publicity (*Straits Times*, 1948). In the 1950s, other agencies had entered the Singapore market: Fortune Advertising Ltd, Marklin Advertising Ltd, Cathay Advertising, GT Advertising & Publicity Service, Papineau Studios, Progress Advertising Ltd and Tan Hock Teck & Co. amongst others (TSFPMA, 1954; 4As, 1958). This section surveys three post-war agencies that had made a significant impact on the Singapore advertising industry: C. F. Young Publicity, Cathay Advertising and Marklin Advertising.

C. F. Young Publicity

C. F. Young arrived from England in 1911 and became a manager at APB. Young was interned during the Japanese occupation, before opening C. F. Young Publicity in 1946. He retired in 1953 and subsequently passed away in 1957 (*Straits Times*, 1957c). Young's nephew M. Hammersley took over the management of the agency in 1953, having acquired it from his uncle. Hammersley renamed it Young Advertising and Marketing Ltd to broaden its services for overseas and local clients. A few years later, he sold majority interest in the company to Royds Overseas Advertising and Marketing Ltd (*Straits Times*, 1959b, 1963a).

Eventually, London Press Exchange acquired Young Advertising. It was renamed LPE Singapore Ltd in 1966. The merger of London Press Exchange and Leo Burnett Chicago in 1969 resulted in Leo Burnett–LPE. In 1970, Leo Burnett merged with Jackson Wain, an Australian agency network that had set up Jackson Wain & Co. (Asia) in Singapore in 1965 to service clients such as Qantas, Procter & Gamble and Horlicks (*Straits Times*, 1965b, 1966a, 1969, 1970).

Cathay Advertising

Founder Emma Kelly from Australia first sold advertising space in Shanghai for Millington Ltd, then moved to Hong Kong to run Millington's office. She established Cathay Advertising in 1946 with its first client HK Telephone Company and subsequently gained the Cathay Airways account (Green, 1987; *Straits Times*, 1965b). Its Singapore branch also commenced operations in 1946. Offices in Kuala Lumpur and Bangkok were subsequently established (Ted Bates, 1974; *Straits Times*, 1956).

Cathay Advertising experienced several changes. It merged with George Patterson Pty Ltd from Australia in 1963. Cathay–Patterson later merged with Ted Bates and Company from New York in 1964, with the Singaporean company claiming to be 'Singapore's largest advertising agency in 1969'. The firm was renamed Ted Bates Limited Singapore in 1974 (Green, 1987; *Straits Times*, 1964; Cathay Advertising, 1969; Ted Bates, 1974).

Marklin

Marklin Advertising had its head office in Hong Kong, with branches in Singapore, Kuala Lumpur and Taiwan (Marklin, 1957, 1967, 1972). Ken Palmer was managing director of Marklin Advertising in the 1950s and President of the Association of Accredited Advertising Agents of Malaya in the 1960s (*Straits Times*, 1966b).

As part of its growth strategy, Marklin aligned itself with the Advertising and Marketing International Network of 38 independent advertising agencies in the United States, Canada, Europe, Australasia and Southeast Asia (*Straits Times*, 1963b). Marklin then became an associate agency of Dentsu Singapore, which had set up a liaison office in 1966 to coordinate research and advertising for its Japanese clients (Tan, 1979).

After 25 years of business, Marklin ceased its Singapore operation in 1976. It came as a surprise to creditors, employees and the industry at large (*Straits Times*, 1976). As a result, media owner Radio & Television Singapore (RTS) introduced a loss-prevention financial system where all advertising agencies, instead of only local firms, had to provide a banker's guarantee equivalent to two months of billings to ensure media bookings (Fong, 1976). This also prompted the major newspapers to implement a banker's guarantee system to ensure media bookings by all advertising agencies (New Nation, 1976).

New advertising era

The banker's guarantee as a criterion for accreditation by media owners hampered financially weak local agencies' ability to buy media. It also strengthened the competitiveness of both international agencies and media-buying companies, which had financial backing from their headquarters. The banker's guarantee for print and television varied: the Singapore News and Publications Ltd as well as the Times Group required a banker's guarantee equivalent to two months of billings, while the Singapore Broadcasting Corporation, previously RTS, mandated a minimum of a US$50,000 banker's guarantee and higher amounts for billings of US$1–3 million (Toh, 1983).

By the 1980s, many international agencies had established operations in Singapore. Grant, Ogilvy & Mather, Lash-Compton (later Saatchi & Saatchi), McCann-Erickson, Leo Burnett, USP Needham, Ted Bates, PTM Thompson (later J. Walter Thompson), Hakuhodo, Kenyon & Eckhart, Young & Rubicam, Dentsu, Doyle Dane Bernbach, D'Arcy MacManus & Masius, and SSC&B: Lintas. Other international advertising agencies also established a presence in Singapore through partnership agreements with local agencies, for example Quantum FCB, Dot & Line Ketchum, Adcom & Grey, CR Grey, Angie-Mui Ayer and BBDO with Batey Ads and Gartshore Kerr Lim before establishing BBDO Singapore in 1987 (Fernandez, 1986; Gwee, 1985; *Business Times*, 1983, 1987, 1988).

The arrival of international agencies did not necessarily result in better practices: a few local admen were frustrated with some 'mediocre expats' in international agencies ('Bean-Eater', 1974; Tan, 1974). One consolation was that more local agencies were on the Ministry of Communications and Information's recommended list for print media projects such as notices, recruitment and tenders (Boey, 1986).

Eventually, many advertising conglomerates established their Asia-Pacific headquarters in Singapore. Singapore is the regional home for the British group of WPP (which includes advertising agencies J. Walter Thompson, Ogilvy & Mather, Young & Rubicam and Grey, and global media networks Mindshare, MEC, MediaCom and Maxus), Omnicom Group (BBDO, DDB and TBWA, and media network OMD); the French Publicis Group (Saatchi & Saatchi, Leo Burnet and Bartle Bogle Hegarty, and media networks Starcom MediaVest and ZenithOptimedia); IPG or the Interpublic Group (McCann and Lowe, and media firms UM and Initiative); the Dentsu group (Aegis and the media networks Carat and Vizeum); and Havas (Havas Worldwide, formerly Euro RSCG, and Havas Media) (Adbrands, 2015).

Singapore has become Asia's broadcast hub. Broadcast networks with regional offices in Singapore include CNBC, Discovery, ESPN Star Sports, HBO, MTV, NBC Universal and Sony Pictures Entertainment (EDB, 2015a). Technology has seen the emergence of digital agencies that are not members of the 4As, such as: We Are Social, iProspect, Goodstuph, VML Qais, Weber Shandwick, Gushcloud, Nuffnang, The Influencer Network, Landor, Uniform and Clicktrue (Manjur, 2015a).

In summary, history has influenced modern advertising in Singapore. Beginning as traders of newspaper space, full-service agencies emerged prior to the Second World War. Pioneering agencies such as Masters Advertising, C. F. Young and Cathay provided the basis for multinational arrivals Ogilvy & Mather, Leo Burnett and Ted Bates. Marklin's collapse and debts triggered the banker's guarantee system to secure media bookings, which gave the competitive advantage to media networks financed by agency conglomerates. Such factors saw Singapore emerge as a regional base for advertising conglomerates, broadcast networks and, later, digital agencies.

Key players and regional affiliations

Singapore advertising has indeed come a long way since the first publication of notices on government, shipping activities, goods for sale and warehouses in the nineteenth century (Lijie and Fanf, 2015; Tan, 1950). This section reviews key industry players in Singapore and then looks at Singapore's advertising affiliations in the region.

Key industry players

The key players in Singapore's advertising industry are:

- the Association of Accredited Advertising Agents Singapore (4As);
- the Singapore Advertisers Association (SAA);
- the Advertising Media Owners of Singapore (AMOS);
- the Consumers Association of Singapore (CASE);
- the Advertising Standards Authority of Singapore (ASAS);
- the Institute of Advertising Singapore (IAS); and
- the educational institutions that nurture talents for the advertising industry.

The 4As is Singapore's oldest advertising association, and was established as the Association of Accredited Advertising Agents of Malaya in 1948. Its membership base has subsequently evolved owing to the changing marketing communication industry. From a base of only full-service advertising agencies, its membership now includes media agencies such as Carat, Havas Media, Initiative, Maxus, MEC, MediaCom, Mindshare, OMD, PHD, Starcom Media, UM and ZenithOptimedia (4As, 2015). Anecdotal estimates suggest that these media networks accounted for 50 per cent of media bookings in Singapore's SG$S2.5 billion advertising industry in 2015 (Personal communication, 2015).

The SAA is a distinctive association for advertisers. It was formed in Singapore in 1952 as the Malayan Advertisers Association. Ordinary members include globally well-known names such as Nestlé, Heineken, Guinness, Tiger Beer, Canon, Lexus, Toyota, StarHub, SingTel, Selangor Pewter, L'Oréal, Nippon Paint and Energizer. Its few associate members include media owners MediaCorp, Singapore Press Holding (SPH) and Reader's Digest as well as advertising agencies McCann and DDB. Top advertisers are NTUC Fairprice supermarket chain, Courts furniture, Dairy Farm, McDonald's and Unilever (Personal communication, 2015).

AMOS is also a unique association. Established in 1973 to represent Singapore media owners, members include the two big players SPH and MediaCorp as well as other media companies such as SingTel, StarHub, Moove Media, JCDecaux Out of Home Advertising and Lighthouse Independent Media (AMOS, 2015).

CASE is a non-profit, non-government organisation that was conceived in 1971 with a mission to 'champion consumers' interests and promote fair trading'. It has signed Memoranda of Understanding with associations covering direct selling, estate agents, moneylenders, pet enterprises, restaurants, clocks and watches, furniture, hotels, jewellers, natural stone, motor workshops, optical trades, optometric, plumbing, radio and electrical traders, renovation contractors, material suppliers, retailers, school transport, vehicle traders, chiropractic and Malay entrepreneurs (CASE, 2015). CASE is part of the Southeast Asian Consumer Council to protect the interest of regional consumers (SEACC, 2015).

ASAS serves as an advisory council to CASE. It was set up in 1976 as the advertising industry's self-regulatory body. ASAS Council includes representatives from government agencies, advertising agencies, advertisers, media owners and related organisations, such as the Media Development Authority and Direct Marketing Association (ASAS, 2015).

Launched in 1990, IAS seeks to develop advertising talent in Singapore. Its origins go back to 1977 when the Joint Education Committee of the 4As, SAA and AMOS collaborated to offer a diploma in advertising (*New Nation*, 1977). IAS has since then focused on facilitating education and ideas exchange through events such as the annual Effie Singapore awards, which has been running since 2004 (Bhalla, 2004); the Singapore Advertising Hall of Fame Awards (for people, company, campaign and team categories); the APPIES (Asian festival of best marketing ideas); and the Career Fair. IAS also runs the Institute of Practitioners in Advertising (IPA) Foundation Certificate of online learning over three months, which culminates in an offline examination towards an entry level industry credential (IAS, 2015).

Advertising and related courses are offered through polytechnics, local private educational institutions, local universities and foreign educational providers. The five polytechnics are Nanyang Polytechnic, Ngee Ann Polytechnic, Republic Polytechnic, Singapore Polytechnic and Temasek Polytechnic. Local private educational institutions include La Salle College of the Arts, Nanyang Academy of Fine Arts, the Management Development Institute of Singapore and the Marketing Institute of Singapore. Local universities are Nanyang Technological University, National University of Singapore, Singapore Management University, Singapore Institute of Technology and SIM University. Foreign educational providers with a presence in Singapore are Curtin Singapore, James Cook University Singapore, Murdoch Singapore, the University of Newcastle Singapore, Glasgow School of Art Singapore, DigiPen Singapore and universities such as RMIT University, which offer international degrees in Singapore through SIM Global Education.

Regional affiliations

Singapore and its neighbours have promoted Asian advertising culture through several avenues. The Asian Advertising Congress brings together the region's advertising professionals, the first congress was staged in 1958 in Tokyo and has since run biennially. The Asian Federation of Advertising Associations was established in 1978 to elevate Asian advertising standards. AdFest has been promoting Asian creative excellence since 1998. The Confederation of Asian Advertising Agency Associations – incorporated in Singapore in 2007 with members from China, Hong Kong, India, Indonesia, Korea, Japan, Malaysia, Singapore and Taipei – has run the APAC Effie Awards since 2013 as part of the New York American Marketing Association and supports Spikes Asia, an awards event collaboration between Haymarket media group and Lions Festivals (AdFest, 2016; AFAA, 2016; C4As, 2016).

Singapore's advertising stakeholders are diverse in nature and possess significant regional and international affiliations extending across associations, educational providers, industry congresses, festivals and awards.

Culture, appeals and campaigns

Singapore has its own culture and advertising practice. This section reviews key aspects of Singapore's unique consumer landscape, and outlines effective advertising appeals and popular campaigns.

Key aspects of consumer culture

Singapore's history and globalisation have contributed to its unique festival, food and materialistic culture. Advertisers often leverage Singapore's multicultural festivals, such as Christmas and Chinese New Year; Vesak Day (celebrated by Buddhists); Thaipusam (a Hindu festival); Deepavali (an Indian light festival); and Hari Raya Haji and Hari Raya Aidilfitri (Muslim celebrations) (YourSingapore, 2016). Singaporean cuisine is a marriage of history and modernisation. Traditional hawker or food centres have been modernised to compete with foreign fast food outlets, speciality restaurants and imported food ingredients. Over 80 per cent of Singaporeans eat at hawker or food centres, 67 per cent patronise restaurants or cafes, 65 per cent buy fast food and 17 per cent shop at speciality supermarkets for foreigners (Weber Shandwick, 2014).

Singapore's history of survival, globalisation, competitiveness and prosperity has influenced the country's materialistic culture. Expressions such as the '5Cs: cash, car, credit card, condominium, and country club', 'Life is not complete without shopping', or 'Everything also I want' have become popular among Singaporeans (Chua, 2003; Coclanis, 2009; Wong, 2014). It is therefore not surprising to see the 5Cs reflected in advertising for private banking, prestige cars, premium credit cards, luxury condominiums and even overseas properties with country club services. Living with multiple credit cards has also become a trend, leading to a mall culture of shopping, socialising and eating, as well as digital purchases of goods and services such as travel, fashion and beauty, entertainment and lifestyle, electronics and general insurance (Paterson, 2014). Related to the materialistic culture is the 'kiasu' culture or the 'afraid to lose out' mentality among Singaporeans. The billion-dollar tuition industry offers an example of this outlook, as evidenced by the number of parents who send their young children for unnecessary extra tuition merely because other parents are already doing so (Chougule, 2016; Ong, 2016).

Significantly, social changes over recent years have prompted a revisitation of the 5Cs. Non-residents now make up 40 per cent of Singapore's population of 5.5 million inhabitants. While some non-residents are skilled foreign talents, others are lower-skilled workers employed in the services, construction and manufacturing sectors (NPTD, 2014). Such diversity has led some to envisage less materialistic revisions of the 5Cs. A 2010 variation listed 'career, comfort, children, consideration and charitability' (Asiaone, 2010). A 2012 survey by the OCBC Bank revealed that 65 per cent of 2,100 respondents did not equate wealth with the traditional 5Cs, preferring 'confidence, career, control, community and a can-do mindset'. A McCann–Erickson 'Strive for More' campaign for OCBC triggered further online discussion about other much-desired 'Cs' in life that included 'character, courage and creativity' (BT Invest, 2012; *Campaign Brief Asia*, 2012). It is therefore refreshing to see a commercial by BBDO advertising agency for Esso LPG that embraces these less material variations of the 5Cs. The commercial depicts Esso LPG being part of a grandmother's life as she raises her two grandchildren in her simple apartment over the years and forms a bond with the deliveryman (*Campaign Brief Asia*, 2015).

Effective advertising appeals

One of Singapore's most effective and longest-running campaigns was the emotive Singapore Girl series of advertisements for Singapore Airlines (SIA). Created in 1972 by Batey Ads (a local creative agency headed by expatriate Australian Ian Batey), the Singapore Girl icon symbolised warmth, grace and charm to distinguish SIA's superior in-flight services (Wong, 2015). Although SIA's new agency TBWA has refreshed the brand by making the customer feel more special and at home, the gentle and caring Singapore Girl remains a central part of the service excellence story (Singapore Airlines, 2013).

The World Advertising Research Centre's annual ranking of best campaigns in the world reveals that emotional and storytelling creative approaches commonly underpin successful advertising (WARC, 2015). The WARC finding is also supported by the Effie Effectiveness Index (EEI). Between 2012 and 2015, the EEI revealed that the Health Promotion Board (HPB) in Singapore has consistently been Singapore's most effective marketer, followed by McDonald's and DBS Bank. HPB campaigns created by DDB Singapore have won the Gold Effie for social messages on dementia, colorectal cancer and quitting tobacco consumption. As a contrast, the EEI for Malaysia for 2012–15 shows Mondelez (marketers of Cadbury), Unilever and Nestle as the most effective marketers (Effie, 2015).

Global brand McDonald's frequently localises its advertising for the Singapore market. A notable example was its collaboration with the Health Promotion Board to promote healthier meals (DDB, 2014). However, in 2015

DDB Singapore reversed the localisation trend by successfully exporting the World's First All-Day Sunrise breakfast campaign. The campaign involved live-streaming of New Year sunrises across the globe – from Gisborne in New Zealand, through Tokyo and Singapore, to Moscow, London and San Francisco (McDonald's, 2015).

WARC notes that humour is also a popular creative approach. Two memorable advertisements using humorous appeal are the Mentos campaign from 2012 and the Durex campaign in 2015. Both are particularly noteworthy in the context of Singapore's no-nonsense success story. The Mentos 'National Night' commercial produced by BBH Asia-Pacific urged Singaporeans to celebrate national day by making love to help solve the country's low birth rate. The Durex 'Apology' online advertisement by Havas Worldwide Singapore apologised to Singaporeans on their country's 50th anniversary for causing low birth rates and encouraged couples to make love without using Durex. Both advertisements successfully generated an impact on social and news media for their capacity to poke fun at the country's low birth rate. While Mentos reported that sales doubled during the campaign period, it remains unclear whether the campaigns directly improved Singapore's birthrate (Mahtani, 2012; Manjur, 2015b).

Whether marketers are appealing to either the traditional or modern 5Cs of consumer culture, it is apparent that emotional, storytelling and humorous creative approaches have actively contributed to the popularisation of brands within the Singapore market. However, marketers entering the market need to pay heed to the Singapore Code of Advertising Practice, which prevents advertising content that is racist, pornographic, sexist or violent, or that discriminates against any religious or ethnic group (ASAS, 2008).

Regional uniqueness

Singapore is a small fish in a big ocean but its location makes it attractive to global marketers who want an easier access to nearby markets. This section looks at the regional market size, its attraction to global companies, and its varied media growth.

Market size

Singapore was one of the founders of the Association of Southeast Asian Nations (ASEAN) in 1967, together with Indonesia, Malaysia, the Philippines and Thailand. The goal of ASEAN is to facilitate a peaceful and prosperous community through cultural, economic, scientific, social and technical cooperation. Today, ASEAN members also include Brunei Darussalam, Cambodia, Lao PDR, Myanmar and Vietnam. ASEAN has a population of over 620 million, about half the size of China or India but larger than the European Union, USA and Japan (ASEAN, 2015). The largest member states by population are Indonesia (252 million), the Philippines (101 million), Vietnam (91 million), Thailand (69 million) and Myanmar (52 million).

ASEAN's economy in 2013 was ranked the seventh largest globally but is likely to be the fourth largest by 2050 as it attracts more globally competitive companies (Vinayak *et al.*, 2014). Based on 2010 data, ASEAN was home to 227 of the world's largest companies, with Singapore having 64 companies followed by Thailand 51, Malaysia 40, Indonesia 33, Vietnam 20 and Philippines 19 (Vinayek *et al.*, 2014).

Singapore is categorised in 'Advanced Asia' with developing economies such as Australia, New Zealand, Japan, South Korea and Hong Kong, while other ASEAN member states such as Indonesia, Malaysia, the Philippines, Thailand and Vietnam are in 'Fast-track Asia' because of rapidly growing economies driven by Western practices and technology (Zenithoptimedia, 2014). The size of the ASEAN market has led to ASEAN+6 economic trade partners: Australia, China, India, Japan, New Zealand and South Korea. Argentina, Canada, Chile, Europe, Pakistan, Russia and the United States are also courting ASEAN. Acclaimed as 'the most label-conscious region in the world'. The region's middle-class segment is estimated to double to 400 million by 2020, which would make ASEAN the third largest middle-class population after China and India (Nielsen, 2015).

Attraction to global companies

Singapore has consistently ranked as the second most competitive economy after Switzerland and ahead of the United States, Germany, Netherlands, Japan, Hong Kong, Finland, Sweden and Britain (Chia, 2015). Many global marketers have set up Asia-Pacific headquarters in Singapore, attracted by the vast regional market, Singapore's central location, its efficient government and its business incentive schemes. Procter & Gamble Singapore is responsible for the firm's Asian perfume manufacturing facility, Leadership Development Centre and a mega innovation centre. Rival Unilever Singapore operates as the regional hub for its Australasia–Southeast Asia cluster and houses a Customer Insight and Innovation Centre. Other famous companies with regional headquarters in Singapore include IBM, Roche, Siemens, Dell, Rolls-Royce and DHL (EDB, 2015b). Among global Fortune 500 companies with regional headquarters in Asia-Pacific, Singapore's share is 41 per cent compared to 34 per cent for its closest competitor Hong Kong (Ghosh, 2015).

Tapping the US$32 billion media sector in ASEAN and the almost 200 million new Internet users, well-known media and entertainment companies have set up in Singapore. Such firms include Disney, Fox, Lucasfilm, Ubisoft and 7,000 content creators in the fields of animation, film, new media, television, trans-media storytelling and video games (STB, 2015). Patent protection has become more efficient through ASEAN's first Patent Search and Examination Authority operation in Singapore (Channel News Asia, 2015).

Varied media growth

Communication connectivity varies across ASEAN member states and compared to other Asia-Pacific countries. New Zealand tops with 91 per cent Internet penetration, followed by Australia, South Korea and Japan at 86–89 per cent. The remaining ASEAN member states have the following Internet penetration: Brunei and Singapore 81 per cent, Malaysia 66 per cent, Thailand 54 per cent, Vietnam 45 per cent, Philippines 44 per cent, Indonesia 28 per cent, Cambodia 25 per cent, Laos 13 per cent and Myanmar 5 per cent (Statista.com, 2015). Smartphone penetration in ASEAN also varies: while Australia has 75 per cent and China 71 per cent, Singapore has 87 per cent, Malaysia 80 per cent, Thailand 49 per cent, Indonesia 23 per cent and the Philippines 15 per cent (Nielsen, 2014). The report on 'Active accounts on the top social network in each country compared to population' also reveals the varying use of social media across ASEAN countries. Compared to the 76 per cent penetration in South Korea and 66 per cent in Hong Kong, the penetration in Singapore is 64 per cent, Malaysia 59 per cent, Thailand 56 per cent, Philippines 47 Per cent, Vietnam 37 per cent and Indonesia 30 per cent (We Are Social, 2016).

There is little linguistic consistency across ASEAN member states; English is only officially used in the Philippines and Singapore. National television networks therefore remain the most popular medium in each nation, followed by the Internet, newspapers, outdoor, magazines and radio (Kantar Media, 2012). Television in Thailand and Indonesia still reaches larger audiences than mobile or Internet media but the gap is narrowing. Elsewhere, the combination of Internet and mobile phones will be a potent force when reaching audiences, especially in Malaysia, Singapore and the Philippines, where mobile plus Internet reach more and younger social media users than television (Nielsen, 2012).

In summary, many global companies find ASEAN an attractive market. By basing their regional headquarters in Singapore, these firms use appropriate media to market to ASEAN consumers and to gain access to the broader region.

Conclusion

Singapore's past has had an abiding impact on its advertising industry. There is a gap in literature on advertising practice in Singapore between the nineteenth century and the 1900s–1930s. Singapore advertising agencies in the 1930s and 1950s have left legacies for Ogilvy & Mather, Leo Burnett and Ted Bates. The debts of Marklin in Singapore sparked a concentrated move by media owners to enforce bankers' guarantees to ensure media bookings, which disadvantaged smaller agencies but made the bigger global advertising groups more competitive. The traditional media sales agent of the nineteenth century remains, but is now operating at both regional and global levels.

Singapore's culture is unique, drawing on a broad range of festivals and culinary traditions. It is also willing to reinvent itself and its values. Advertising reflects these norms through emotional, storytelling or humorous creative approaches. However, national concepts are also influenced by broader regional influences. There are many stakeholders in the Singaporean advertising industry, which are developing stronger regional affiliations. The ASEAN market is substantial and attracts global companies to operate out of Singapore and to use the right media mix to target their consumers.

Digging deeper into the digital archives of old publications may uncover new discoveries about Singapore's advertising history – much like physical restoration to the Cathedral of the Good Shepherd in Singapore, which uncovered a time capsule from 1843. Containing currencies from Britain, France, Spain and Vietnam as well as newspapers such as the *Bengal Catholic Herald*, the *Madras Catholic Expositor*, the *Singapore Free Press* and the *Straits Messenger*, the capsule revealed that Singapore has long been at the crossroads of the region's commercial and media industries. (Zaccheus, 2016).

References

4As (1958) 'The Association of Accredited Advertising Agents of Malaya', *Straits Times*, 29 April, p. 11.

4As (2015) *Membership*, Available at: www6.admarcom.sg/Content/Page.aspx?cp=198 (accessed 14 November 2016).

AdAge (1999) *Ad Age Advertising Century: Timeline.* Available at: http://adage.com/article/special-report-the-advertising-century/ad-age-advertising-century-timeline/143661/ (accessed 14 November 2016).

AdBrands (2015) *The Top 50 Marketing Groups Worldwide by Revenues.* Available at: www.adbrands.net/agencies_index.htm (accessed 17 February 2017).

Adfest (2016) *About Adfest.* Available at: www.adfest.com/About_us_aboutadfest.php (accessed 14 November 2016).

AFAA (2016) *Asian Federation of Advertising Associations.* Available at: http://afaaglobal. org (accessed 14 November 2016).

AMOS (2015) *Members.* Available at: www.amos.org.sg/members.html (accessed 14 November 2016).

Anderson, M. H. (1984) *Madison Avenue in Asia: Politics and Transnational Advertising.* Madison, NJ: Fairleigh Dickinson University Press.

APB (1931) 'Notice', *The Singapore Free Press and Mercantile Advertiser*, 16 January, p. 9.

APB (1940) 'To these our clients', *Straits Times*, 2 January, p. 16.

ASAS (2008) *Singapore Code of Advertising Practice.* Available at: https://asas.org.sg/Portals/0/Images/ASAS/docs/SCAP%202008.pdf?ver=2014-05-16-093651-153 (accessed 14 November 2016).

ASAS (2015) *Introduction.* Available at: https://asas.org.sg/About (accessed 17 February 2017).

ASEAN (2015) *Association of Southeast Asian Nations.* Available at: www.asean.org (accessed 14 November 2016).

Asiaone (2010) *Singapore's SM Goh Reinvents 'Singapore Dream'.* Available at: http://news.asiaone.com/News/AsiaOne+News/Singapore/Story/A1Story20100808-231056.html (accessed 14 November 2016).

Bean-Eater (1974) 'Mediocre expats and our frustrated admen', *Straits Times*, 31 May, p. 14.

Bhalla S. T. (2004) 'Effie comes to town', *Today*, 22 March, p. 19.

Boey, K. Y. (1986) 'Government bodies have more agencies to turn to', *Business Times*, 22 July, p. 3.

BT Invest (2012) *S'poreans Chasing New 5 Cs.* Available at: www.btinvest.com.sg/
wealth/wealth-planning/sporeans-chasing-new-5-cs-20121012/ (accessed 14 November
2016).

Business Times (1983) 'Quantum ties up with American advertising agency', *Business
Times*, 21 September, p. 3.

Business Times (1987) 'BBDO eyeing global accounts following name change', *Business
Times*, 6 May, p. 7.

Business Times (1988) 'Reshuffle at Dot & Line', *Business Times*, 13 January, p. 9.

C4As (2016) *The Confederation of Asian Advertising Agency Associations.* Available at:
http://c4as.org (accessed 17 February 2017).

Campaign Brief Asia (2012) *OCBC and McCann Worldgroup Singapore encourage Singaporeans to Strive for More.* Available at: www.campaignbrief.com/asia/2012/10/
ocbc-and-mccann-encourage-sing.html (accessed 17 February 2017).

Campaign Brief Asia (2015) *Esso LPG Brings People Together One Meal at a Time in
'Connection' Film by BBDO Singapore.* Available at: www.campaignbriefasia.
com/2015/07/esso-lpg-brings-people-togethe.html (accessed 14 November 2016).

CASE (2015) *Friends & partners.* Available at: www.case.org.sg/friendsandpartners.aspx
(accessed 14 November 2016).

Cathay Advertising (1969) 'So you'd like to get into advertising', *Straits Times*, 23
August, p. 8.

Channel News Asia (2015) *Singapore Begins Operations as ASEAN's First International
Patent Search, Examination Authority.* Available at: www.channelnewsasia.com/news/
business/singapore/singapore-begins/2088536.html (accessed 14 November 2016).

Chia, Y. M. (2015) 'Singapore remains world's second-most competitive economy',
Straits Times, 30 September.

Chougule, A. (2016) *'Kiasu' Culture is Fatal to National Identity*, 12 April, Yahoo News.
Available at: https://sg.news.yahoo.com/kiasu-culture-fatal-national-identity-043408633.
html (accessed 17 February 2016).

Chua, B. H. (2003) *Life is not Complete Without Shopping: Consumption Culture in Singapore.* Singapore: Singapore University Press.

Coclanis, P. A. (2009) 'Everything also I want: Another look at consumer culture in contemporary Singapore', *Business & Economic History Online*, 7. Available at: www.
thebhc.org/node/839 (accessed 17 February 2017).

Cornelius-Takahama, V. (2001) 'Singapore chronicle', *Singapore Infopedia*. Available at:
http://eresources.nlb.gov.sg/infopedia/articles/SIP_513_2005-01-06.html (accessed 14
November 2016).

Crawford, R. (2015) 'Relocating centers and peripheries: Transnational advertising agencies and Singapore in the 1950s and 1960s', *Enterprise & Society*, January, pp. 1–23.

DDB (2014) *'Go Light and Go Yummy', McDonald's Partners Health Promotion Board.*
Available at: www.ddb.com.sg/?p=2849 (accessed 14 November 2016).

EDB (2015a) *Media and Entertainment.* Available at: www.edb.gov.sg/content/edb/en/
industries/industries/media-and-entertainment.html (accessed 14 November 2016).

EDB (2015b) *Case Studies: Businesses in Singapore.* Available at: www.edb.gov.sg/
content/edb/en/case-studies.html (accessed 14 November 2016).

EDMSMA (1906) 'Notice: The best advertising medium', *Eastern Daily Mail and Straits
Morning Advertiser*, 6 October, p. 4.

Effie (2015) *Effie Effectiveness Index: Most Effective Marketers.* Available at: www.
effieindex.com/ranking/?rt=6 (accessed 14 November 2016).

eResources (2014) *The 1819 Singapore Treaty.* Available at: http://eresources.nlb.gov.sg/infopedia/articles/SIP_2014-05-16_133354.html (accessed 14 November 2016).

eResources (2015) *Newspaper SG.* Available at: http://eresources.nlb.gov.sg/newspapers/FAQ/EN.aspx (accessed 14 November 2016).

eResources (2016) *History SG.* Available at: http://eresources.nlb.gov.sg/history/time-line/1299-1599 (accessed 14 November 2016).

Fong, K. (1976) 'Ad firms hit by RTS new ruling', *New Nation*,1 September, p. 3.

Fernandez, M. (1986) 'The woman who "married" ad firm to US agency', *Straits Times*, 4 February, p. 22.

Frith, K. T. (1996) *Advertising in Asia: Communication, Culture and Consumption.* Iowa City, IA: Iowa State University Press.

Ghosh, A. (2015) *Race To Be the Preferred Asian HQ Location.* Available at: www.pwc.com/sg/en/singapore-budget-2015/budget-2015-01.html (accessed 14 November 2016).

Green, A. (1987) *Emma Kelly Founder of Cathay Advertising.* Available at: http://cathay-advertisingltdhongkong.blogspot.com.au/2013/11/elma-kelly-founder-of-cathay-advertising.html (accessed 14 November 2016).

Gwee, M. (1985) 'Agency ties up with US group', *Business Times*, 20 December, p. 3.

HAT (2011) *S H Benson: History.* Available at: www.hatads.org.uk/catalogue/agencies/21/S-H-Benson/ (accessed 17 February 2017).

IAS (2015) *An Industry Built on Ideas People Rebuilds Itself Constantly.* Available at: www.ias.org.sg (accessed 17 February 2017).

John Little (2015) *About us.* Available at: www.johnlittle.com.sg/corporate.php (accessed 14 November 2016).

Kantar Media (2012) *Global Adex.* Available at: www.kantarmedia.com/global-offer/global-adex (accessed 14 November 2016).

Lijie, H. and Fanf, J. (2015) *Front Page Stories of Singapore since 1845.* Singapore: Straits Times Press.

McDonald's (2015) *The World's First All-Day Sunrise.* Available at: www.getupandgo.sg.

Mahtani, S. (2012) 'Thursday's the day to go all the way for civic duty in Singapore'. *The Wall Street Journal.* Available at: www.wsj.com/articles/SB10000872396390443545504577567052477900124 (accessed 14 November 2016).

Manjur, R. (2015a) 'Top agencies who know how to market themselves on social media'. *Marketing Interactive.* Available at: www.marketing-interactive.com/top-digital-agencies-know-market-themselves-social-media/ (accessed 14 November 2016).

Manjur, R. (2015b) 'Look Durex cuts through SG50 marketing clutter with this hilarious ad'. *Marketing Interactive.* Available at: www.marketing-interactive.com/look-durex-cuts-sg50-ad-clutter-brilliant-marketing-stunt/ (accessed 14 November 2016).

Marklin (1957) 'Marklin Advertising Ltd', *Straits Times*, 16 March, p. 12.

Marklin (1967) 'Marklin Advertising Limited require an experienced art director for their office in Taiwan', *Straits Times*, 20 February, p. 16.

Marklin (1972) 'Advertising executives Hong Kong', *Sydney Morning Herald*, 27 April, p. 13.

New Nation (1976) 'Ad agents must give bank guarantees', *New Nation*, 14 September, p. 2.

New Nation (1977) *Diploma Course for Ad-Men*, 9 February, p. 4.

Nielsen (2012) *The Asian Media Landscape is Turning Digital: How can Marketers Maximise their Opportunities?* Available at: www.nielsen.com/content/dam/corporate/au/en/reports/2012/changing-asian-media-landscape-feb2012.pdf (accessed 14 November 2016).

Nielsen (2014) *The Asian Mobile Consumer Decoded.* Available at: www.nielsen.com/ph/en/insights/news/2014/asian-mobile-consumers.html (accessed 14 November 2016).

Nielsen (2015) *ASEAN 2015: Seeing Around the Corner in a New Asian Landscape.* Available at: www.nielsen.com/content/dam/nielsenglobal/apac/docs/reports/2014/Nielsen-ASEAN2015.pdf (accessed 14 November 2016).

NLB (2016) *OneSearch.* Available at: http://search.nlb.gov.sg (accessed 14 November 2016).

NPTD (2014) *2014 Population in Brief.* Available at: www.nptd.gov.sg/portals/0/news/population-in-brief-2014.pdf (accessed 14 November 2016).

Observer (1914) 'Unsightly advertising', *Observer*, 27 June, p. 11.

Ong, J. (2016) 'Singapore should kill "kiasu" culture: NMP Kuik Shiao-Yin', *Channel News Asia*, 5 April, .

Paterson, K. (2014) *Mall Culture Puts Singapore Ahead of Global Ecommerce Game.* Singapore: Digital Market Asia.

ROC (1960) 'Government records', National Archives of Singapore, 4 April.

SCMP (1979) 'Death of an advertising pioneer', *South China Morning Post*, 8 July.

SEACC (2015) *Southeast Asian Consumer Council*, Available at: www.seaconsumers.org/?page_id=72 (accessed 14 November 2016).

Singapore Airlines (2013) *Singapore Airlines launches new brand campaign.* Available at: www.singaporeair.com/jsp/cms/en_UK/press_release_news/ne130902.jsp (accessed 14 November 2016).

Singapore Tourism Board (2016) *Faces of Singapore.* Available at: www.yoursingapore.com/en_au/about-singapore/people-of-singapore.html (accessed 14 November 2016).

Statista.com (2015) *Internet Penetration in Asia Pacific as of 1st quarter 2015, By Country.* Available at: www.statista.com/statistics/281668/internet-penetration-in-southeast-asian-countries/ (accessed 14 November 2016).

STB (2015) *4 Reasons Singapore is Poised for Success as a Global Hub for Content Creators.* Available at: http://mashable.com/2015/10/22/singapore-digital-media/#I5WHgw6_OaqK (accessed 14 November 2016).

Straits Chinese Herald (1894) 'Latest advertisements', *Straits Chinese Herald*, 9 March, p. 2.

Straits Observer (1876a) 'Subscription to the *Straits Observer*', *Straits Observer*, 23 May, p. 1.

Straits Observer (1876b) 'Mr Andrew Wind, Advertising and Subscription Agent', *Straits Observer*, 18 July, p. 2.

Straits Times (1848) 'L'Observateur Francais: A French journal', *Straits Times*, 8 January, p. 6.

Straits Times (1914) 'The advertising agent', *Straits Times*, 16 June, p. 3.

Straits Times (1931) 'Publicity Co. and E. G. Mozar', *Straits Times*, 1 December, p. 15.

Straits Times (1933a) 'Have you ordered your copy of the 1933 Directory and Chronicle?' *Straits Times*, 6 March, p. 16.

Straits Times (1933b) 'Jewel box of advertising exhibition: Singapore publicity effort creates wide interest', *Straits Times*, 21 August, p. 6.

Straits Times (1934) 'British trade fair', *Straits Times*, 25 April, p. 14.

Straits Times (1937) 'Advertising man arrives. To inspect new Singapore branch', *Straits Times*, 8 December, p. 12.

Straits Times (1948) 'Advertising Association', *Straits Times*, 6 May, p. 10.

Straits Times (1949a) 'Leave in E. Africa', *Straits Times*, 12 February, p. 4.

Straits Times (1949b) 'Master's 21 years of advertising in Malaya', *Straits Times*, 6 September, p. 4.

Straits Times (1950) 'An ex-internee', *Straits Times*, 18 May, p. 8.

Straits Times (1956) 'Cathay Ltd gets new chief in Singapore', *Straits Times*, 17 February, p. 12.

Straits Times (1957a) 'Notices: Millington Ltd', *Straits Times*, 15 April, p. 12.

Straits Times (1957b) 'Masters get new expert', *Straits Times*, 17 December, p. 14.

Straits Times (1957c) 'Mr. Young, Singapore publicity man, dies at 66', *Straits Times*, 8 November, p. 9.

Straits Times (1958) 'Singaporean dies in UK', *Straits Times*, 20 February, p. 10.

Straits Times (1959a) 'Colony advertising agency reformed', *Straits Times*, 16 January, p. 14.

Straits Times (1959b) 'Advertising agency's marketing service', *Straits Times*, 17 April, p. 16.

Straits Times (1960a) 'Masters appoint Malayan manager', *Straits Times*, 19 April, p. 12.

Straits Times (1960b) 'Masters form new market division', *Straits Times*, 30 September, p. 10.

Straits Times (1961) 'Changes in Benson's Malaya, HK companies', *Straits Times*, 15 December, p. 18.

Straits Times (1963a) 'Advertising director is retiring', *Straits Times*, 5 February, p. 14.

Straits Times (1963b) 'Advertising agencies' big link-up', *Straits Times*, 6 April, p. 14.

Straits Times (1964) '4th Asian office for Cathay Advertising', *Straits Times*, 10 April, p. 12.

Straits Times (1965a) 'Death of an advertising pioneer', *Straits Times*, 10 September, p. 9.

Straits Times (1965b) 'Visitor from parent company in Australia', *Straits Times*, 2 February, p. 14.

Straits Times (1966a) 'Advertising agency changes its name', *Straits Times*, 30 March, p. 12.

Straits Times (1966b) 'Palmer is again Advertising Assn chairman', *Straits Times*, 22 January, p. 4.

Straits Times (1969) '4th largest in world', *Straits Times*, 25 June, p. 14.

Straits Times (1970) 'Merger of two ad agencies', *Straits Times*, 9 November, p. 13.

Straits Times (1971a) 'Looking into the future', *Straits Times*, 29 October, p. 34.

Straits Times (1975) 'Elliott's visit to S'pore', *Straits Times*, 17 September, p. 14.

Straits Times (1976) '30 lose jobs as Marklin closes down', *Straits Times*, 2 July, p. 13.

Tan, L. (1979) 'Dentsu charge into market', *Business Times*, 28 December, p. 1.

Tan, L. C. (1974) 'Admen split on the role of expats', *Straits Times*. 4 June, p. 12.

Tan, S. C. (1950) 'The first newspaper in the colony', *Straits Times*, 5 January, p. 6.

Ted Bates (1974) 'Introducing a new name to Singapore', *Straits Times*, 18 April, p. 9.

Thulaja, N. R. (2005) 'Singapore Infopedia', *Singapore Free Press*. Available at: http://eresources.nlb.gov.sg/infopedia/articles/SIP_88_2005-02-03.html (accessed 14 November 2016).

Toh, S. F. (1983) 'Bankers guarantee: Ad agencies in a tight spot', *Singapore Monitor*, 7 February, p. 9.

TSFP (1949) '21st birthday party', *Singapore Free Press*, 10 September, p. 5.

TSFP (1952) 'She will write about Malaya', *Singapore Free Press*, 20 May, p. 5.

TSFPMA (1835) 'The Singapore Free Press and the men who have made it', *Singapore Free Press and Mercantile Advertiser*, 8 October, p. 1.

TSFPMA (1932) 'Mrs. Beatrice Thompson', *Singapore Free Press and Mercantile Advertiser*, 15 April, p. 14.

TSFPMA (1936) 'Man who pioneered radio in China and fostered art of advertising', *Singapore Free Press and Mercantile Advertiser*, 1 April, p. 2.

TSFPMA (1954) 'Singapore plastic fabricators are proud', *Singapore Free Press and Mercantile Advertiser*, 28 September, p. 5.

Vinayak, H. V., Thompson, F. and Tonby, O. (2014) *Understanding ASEAN: Seven Things You Need to Know*. Available at: www.mckinsey.com/insights/public_sector/understanding_asean_seven_things_you_need_to_know (accessed 14 November 2016).

WARC (2015) *WARC 100: The World's Best Marketing Strategies*. Available at: www.warc.com/warc100.100 (accessed 14 November 2016).

WeAreSocial (2016) *Special Reports: Digital in 2016*. Available: http://wearesocial.com/sg/special-reports/digital-2016 (accessed 14 November 2016).

Weber Shandwick (2014) *Food Forward Trends Report*. Singapore: Weber Shandwick.

Weekly Sun (1913) 'Union Times, Chinese daily newspaper', *Weekly Sun*, 9 August, p. 2.

Wong, D. (2014) *New 5 Cs That Define Singaporean success*. Available at: https://sg.news.yahoo.com/blogs/singaporescene/new-5-cs-that-define-singaporean-success-023721747.html (accessed 14 November 2016).

Wong, K. (2015) *The Singapore Girl: From an Experiment to an Icon*. Available at: www.channelnewsasia.com/news/singapore/the-singapore-girl-from/2010584.html (accessed 14 November 2016).

YourSingapore (2016) *Festivals & Events*. Available at: www.yoursingapore.com/en_au/festivals-events-singapore.html (accessed 14 November 2016).

Zaccheus M. (2016) 'Rare finds at S'pore's oldest Catholic church', *Straits Times*, 30 June, p. 4.

Zenithoptimedia (2014) *Executive Summary: Advertising Expenditure Forecasts December 2014*. Available at: www.zenithoptimedia.com/wp-content/uploads/2014/12/Adspend-forecasts-December-2014-executive-summary.pdf (accessed 14 November 2016).

13 China

Unique approaches to advertising in a globalising world

Julie Bilby and Kunal Sinha

Introduction

The defining characteristic of China's advertising industry is *speed*. Everything happens in a hurry, and, as is often the case with things done in haste, essentials may sometimes be overlooked. China leads the world in its uptake of digital communication and e-commerce, and, after only three decades, is the world's second largest and fastest growing advertising industry. Yet, according to industry experts, it is possible that the fundamentals of brand building and consumer engagement may have been neglected in the Chinese advertising industry's haste to grow.

This chapter looks at each of these critical factors in turn:

- the nature and scope of advertising in China;
- key influences on Chinese advertising practice;
- the role of advertising in the globalisation of Chinese culture; and
- China's contribution to the global advertising industry.

It concludes by presenting examples of various advertising campaigns – local, 'glocal' and global see how they performed in the Chinese marketplace.

All in all, the authors seek to paint a picture of the dynamic advertising industry in China, bearing in mind that a snapshot of the industry even five years ago would bear little resemblance to the Chinese industry today. The challenge is to identify and present the *enduring* characteristics of the unique Chinese advertising landscape.

Nature and scope of advertising in China: the role, value and characteristics of Chinese advertising

The Chinese advertising industry is constantly evolving and transforming in response to the complex, dynamic marketplace it serves. As Graham Fink, Chief Creative Officer, Ogilvy & Mather China, suggests, the Chinese advertising industry operates 'slightly faster than the speed of light' (Reeves, 2015, p. 1). This pace of change is both impressive and daunting – especially to outsiders trying to get a handle on what's happening in China. Even the most experienced global corporations may find themselves perplexed by the cultural challenges of operating in China (Sinclair, 2008). Yet, as home to one-fifth of the world's population, with the second largest economy in the world, it is very hard for businesses to ignore China (Reeves, 2015).

From complete eradication during the Maoist era to slow beginnings under a centrally controlled government from 1979, advertising in China has grown extremely rapidly. Thirty years later, it is the second largest and fastest growing advertising industry in the world (Anon., 2015a; Reeves, 2015). Advertising in China is often described as having 'leapfrogged' many of the key phases and challenges that Western advertising experienced. This is seen as both a positive and a negative. China, in its highly pragmatic and efficient way, avoided many pitfalls by shrewdly observing and learning from the experience of others. However, the fledgling Chinese industry also missed out on some key marketing and advertising principles, including brand building and consumer engagement. China has a growing presence in international creative award shows, yet still lags behind the rest of the world in effectiveness awards and enduring advertising success stories.

Industry players

Multinational advertising agencies first entered China in the early 1980s in joint venture arrangements with Chinese companies – a Chinese government requirement which remained in place until 2005 (O'Barr, 2007). Japanese-owned Dentsu was the first foreign agency admitted to China in 1979, followed by Ogilvy & Mather, J. Walter Thompson and McCann Erickson in the 1980s, and a flurry of other multinational companies in the 1990s (Sinclair, 2012). Their workforces were almost exclusively expatriate, as native-born Chinese generally lacked sufficient advertising and marketing skills, education or thinking. These were completely foreign concepts after decades of a closed communist regime with no free market or competition.

Until recently these large multinational agencies and their global clients dominated the Chinese industry landscape. However, the number of 'home grown' agencies has increased enormously. These agencies tend to be more specialised and more reactive than the foreign-owned companies. They are also more attuned to the local consumer and more familiar with the complexities of doing business in China. Multinational agencies (MNCs) that used to be focused on brand building are now finding themselves having to diversify into less familiar territory (e.g. branded content, user-generated content, social and digital media), and not always successfully. The distinction between 'local' and 'foreign' agencies is becoming increasingly blurred, especially as many local agencies have become acquisition targets for MNCs.

In 2015, there were over 105,700 advertising agencies in China, employing around three million people, with an estimated payroll of US$23.1 billion. Between 2010 and 2015, the Chinese advertising industry experienced revenue growth of 20.2 per cent annually and, by 2015, the industry was estimated to have generated US$102.8 billion in revenue. Total industry assets were estimated to be worth US$66.1 billion in 2015, an increase of 11.8 per cent from 2014 (Anon., 2015a). However, growth in localised advertising markets has effectively stagnated. Local advertising companies have tended to be geographically scattered, small-scale operations with relatively unsophisticated management expertise. However, it appears that this situation is changing as more local personnel gain international-standard training (Anon., 2015a). Expatriates nevertheless continue to feature prominently in senior positions in the larger multinational advertising agencies. As Clift and Tiltman (2013, p. 2) explain, 'China's ad industry [still] welcomes the active involvement of the advertising elite from all around the world'. Many senior posts are held by people from Taiwan, Hong Kong or Singapore. Such individuals are employed by global agencies on account of their proficiency with Chinese language and culture, as well as their Western education and business background (Lo and Yung, 1988).

Clients and products

The first advertising clients in China, post 1979, were global corporations that arrived to take advantage of the newly open, and seemingly limitless, Chinese market. The first advertising agencies were multinationals serving clients such as Procter & Gamble, Unilever and Volkswagen. Over the years, there has been a shift away from foreign domination of the market. Today, the main clients of both foreign-owned and local agencies tend to be increasingly large Chinese corporations (Sinclair, 2008). A look at China's largest advertisers reveals that four of the top ten are Chinese owned (AdBrands, 2015). Procter & Gamble remains in first position amongst China's most popular consumer goods brands, followed closely by Chinese dairy brands Yili and Mengniu. In fact, 11 of the 21 most valuable fast moving consumer goods (FMCG) companies – each reaching over 100 million urban Chinese households – are Chinese (Nylander, 2015).

Until recently, Chinese clients were seen as more risk-averse and conservative than those in developed markets (Sinclair, 2008), but it appears that the pendulum has recently swung to the opposite extreme: 'new is better'. Clients are demanding more of the 'new' from their agencies, especially in user-generated content and social media. This challenges the traditional agency emphasis on branding and strategy. Advertising agencies in China have had to rethink their operations and core business in order to better service their clients (Thoughtful Media, 2015a). Large foreign-owned agencies are expanding into unfamiliar territories. However, there is an increasing realisation (particularly as Chinese economic growth flattens and stabilises) of the need to return to high-quality strategy and creative, and to welcome cooperation with smaller specialist agencies rather than competing with them.

Advertising appeals and benchmarks of success

The main determinant of success in Chinese advertising is quantitative measurement of response to advertising activity, especially in the form of short-term sales. Most clients are reluctant to pay for creative advertising, instead demanding work that is highly rational, literal and sales-driven. In fact, it appears to be a commonly held view that Chinese consumers are unlikely to respond to creativity (Broadbent, 2013) and that devices such as analogies may not be understood by a Chinese audience (Reeves, 2015). On the other hand, celebrity endorsements are used extensively, whether or not they are relevant to the brand. In fact, the same celebrity can often be seen in advertisements for competing brands. As a consequence, most Chinese advertising lacks creativity, and is heavily reliant on product information and repetition to communicate (Broadbent, 2013; Man and Piepalius, 2013). Such trends stand at odds with the growing body of research which suggests that Chinese audiences actually do appreciate and respond to advertising creativity (e.g. Broadbent, 2013; Bilby *et al.*, 2016).

However, there are signs of change in the industry. Growing numbers of case studies reveal 'brave' clients who are willing to invest in creative, integrated advertising communication strategies. For instance, Lee Jeans ran a social activation campaign in China in 2009 to celebrate the company's 120th anniversary, giving away 120 pairs of bespoke jeans with gold rivets. To win a pair of these jeans, consumers were invited to participate in an online game that lasted 120 hours, requiring them to search online or in-store for information about the brand's heritage. In this way, Lee responded to the needs of the young Chinese market by presenting information about the brand and its 'pedigree' through a subtle yet creative approach.[1]

Similarly, luxury brands intent on establishing a market in China are seeking to stimulate desire and provide brand and product information in innovative ways (Liu *et al.*, 2016). Chanel, for example, recently chose 15-year-old Willow Smith – daughter of US actor Will Smith – as their brand ambassador. As a pre-millennial digital native, Smith's fashion eclecticism appeals to younger Chinese, especially the *fu er dai* (second generation rich), who are experimenting with and developing their own sense of style (Clode, 2016).

As far as specific appeal types, advertising in China tends not to deviate from strongly held cultural values such as filial duty, whereby children are expected to show respect towards parents and elders. Parents, likewise, are consistently portrayed as providing the very best that money can buy for their children (or, more often, their only child). Families are frequently shown gathering together, several generations under the one roof, for festivals and special celebrations such as New Year. It is rare that social norms are challenged in Chinese advertising, although it is anticipated that this will change as the market becomes more sophisticated and even cynical towards advertising. For instance, a Volkswagen Sagitar advertisement that depicted a wife hitting her husband with a frying pan for buying an 'expensive' car initially attracted a great deal of criticism for showing disrespectful values.[2] On the other hand, Lynx ran a highly successful online campaign for men's shower products featuring 'little brother' (a Chinese euphemism for male body parts), encouraging men to use body washes that were specifically designed for the male physique.[3]

There are also signs of change in the types of audiences being targeted with advertising messages. Up until recent years, there has been a preoccupation with the youth market in China. However, the senior market represents a growing opportunity for brands and services prepared to invest in understanding and reaching it. As demographics and lifestyles change, the 'senior wallet' will grow in value and importance. In fact, this demographic is often charged with the responsibility of making big life decisions such as finding housing and even marriage partners on behalf of their time-poor children (Sinha, 2015). A recent example of advertising targeting this older demographic is a microfilm created for the Yili dairy brand, documenting the travels of an elderly Chinese couple who backpacked through 46 countries between 2008 and 2012.[4]

Key influences in Chinese advertising practice

There are many challenges to advertising practice in China, particularly as the industry is under constant pressure to respond to the market's dynamic conditions of the market as well as society in which it operates. These challenges include:

- the size and complexity of the Chinese marketplace, with vast differences between regions and tiers;
- the rapid pace of cultural, social and economic change;
- the influence of government and censorship;
- the unprecedented uptake of digital media by Chinese consumers; and
- brand building and trust issues.

Size and scope of China market

The notion of a single Chinese market is completely unrealistic. Made up of 56 distinct cultural groups (Ouyang *et al.*, 2000) spread across 34 administrative regions (Swanson, 2015) with vastly different geographic, climactic and economic conditions, China presents numerous barriers to building a national market. In fact, China is better understood as multiple complex markets rather than a single entity (Cui and Lui, 2000; Song *et al.*, 2015). Its vast physical size and huge population provide challenges at every level of the marketing process, from distribution and quality assurance to advertising of goods and services. Additionally, from a consumer perspective, there is extreme differentiation across China in terms of demographic and sociological characteristics (Sinclair, 2008). There is much excitement around the idea of an emerging middle class (e.g. Kuo *et al.*, 2015; Scutt, 2015), yet there are vast gaps between the purchasing power and attitudes towards brands across regional and socioeconomic strata (Sinclair, 2008).

City tiers and market segmentation

A unique feature of the Chinese marketing landscape is the system of city tiers, introduced by the Chinese government in the 1980s as a means of prioritising infrastructure and urban development throughout the nation (Starmass, 2011). Although city tiers were never intended to serve as anything other than an administrative ranking system, they have become a useful proxy for segmenting the enormous Chinese populace.

Tier one cities such as Beijing, Guangzhou and Shanghai, form the frontline of China's economic engagement with the rest of the world. Tier two cities include provincial capitals and large cities such as Qingdao, Dalian and Shenzhen (Nielsen, 2010) that are rapidly catching up in terms of economic importance and infrastructure development. Tier three and four cities such as Ningbo, Guilin and Lanzhou (Nielsen, 2010) are less economically developed and more traditional in terms of cultural values and lifestyle (Sinclair, 2008; Liu *et al.*, 2011). The rural tier five and six towns and cities remain significantly underdeveloped with vastly different consumer cultures, values and demographics to the rest of China, and yet they represent an immense opportunity for 'companies that can tap into local and regional psyches and lifestyles' (WPP, 2009, p. 1).

Rapid social and cultural change

China's rise in the past three decades has been on the back of breakneck urbanisation. More than half of the population now live in cities, with migration from the countryside expanding the urban population by 500 million. As a result, China has many large cities: over 100 have more than one million inhabitants; six supersized cities have populations of more than ten million (Fang, 2015).

China's middle class is expected to grow by 326 million by 2030, bringing the total middle-class urban population to around 854 million. This is good news for the advertising industry, with growth anticipated to lift consumption share of GDP to around 50 per cent by 2030, from 36 per cent in 2014 (Scutt, 2015). This new middle class is far more familiar with global cultures and brands than the previous generation. Spurred on by the relaxation of travel restrictions, and encouraged by the quick adoption of Chinese payment gateway Unionpay, 116 million Chinese tourists travelled overseas in 2015, with the number projected to rise to about 242 million in 2024. These travellers have deep pockets, spending US$229 billion overseas in 2015, and averaging two trips abroad per year (Dasgupta, 2015).

Urbanisation, wealth and exposure to international lifestyles have huge consequences for brand preference and consumption behaviours of the Chinese population. Consumers will often pay a premium for foreign brands, not only to ensure quality but also to display their status and the fact they are well-travelled. Familiarity with global brands has also made Chinese consumers more discerning about a brand's origins (Nelson, 2011). For instance, US brands are associated with technology and innovation; French brands with luxury and trendiness; German brands with safety and quality; and Australian food brands with health and natural ingredients (Gu, 2015).

Changing economic environment

In spite of the slowing of China's economic growth since 2015, estimates suggest that China's consumer economy will expand by US$2.3 trillion by 2020, some 81 per cent of which is expected to come from households with annual income over US$24,000 (Kuo *et al.*, 2015). Chinese advertising spend is expected to continue to grow steadily while China remains a dynamic and exciting prospect for marketers (Yeh and Zhang, 2013; Reeves, 2015).

Media consumption across China

There is little question that China has leapt straight into the digital age with 632 million Internet users and 480 million smartphone owners (Anon., 2015b). It has also raced ahead of the rest of the world in embracing e-commerce and consumer-to-consumer (C2C) marketing. For example, the Chinese mobile phone app *WeChat* not only has email and texting functionality, it is also used to settle bills at restaurants, book and pay for services such as home cleaning, make donations to charity and even buy cars (Doland, 2015a). As Graham Fink reflects (in Reeves, 2015), social media in China is more than just a means of communicating; it also reflects a way of life. Face to face, most Chinese come across as humble and reserved. On social media they become far more noisy, brash and demanding – altogether transforming their personalities.

In defiance of the perceived trend in other parts of the world (Brennan, 2013; Hagen, 2014), television remains a very popular choice of media in China (Garton and Liu, 2012). Chinese television currently represents the highest single category of advertising spending (Yeh and Zhang, 2013). It has the highest penetration of any media form, and is considered the most effective means of reaching the mass of lower tier consumers (Garton and Liu, 2012). However, television coverage is also highly decentralised. There are more 3,000 channels across China (compared with 2,000 in the US), making it virtually impossible to launch a truly national television campaign. Even advertising on the national channel, CCTV, does not guarantee effective coverage in every region. Viewers in Shanghai and Guangzhou, for example, prefer local stations broadcasting in their own dialects (Sinclair, 2008). Branded content has also emerged as a significant tactic for brands on television. China's first ever branded content reality show, *The Sephora Beauty Academy*, was broadcast in 2011 on one of the country's biggest satellite channels Dragon TV and on the video website Tudou. The programme followed 12 aspiring make-up and beauty artists from across China as they competed to become the brand's first Asian beauty ambassador.[5] As this example shows, it is not a case of *either* television *or* online as the dominant media form in China, but rather both working in tandem (e.g. digital TV available on mobile phones or interactive QR codes embedded in TV shows) (Hagen, 2014).

Influence of government and censorship

The central government in China continues to play a decisive role in regulating advertising communication. For example, in 2014, the State Administration for Press, Publication, Radio, Film and Television (SARFT) banned the use of puns and wordplay in advertising, promising to punish those found in violation of the rules of 'proper language'. This is in spite of the fact that the Chinese language is rich in idiom and double entendre (Chan, 2014). Additionally, it was recently declared illegal to use superlatives such as 'the biggest', 'the best' or 'the most' in Chinese advertising (Reeves, 2015). Nevertheless, such constraints have not necessarily stifled creativity. In many cases, they have encouraged more lateral solutions as advertisers are forced to be more nuanced, and less literal, in their ways of communicating (Reeves, 2015).

Building brands; building trust

While Chinese consumers could only recognise two luxury brands in 2008 (Atsmon and Dixit, 2009), this figure had doubled by 2011 (Atsmon *et al.*, 2011). By 2013, a survey of middle-class consumers across China found that respondents could recognise up to 59 brands (KPMG, 2013). This exponential growth in brand recognition has been due, in large part, to word of mouth, which has become a powerful means of knowledge dissemination for brands in China. In particular, brands are increasingly harnessing e-Word of Mouth, with top bloggers – seen as fashion leaders and trendsetters – primed and paid by brands to spread the word.

Brand trust continues to represent a big issue for Chinese consumers. Contamination problems (e.g. milk powder) and counterfeiting issues (e.g. technology products) have made would-be purchasers cautious and disinclined to trust brands (Tanner, 2014; Anon., 2015a). Yet, once trust has been established, a brand is free to cross and transcend categories. Trusted brands represent a seal of quality assurance; such brands may enjoy greater extendibility in China than in the West. For example, Tesco, a UK food retailer, also successfully markets financial services, clothing and electronics in China (Bastin, 2011). Danone is known as a yoghurt brand in France, but in China it represents dairy products, biscuits and beverages (Melewar *et al.*, 2006). This is not to say that Chinese consumers are naïve – in fact, they are some of the smartest shoppers in the world, with Chinese consumers doing significantly more pre-purchase research than their Western counterparts (Anon., 2015c; Tanner, 2014). The bottom line is that brands must be able to withstand intense scrutiny and subsequent word of mouth in order to succeed in China.

The role of advertising in the globalisation of Chinese culture

If we take globalisation to mean inclusion with the rest of the world, then advertising has undoubtedly played a part in China's global engagement. Advertising has, to some extent, exposed Chinese consumers to foreign products and lifestyles, although, according to Sinclair (2008), consumers living outside the larger, more cosmopolitan Chinese cities continue to purchase products on the basis of price and reliability rather than an intangible brand image imparted by advertising. Yet, as Sinclair suggests, this may still be more about income distribution and purchasing power on the part of regional consumers than about susceptibility to advertising images and appeals.

Globalisation, or 'modernisation', has been on China's political agenda since 1979 (Anderson, 1981). Coupled with this push to modernise was a realisation that advertising could be harnessed as a tool for social change. Thus, Chinese authorities cautiously 'permitted advertising to influence how the country communicates with itself and the rest of an increasingly interdependent world' (ibid., p. 10). Globalisation has subsequently led to China renegotiating its place in the world (Song and Lee, 2012). Aspects of global culture have been adapted to Chinese values and traditions, resulting in a 'cultural hybridity' that has impacted on many areas of life including purchase and consumption, travel, brand preferences, tastes and desires (Zhang and Harwood, 2004;, Cui *et al.*, 2012), gender representation (Shao *et al.*, 2014), and sexual imagery in media (Wan *et al.*, 2014).

Ikea is one example of a global corporation that has merged into Chinese society with great success. Shopping at Ikea China can be likened to being in an amusement park without rides, where shoppers enjoy inexpensive hot dogs and ice cream and are free to fall asleep on the beds (Doland, 2015b). Starbucks, on the other hand, was accused of cultural insensitivity and foreign imperialism by an online protest group and forced to close a store in the Forbidden City, one of China's most historic sites, in 2007 (O'Barr, 2007). In the meantime, the Chinese government continues to closely monitor and regulate the nation's advertising and commercial activities, but, according to O'Barr, China also demonstrates that advertising can co-exist with socialism and play a key cultural and economic role in a non-Western society.

China's place in the global advertising industry

Historically, China had a massive impact on global culture. Up to the fifteenth century, China was a huge player in global events and innovation (Balmer and Chen, 2015). In recent history, China's place as a global force was hugely diminished, but there is little doubt that China is now rapidly gaining international significance as an economic and political power (Bajoria, 2009; Swanson, 2015).

In terms of international advertising recognition, however, China has a long way to go. According to industry experts, Chinese advertising creativity has yet to find its voice, and so has not had a significant impact on global advertising practice (Bilby *et al.*, 2016). Much of the work produced in China is literal and rational, analogies don't always work and celebrities are used without regard for brand relevance. Additionally, many of China's most effective advertising concepts don't translate well culturally or linguistically (Reeves, 2015).

In spite of this, Chinese work is beginning to attract attention at international advertising festivals. For example, in 2015, China ranked eighth in the world at One Show with 54 winning entries. It also led Asia for the number of winning press advertisements at Cannes. Furthermore, 2015 saw Greater China winning 50 of the 315 medals awarded at AdFest (Thoughtful Media, 2015c, 2015b). In recognition of the exceptional growth of China's advertising industry, the Cannes Lions International Festival of Creativity introduced a 'China Day' in 2013, consisting of series of forums presented by some of China's industry thought leaders and creative agency heads (Anon., 2013). It is worth noting that, 'while the West has been advertising for much longer, the Chinese ad industry – and local brands – don't deserve to be patronised. Their best work is some of the best in the world' (Reeves, 2015, p. 3).

Chinese advertising campaigns: local, 'glocal' and global

Local campaigns

With China's cities experiencing severe air pollution, the air-purifier market is booming. A search on Taobao turns up 101,800 air-purification products from at least 23 brands including Sharp, TCL, Philips, Haier and Xiaomi. Xiao Zhu, an air purifier brand that was barely a year old, wanted to stand out in this congested market. Xiao Zhu's creative agency, Young & Rubicam, decided to expose China's worst polluters by using the smoke spewing from factories in Hangzhou and Shanghai as an outdoor medium. Images of choking, crying children were projected onto the smoke plumes, along with the Xiao Zhu logo and a message: 'Don't let a future of asphyxia happen'.[6] The video documenting this stunt delivered more than 17.3 million views and resulted in a 38 per cent increase in brand awareness within a week of its launch. Sales increased by 20 per cent in the quarter and the campaign went on to win seven Lions at the Cannes Festival, including Gold in the Outdoor category (Chan, 2015).

While celebrity endorsement is rampant in Chinese advertising, some local brands are breaking out and connecting with their customers at an emotional level. For instance, Su Ning, a large electronics retailer, ran a TV advertisement showing a service engineer marooned on a desert island. The engineer writes messages, puts them in bottles and tosses them into the sea. A holidaying couple discovers one of these bottles on a faraway beach; the message inside has a phone number and a request to call the engineer and remind him of a customer's service appointment.[7] The advertisement works through its ironic humour as it exaggerates the marooned employee's dedication, a value that is cherished in China.

'Glocal' campaigns

Due to its enormous size and diverse population, it is generally necessary for multinational organisations to treat China as a separate market, or as a series of markets. As a consequence, many global campaigns are adapted – or 'glocalised' – specifically for Chinese consumers. This has met with mixed success over the years, but the following case studies represent some of more effective examples.

In a society where children are often raised by their grandparents, an innovative mobile phone campaign for Durex condoms highlighted the need for young Chinese adults to behave responsibly. The Durex 'Baby app' allowed users to experience life as a new parent – feeding and playing with 'their baby', soothing it and changing its diapers. Users were also able to share special moments with the baby through extensive social network integration. The app quickly became iTunes' fifth most popular download in China whilst generating participation and word of mouth for the Durex brand.[8]

In 2012, Volkswagen undertook a two-year co-creation programme in China. Primarily aimed at young Chinese 20- to 30-year-olds who are hungry for self-expression and a degree of individualism, Volkswagen invited participants to reinvent the 'people's car'. Individuals and communities were engaged online and offline in the process of designing and building 'a car created by the people for the people'. As a result, over 260,000 ideas were submitted, the campaign website received more than 35 million visits, and the brand was followed by 3.1 million people. The campaign by BBDO/Proximity China won a Gold and two Bronze Lions at the Cannes Festival, and picked up many more awards at Spikes, the One Show and the London Festival.[9]

Global campaigns

There are a few examples of global campaigns that have performed well in China without any need for local adaptation. Nike, for instance, has been able to capitalise on the huge popularity and recognition of basketball superstars Michael Jordan, Lebron James and Kobe Bryant by deploying them as brand ambassadors in advertising, point-of-sale and events in China. Nike Air Jordan shoes have subsequently become desired fashion items in major Chinese cities, where the shoe is viewed as a status symbol and a sign of up-and-coming wealth (Anon., 2016).

Nike is likewise successfully employing a global marketing strategy to promote women's fitness wear in China, as well as elsewhere in the world. The brand's fitness tracker Nike+ app is as popular in China as it is in Europe, as women users are encouraged to share their training experiences on social media using the BetterForIt hashtag (O'Reilly, 2015).

The global Snickers 'You're not yourself when you're hungry' advertising campaign has also enjoyed success in China. One of its latest advertisements for the Chinese market is the result of collaboration across the Mars Food–BBDO global network. This ad features Mr Bean as a kung fu master who does not perform at his best until his hunger is relieved by a Snickers bar. Close involvement between Chinese and UK counterparts ensured that the cultural nuances of each market, such as remaining true to period kung fu costumes, were observed (Green, 2014).

As the Snickers example illustrates, China is slowly but surely gaining recognition as a source of creative ideas for global advertising campaigns. Similarly, as part of Coca-Cola's global 'Open Happiness' campaign, Ogilvy & Mather Shanghai designed a poster in which a hand passing a bottle of Coca-Cola was depicted in the form of Coke's iconic white ribbon, in response to a simple brief: Share a Coke.[10] The poster won a Grand Prix in the Outdoor category at the Cannes Lions, and was rolled out globally. It also inspired a major marketing push in Latin America where the ribbon was replaced by a 'fist bump', representing a universal sign of friendship. The image appears on packaging, advertising and merchandising as part of a campaign called #VerdaderoAmigo, or #TrueFriendship.[11]

Conclusion

This chapter has presented a picture of the vibrant Chinese advertising industry, situating it in the global advertising environment while communicating its unique character. Considering its relative youth and the restrictions under which it operates, the progress and growing list of achievements of China's advertising industry are impressive. Whilst brand building and consumer engagement may have been somewhat overlooked in China's rapid growth phase, there is a sense that operating in a slower economy with increasingly sophisticated consumers will see a return to, and reliance on, sound business principles – coupled with greater innovation and creativity. It will be fascinating to watch the Chinese advertising industry mature and increasingly take its place as a serious and influential global player.

Notes

1 Lee Jeans 120th anniversary China campaign, 2009. Available at: www.coloribus. com/adsarchive/promo-casestudy/lee-the-gold-button-15574255/.
2 Volkswagen Sagitar advertisement, 2012. Available at: www.youtube.com/ watch?v=OjJVqxA4lGM.
3 Lynx 'Little Brother' advertisement, 2013. Available at: www.coloribus.com/ads archive/viral/lynx-little-brother-19151705/.
4 Lynx 'Little Brother' advertisement, 2013. Available at: www.coloribus.com/ads archive/viral/lynx-little-brother-19151705/.
5 Sephora Beauty Academy in China case study, 2011. Available at: www.youtube. com/watch?v=AmROlqC1yTA.
6 Xiao Zhu case study, 2015. Available at: www.campaignlive.com/article/china-air-purifier-brand-takes-political-risks-winning-campaign/1357515.
7 Su Ning advertisement, *The Ad Show*, 2009. Available at: www.youtube.com/ watch?v=D5n7ijTSSTA.
8 Durex 'Baby app' case study, Fugumobile, 2014. Available at: http://fugumobile. mobi/home/?p=941.

9   Volkswagen 'People's car project' social media case study, 2013. Available at: http://cargocollective.com/JojoZ/Gold-Lion-Awarded-The-People-s-Car-Project-Volkswagen.

10 Volkswagen 'People's car project' social media case study, 2013. Available at: http://cargocollective.com/JojoZ/Gold-Lion-Awarded-The-People-s-Car-Project-Volkswagen.

11 Fist bump for friendship' campaign, 2015. Available at: http://theonecentre.com/bar/blog/coca-cola-embraces-fist-bump-for-teen-focused-campaign.

References

AdBrands (2015) 'China's top advertisers in 2014', *AdBrands.net*. Available at: www.adbrands.net/cn/index.html (accessed 14 November 2016).

Anderson, M. H. (1981) 'China's 'Great Leap' toward Madison Avenue'. *Journal of Communication*, 31(1), pp. 10–22.

Anon. (2013) 'Cannes Lions introduces China Day', *ACN Newswire*, pp. 1–2. Available at: www.acnnewswire.com (accessed 14 November 2016).

Anon. (2015a) 'Advertising agencies in China: Market research report', *Ibisworld*, pp. 1–2, Available at: www.ibisworld.com/industry/china/advertising-agencies.html (accessed 14 November 2016).

Anon. (2015b) 'BrandZ Top 100 most vaulable Chinese Brands: Chinese brands come of age', *Millward Brown Asia Report*, pp. 1–127. Available at: www.millwardbrown.com/docs/default-source/global-brandz-downloads/china/BrandZ_2015_China_Top100_Report_EN.pdf (accessed 14 November 2016).

Anon. (2015c) 'Smart shoppers: 9 in 10 Chinese consumers research products before they buy', *TNS Press release*, 1 December. Available at: www.tnsglobal.com/node/115321 (accessed 14 November 2016).

Anon. (2016) 'Nike bets on China, despite downturn', *WARC*, Available at: www.warc.com/LatestNews/News/Nike_bets_on_China,_despite_downturn.news?ID=36011 (accessed 14 November 2016).

Atsmon, Y. and Dixit, V. (2009) 'China's confident consumers: A survey highlights how fast the market is changing', *McKinsey Quarterly*, 4 November, pp. 1–5.

Atsmon, Y., Dixit, V. and Wu, C. (2011) 'Tapping China's luxury-goods market', *McKinsey Quarterly*, 2 April, pp. 1–5.

Bajoria, J. (2009) 'China's role in the world', *Council on Foreign Relations*. Available at: www.cfr.org (accessed 14 November 2016).

Balmer, J. M. T. and Chen, W. (2015) 'China's brands, China's brand development strategies and corporate brand communications in China', *Journal of Brand Management*, 22(3), pp. 175–93.

Bastin, M. (2011) 'How far can you stretch your brand?' *China Daily*, 18 November, pp. 1–2.

Bilby, J., Reid, M. and Brennan, L. (2016) 'The future of advertising in China', *Journal of Advertising Research*, pp. 1–14. DOI: 10.2501/JAR-2016-000.

Brennan, D. (2013) 'TV's not dead', *Market Leader*, Quarter 3, pp. 1–8.

Broadbent, T. (2013) 'Communication: Dawn of creation for Asia', *Market Leader*, Quarter 1, pp. 1–6.

Chan, J. (2014) 'Will Chinese crackdown on advertising puns stifle creativity?' *Campaign*, pp. 1–16. Available at: www.campaignlive.com/article/will-chinese-crackdown-advertising-puns-stifle-creativity/1325070 (accessed 14 November 2016).

Chan, J. (2015) 'In China, air-purifier brand takes political risks', *Campaign*. Available at: www.campaignlive.com/article/china-air-purifier-brand-takes-political-risks-winning-campaign/1357515 (accessed 14 November 2016).

Clift, J. and Tiltman, D. (2013) 'VW, PepsiCo, SinoMedia and Beijing Dentsu: China Day at the 2013 Cannes Lions', *WARC*. Available at: www.adweek.com (accessed 14 November 2016).

Clode, J. (2016) 'Why Willow Smith is great for Chanel in China', *Social Brand Watch*, pp. 1–3. Available at: http://socialbrandwatch.com/willow-smith-chanel-s-latest-ambassadress (accessed 14 November 2016).

Cui, G. and Lui, Q. (2000) 'Regional market segments of China: Opportunities and barriers in a big emerging market', *Journal of Consumer Marketing*, 17(1), pp. 55–72

Cui, G., Yang, X., Wang, H. and Liu, H. (2012) 'Culturally incongruent messages in international advertising', *International Journal of Advertising*, 31(2), pp. 355–76.

Dasgupta, S. (2015) 'Chinese tourists defy slowing economy to travel abroad', *Voice of America*, pp. 1–2. Available at: www.voanews.com/content/chinese-tourists-abroad-defy-slowing-economy/2993418.html (accessed 14 November 2016).

Doland, A. (2015a) 'How agencies are adapting to China's e-commerce boom', *Advertising Age*. Available at: http://adage.com/article/global-news/agencies-adapting-china-s-e-commerce-boom/301503/ (accessed 14 November 2016).

Doland, A. (2015b) 'Defying tough times, these four foreign brands are successful in China', *Advertising Age*, pp. 1–4. Available at: http://adage.com/article/global-news/foreign-brands-successful-china/299242/ (accessed 14 November 2016).

Fang, L. (2015) 'The great sprawl of China', *The Economist*, 24 January, Urbanisation pp. 1–4. Available at: www.economist.com/node/21640396/print (accessed 14 November 2016).

Garton, S. and Liu, J. (2012) 'China's lower tier markets', *Admap Magazine*, China Supplement, March, pp. 1–7.

Green, R. (2014) 'BBDO China transports Mr Bean to ancient China for global collaboration Snickers campaign', *Campaign Brief Asia*, 6 October, pp. 1–3.

Gu, L. (2015) 'Chinese spending habits', *Mintel Reports*, April. Available at: http://store.mintel.com/chinese-spending-habits-china-april-2015 (accessed 14 November 2016).

Hagen, D. (2014) 'TV planning: Convergent behaviour', *Admap Magazine*, January, pp. 26–7.

KPMG (2013) 'Chinese luxury consumers are increasingly purchasing overseas: Cosmetics, watches and bags are their top choices, finds KPMG survey', *KPMG News Feed*, 22 January, pp. 1–3. Available at: www.kpmg.com/cn/en/pressroom/pressreleases/pages/press-20130122-chinese-luxury-consumers.aspx (accessed 14 November 2016).

Kuo, Y., Walters, J., Gao, H., Wang, A., Yang, V., Yang, J., Lyu, S. and Wan, H. (2015) *The New China Playbook: Young, Affluent, E-Savvy Consumers Will Fuel Growth*, bcg.perspectives. Available at: www.bcg.com.cn/en/files/publications/.../BCG-The-New-China-Playbook-Dec-2015.pdf (accessed 17 February 2017).

Liu, S., Smith, J. R., Liesch, P. W., Gallois, C., Ren, Y. and Daly, S. (2011) 'Through the lenses of culture: Chinese consumers' intentions to purchase imported products', *Journal of Cross-Cultural Psychology*, 42(7), pp. 1237–50.

Liu, S., Perry, P., Moore, C. and Warnaby, G. (2016) 'The standardization–localization dilemma of brand communications for luxury fashion retailers' internationalization into China', *Journal of Business Research*, 69(1), pp. 357–64.

Lo, T. W.-C. and Yung, A. (1988) 'Multinational service firms in centrally planned economies: Foreign advertising agencies in the PRC', *Management International Review*, 28(1), pp. 26–33.

Man, P. and Piepalius, S. (2013) 'Lynx: Launching the Lynx effect in China', *WARC: Prize for Asian Strategy*, pp. 1–9. Available at: www.warc.com (accessed 7 March 2017).

Melewar, T. C., Badal, E. and Small, J. (2006) 'Danone branding strategy in China', *Journal of Brand Management*, 13(6), pp. 407–17.

Nelson, C. (2011), 'Understanding Chinese consumers', *China Business Review*, pp. 1–14. Available at: www.chinabusinessreview.com/understanding-chinese-consumers (accessed 14 November 2016).

Nielsen (2010) *Chinese Take-Away* (2nd edn). Shanghai: The Nielsen Company.

Nylander, J. (2015) 'Top 21 winning brands In China', *Forbes*, 6 December, pp. 1–2. Available at: www.forbes.com/sites/jnylander/2015/12/06/top-21-winning-brands-in-china/#74614f4b3f4f (accessed 14 November 2016).

O'Barr, W. M. (2007) 'Advertising in China'. *Advertising & Society Review*, 8(3). Available at: https://muse.jhu.edu/article/221972 (accessed 17 February 2017).

O'Reilly, L. (2015) 'Nike is launching its biggest ever women's push', *Business Insider, Australia*, 13 April, pp. 1–9.

Ouyang, M., Zhou, D. and Zhou, N. (2000) 'Twenty years of research on marketing in China: A review and assessment of journal publications', *Journal of Global Marketing*, 14(1–2), pp. 187–201.

Reeves, A. (2015), 'The state of Chinese advertising', *Beakstreet Bugle.com*, pp. 1–8. Available at: http://beakstreetbugle.com/articles/view/468/the-state-of-chinese-advertising-market-2015 (accessed 14 November 2016).

Scutt, D. (2015) 'China's rising middle class will create opportunities the world has never seen before', *Business Insider*. Available at: www.businessinsider.com/chinas-rising-middle-class-will-create-opportunities-the-world-has-never-seen-before-2015-5?r=UK&IR=T (accessed 14 November 2016).

Shao, Y., Desmarais, F. and Weaver, C. K. (2014) 'Chinese advertising practitioners' conceptualisation of gender representation'. *International Journal of Advertising*, 33(2), pp. 329–50.

Sinclair, J. (2008) 'Globalization and the advertising industry in China', *Chinese Journal of Communication*, 1(1), pp. 77–90.

Sinclair, J. (2012), *Advertising, the Media and Globalisation*. London: Routledge.

Sinha, K. (2015) 'Thrifty at sixty? Perspectives on senior inclusion and value in Chindia', *WARC Exclusive: Aging Asia Series*, pp. 1–13. Available at: www.warc.com (accessed 7 March 2017).

Song, G. and Lee, T. K. (2012) ' "New Man" and "New Lad" with Chinese characteristics? Cosmopolitanism, cultural hybridity and men's lifestyle magazines in China'. *Asian Studies Review*, 36(3), pp. 345–67.

Song, J., Sawang, S., Drennan, J. and Andrews, L. (2015) 'Same but different? Mobile technology adoption in China'. *Information Technology & People*, 28(1) pp. 107–32

Starmass (2011) 'Chinese first tier cities, second tier cities and tiered cities in China', *Starmass.com*. Available at: www.starmass.com/china-review/businss-tips/chinese-tiered-cities.htm (accessed 14 November 2016).

Swanson, A. (2015) '7 simple questions and answers to understand China and the U.S.', *Washington Post*. Available at: www.washingtonpost.com/news/wonk/wp/2015/09/22/everything-you-need-to-know-about-china-and-the-u-s/ (accessed 14 November 2016).

Tanner, M. (2014) 'In China, even zoo animals can be fakes: Chinese consumers and trust issues', *Advertising Age*. Available at: http://adage.com/article/guest-columnists/brands-build-trust-chinese-consumers/293964/ (accessed 14 November 2016).

Thoughtful Media (2015a) 'The future of advertising in China', N. Madden (ed.), *Thoughtful China*, 16 March. Available at: www.youtube.com/watch?v=309OJaCuVgo (accessed 14 November 2016).

Thoughtful Media (2015b) 'China's performance at Ad Fest 2015', *Thoughtful China*, 5 May. Available at: www.youtube.com/watch?v=Rcpvq83ZSGQ (accessed 14 November 2016).

Thoughtful Media (2015c) 'China's performance at The One Show and Cannes', *Thoughtful China*, 4 August. Available at: www.youtube.com/watch?v=yQ84hP67Qd0 (accessed 14 November 2016).

Wan, W. W. N., Luk, C.-L. and Chow, C. W. C. (2014) 'Consumer responses to sexual advertising: The intersection of modernization, evolution, and international marketing'. *Journal of International Business Studies*, 45(6), pp. 751–82.

WPP (2009) 'China beyond study offers insights in China's 4th–6th tier towns'. Available at: www.wpp.com/wpp/press/2009/jun/23/china-beyond-study-offers-insights-in-chinas/ (accessed 14 November 2016).

Yeh, J. and Zhang, M. (2013) 'Taking the pulse of China's ad spending', *McKinsey Quarterly*, June. Available at: www.mckinsey.com/industries/media-and-entertainment/our-insights/taking-the-pulse-of-chinas-ad-spending (accessed 17 February 2017).

Zhang, Y. B. and Harwood, J. (2004) 'Modernization and tradition in an age of globalization: Cultural values in Chinese television commercials', *Journal of Communication*, 54(1), pp. 156–72.

14 Australasian advertising and the world

Jackie Dickenson and Robert Crawford

Australasia

Australasia is a sub-region of the Asia-Pacific region and comprises the countries of Australia, New Zealand and numerous Pacific Islands, including Papua New Guinea. Australia and New Zealand have well-established advertising industries which dominate advertising activity in the region. The Australian advertising industry is the larger of the two industries, reflecting Australia's significantly bigger population – 23.5 million people compared to New Zealand's 4.65 million. In 2014 advertising revenue was AU$12.8 billion in Australia and NZ$2.386 billion in New Zealand (Zenith Optimedia, 2015). In Australia 7,890 businesses employed 19,110 people in the marketing communications field – the top 150 agencies make up the bulk of this work, employing some 6,000 (Australian Bureau of Statistics, 2015; Communications Council, 2015; IBISWorld, 2015). The New Zealand advertising industry employed 4,840 people in at least 245 businesses (Yellow, 2016). By way of contrast, some 30 communications agencies operate in Papua New Guinea (Commonwealth Network, 2016).

The major global networks – WPP, Omnicom, Interpublic, Dentsu Aegis, TBWA, Publicis Groupe, M&C Saatchi, Havas Worldwide and the Enero Group – are all represented in the region (Campaign Brief, 2012). WPP operates in the region as WPP AUNZ. Its stable includes GPY&R, Grey, JWT, Ogilvy (WPP, 2016). Omnicom's BBDO, DDB and TBWA all operate in the region. In Australia TBWA trades as Whybin/TBWA, while BBDO's operations are known as Colenso BBDO in New Zealand and Clemenger BBDO in Australia (Clemenger BBDO, 2016; Colenso BBDO, 2014; Omnicom Group, 2016; TBWA, 2016). Interpublic is represented by McCann. Publicis Groupe operates Saatchi & Saatchi (Saatchi & Saatchi, 2016a, 2016b) and Leo Burnett (the region's leading creative agency) in both markets, but Publicis Mojo in Australia alone. BWM (Australia) and Haystac (New Zealand) represent the Dentsu Aegis network in the region. M&C Saatchi withdrew from New Zealand in 2014, but remains open in Australia (Venuto, 2014). The Enero Group is represented by BMF in Australia alone. FCB Global closed its Australian operations in 2014 and is now represented only in New Zealand (Grey, 2016). Branches of these agencies are located predominantly in the Australian cities of Sydney and Melbourne, and in

New Zealand's largest city, Auckland, as well as its capital, Wellington. Each country also has additional centres of commercial activity.

Each industry supports a number of sizeable independent agencies. In Australia, Cummins & Partners, Joy, AJF Partnership, and The Monkeys (agency of the year in 2014) are notable. The Monkeys formed in 2006, seeing 'an opportunity to broaden the concept of what an agency can offer beyond traditional advertising' (Dunn, 2013). Cummins & Partners have recently embarked on attaining their own global network, buying agencies in Toronto and New York (Cummins & Partners, 2015; Wander, 2015). In New Zealand, notable independent agencies include the Alt Group, Joy and True. The first market research companies began opening in Australia just before the Second World War, but only took off in the 1950s and 1960s. In New Zealand similar firms commenced operations only in the 1960s. The key firms operating in the region include McNair Ingenuity, A. C. Neilson, Ipsos, Colmar Brunton and TNS Kantar.

Media agencies have long been key players in the region's advertising industry. For 2014/15 the Omnicom-owned OMD had billings of AU$1.33 billion, which just nudged out Denstu-Aegis's Carat with AU$1.3 billion. In third place was Group M's Mediacom with AU$1.23 billion. Group M's agencies collectively billed AU$2.844, making it the high-billing holding group in Australia (Christensen, 2015). New Zealand's OMD not only dominated the local media market, Campaign Asia awarded it top media agency in the region for 2013, 2014 and 2015. Group M's arrival in New Zealand in 2015 indicates a desire to challenge its dominance. Local retailers dominate the advertising spends in both countries: Woolworths and Wesfarmers in Australia, and Foodstuffs in New Zealand (StopPress, 2014). Of the global brands, the British manufacturer Reckitt Benckiser (Dettol, Vanish, Mortein) is the fifth biggest spender while the fast food giant McDonalds is the biggest spender of the US brands (Adbrands, 2015).

According to the Hofstede system of cultural measurement, both Australia and New Zealand are highly individual and masculine cultures, thus direct advertising appeals are likely to be more successful (Hofstede, 2016). GLOBE places both countries within the Anglo cluster (Gupta and Hanges, 2004), which reflects the region's history from the end of the eighteenth century when Britain colonised Australasia. The common heritage of Australia and New Zealand is reflected in their (slightly varied) Westminster-style democracies, although the two nations have different relationships with their respective indigenous populations: the New Zealanders signed a treaty with the indigenous Maoris in 1840, but Australia is yet to sign a treaty with indigenous Australians. Non-British immigration to both countries has been a significant development since the Second World War with neighbouring regions overtaking Britain as the most popular source of migrants. Advertising imagery in both countries has been slow to reflect their increasingly multicultural populations.

The cultural, economic and political connections between these former British colonies have been historically strong. Such links have also influenced the development of the advertising industry in both countries. As elsewhere in the world, advertising emerged in the region as a separate industry from the newspaper industry in the second half of the nineteenth century. Charles Haines opened New Zealand's first full service agency in 1891, while John Ilott established his shop the following year (Phillips, 2013). Full service agencies arrived later in Australia. Sydney's first full service agency – Miller's – opened in 1902, shortly followed by the Weston Company (Crawford, 2008). The Paton Advertising Service commenced operations in Melbourne in 1904. Advertising expenditure gradually increased before taking off in the 1920s. Frank Goldberg established his agency in Wellington in 1925 and quickly became a regular traveller to Australia (Lawson, 2016). His decision to relocate to Sydney in 1928 meant that Goldberg Advertising was the first foreign agency to commence operations in Australia. J. Walter Thompson was the first American agency to enter the region, opening offices in Melbourne, Sydney and Wellington in 1930. When the Depression forced the Wellington branch to close a year later, various staff members moved across to Sydney (Crawford, 2016).

After the Second World War, both countries enjoyed rapid economic growth. Consumer prosperity coupled with the arrival of commercial television attracted the interest of multinational advertising agencies (Crawford and Dickenson, 2016). Local content restrictions on television commercials also compelled overseas agencies to establish Australian operations. McCann Erickson's arrival in 1959 was followed by FCB and Ted Bates in 1964, Ogilvy & Mather in 1967, Y&R in 1968, Leo Burnett in 1970 and Saatchi & Saatchi in 1985. International interest in New Zealand was curtailed by legislation, which prevented overseas agencies from buying more than a 49 per cent share of any local agency. Unlike Australia, New Zealand did not have local content restrictions on advertisements, enabling overseas firms to broadcast imported British, American or Australian commercials on New Zealand television. Over the 1980s and 1990s, restrictions on foreign ownership of New Zealand agencies were relaxed while Australian local content restrictions were dismantled. Both shifts would bring the region into closer alignment with one another as well as the global networks and their international strategies. In New Zealand, 2006 was a particularly challenging year with the closure of a number of independent agencies (Medcalf, 2006). The challenges posed by digitisation have impacted on the structure, operations and output of agencies in both countries (McNickel, 2002). While Australian and New Zealand agencies have met these changes with a mix of innovation and pragmatism, adapting to the emerging digital field and finding relevant and creative solutions to client problems has remained an ongoing issue.

The role of the region in the globalisation of culture

Both Australia and New Zealand foster a culture of irreverence, which is, arguably, a legacy of their colonial heritages, and is reflected in their advertising styles.

The 1999 'Bugger' campaign for Toyota Hilux illustrates this style. Created by Saatchi & Saatchi New Zealand, the commercials depicted a series of calamities on a homestead, which were followed by the victim laconically stating

'Bugger!' While the campaign attracted some complaints in New Zealand for its use of obscene language, it nevertheless proved to be highly popular (NZON-SCREEN, 2016a). The campaign was successfully transferred to Australia, where it was readily 'adopted' as a local advertisement. Overall, the region utilises a combination of English and US approaches, the former from the British past, the latter a result of a relatively uncomplicated process of globalisation. The most successful tourism campaigns in both countries reflect these connections, reaching out to global audiences while expressing highly nationalised ideas and images. The 1984 'Come and Say G'day' campaign placed Australia on the tourist itinerary. Featuring a fresh-faced Paul Hogan, the campaign welcomed the world to Australia's laid-back lifestyle and revelled in its stunningly beautiful sights. Coinciding with the enormous success of the film *Crocodile Dundee* (also starring Hogan) the campaign saw tourism numbers skyrocket, as Australia moved from being a distant and unfamiliar continent to become a desirable destination. Subsequent campaigns seeking to update the campaign but retain the same structure have met with less success. A more innovative campaign was the 2009 'Greatest Job in the World' advertisement, which invited applicants to submit video résumés for a well-paid job that required little more than lazing on a tropical island and posting regular updates on social media. With 35,000 applications from over 200 countries, the campaign put Australia back on the map in an engaging way. The '100% Pure' campaign established a broader and more sustained appeal for New Zealand on the global market (100% Pure New Zealand, 2016). Launched in 1999, the simple, clear and transferable slogan succinctly articulated New Zealand's uniqueness to the audience. It also successfully repositioned New Zealand from a relatively obscure place to a hip destination, which offered pure nature as well as pure adventure (Tourism New Zealand, 2009a). Aided by the success of the *Lord of the Rings* film trilogy, the New Zealand brand attracted a growing number of visitors. Between 1999 and 2008, visitor numbers grew from 1.6 million to 2.4 million (Tourism New Zealand, 2009b), while the value of the New Zealand brand was estimated to be US$13 billion. The campaign also collected multiple local and international awards.

Noting that like-minded social classes in different countries tend to cut across national identity and aid the process of homogenisation in the exporting of American culture, John Sinclair (1987) offers a further explanation for the similarities between Australian and New Zealand advertising. Combined with relatively weak national identities and an already-expanding consumer society, the ascendency of the middle classes in Australia and New Zealand made it relatively easy for American corporations to enter each market. From the 1970s, US fast food chains – Pizza Hut, Kentucky Fried Chicken and McDonalds – faced little resistance across the region. In New Zealand, as Brailsford (2003) notes, these global fast food brands 'just slotted in' and have since consistently outspent local competitors on television. The impact of these campaigns is reflected in the response to the 1975 campaign for Kentucky Fried Chicken featuring an animated brother and sister singing 'and Hugo said you go'. Despite being created and produced in Australia, the campaign for the multinational fast food chain has been included in NZ On Screen, an 'online showcase of New Zealand television, film and music video' (NZONSCREEN, 2016b). In another example of the interplay between local and global cultures, the 1974 American commercial singing 'Baseball, hot dogs, apple pie and Chevrolet' was remade in Australia with the lyrics 'Football, meat pies, kangaroos and Holden cars'. For New Zealand audiences, 'kiwi birds' replaced the Australian national symbol. More recent local contributions to global campaigns were the locally produced variations of the Snickers 'You're not you when you're hungry' campaign featuring Betty White from 2010. In 2012 the New Zealand commercial featured controversial broadcaster Paul Henry, while the 2013 Australian remake featured Ray Meagher (better known as the volatile 'Alf' from the Australian television soap *Home and Away*) (Boon, 2013).

The region's contribution to the global industry

The region's advertising industry punches well above its weight, especially in creative performance. In the 2015 Global Creativity Index, Australia topped the table and New Zealand came in third, after the United States (Florida *et al.*, 2015). This strength in creativity is reflected in the region's performance at global creative advertising awards: in 2014 Australia ranked fifth in the world for the number of creative awards won and New Zealand was fourteenth (Directory, 2015). That a country with a population less than one-fourteenth the size of the United States can win more creative awards is remarkable. New Zealand's achievement is even more impressive: its population is some 69 times smaller than that of the United States. New Zealand advertising is generally regarded as creatively superior to Australian advertising, both locally and internationally (Hicks, 2012). The creative excellence of the region's advertising industries, especially that of New Zealand, is explained by some as the result of necessarily small budgets requiring a firmer concentration on strong ideas: 'Without the eye-watering budgets that some UK agencies have, New Zealand shops tend to focus on the purity of ideas' (Talbot, 2012). As such, there seem to be fewer barriers to creative ideas. New Zealand also benefits from a world-renowned film production industry, which gained significant and, so far, lasting momentum from the production of the *Lord of the Rings* series and the two *Hobbit* movies in the country.

Australia and New Zealand have also emerged as useful test markets for global brands. In 2016, they were used as test markets (alongside the US) for the online game Pokémon Go. Other successful tests conducted in Australia include McDonald's McCafé and Tesla Powerwall batteries. New Zealand has also been a popular market for apps: Facebook trialled Snapchat-like disappearing messages as well as a tool to promote the user's status updates to friends – both plans were shelved in light of negative responses from New Zealand consumers (*The Economist*, 2015). Speaking about the reasons why Australia has been used as a test market, Michael Silverstein, managing director of the Boston

Consulting Group, claimed that Australians' hunger for new experiences and products made them a 'good proxy for white, Christian America', a point that many citizens of the largely secular Australia might challenge! The size and quality of Australia's infrastructure in terms of media, distribution channels and talent similarly made it a desirable test market (Fry, 2015). Perhaps a more important consideration is the region's distance from the rest of the world – failures in this far flung region need not damage the global brand. For agencies servicing these brands, the test markets also provide a unique opportunity to test their advertising.

Glocal/global campaigns

The performance of the global brand Coca-Cola in the Australasia region reveals the singular characteristics of each of the markets and sheds light on responses to the current challenges posed by new technologies. The entry of McCann Erickson to the Australasia region in 1959 was, in large part, prompted by the requirements of its global clients, most notably Coca-Cola (Crawford, 2016). Unable to screen its global campaigns on Australian television on account of local content restrictions, McCann Erickson's local operation simply had them reshot locally, frame for frame. As this process was laborious and could produce sub-standard results, McCann Erickson's Sydney office was given an opportunity to create and produce its own commercials. For decades, Australia along with Japan would have the distinction of being the only markets outside of the US where Coke commercials were locally created. Over the next decades, the soft drink brand pursued a global strategy/local execution across the region. One of its first successes was the 'Beach Ball' advertisement, which first aired in 1964. Making the most of Australia's sunny climate and beautiful beaches, the advertisement connected Coca-Cola to youth, fun and summer. Such themes, as well as the giant beach ball itself, would become a mainstay of Coke advertising campaigns in Australia over the 1970s and 1980s (Coke's 2009 campaign nostalgically reprised this formula, albeit with a giant translucent Coke bottle in place of the beach ball) (Burrowes, 2009). By the time of the 1991 Sky Surfer campaign, the locus of action had been relocated from the beach to Australia's 'Red Centre'. Featuring action shots of the new adrenaline-pumping sport of sky surfing, the commercial was shot by a New Zealander (whose credits would later include the Toyota 'Bugger' advertisement). It would stand out as one of the first non-American Coke campaigns to be screened globally.

The region continues to make a very real contribution to Coca-Cola's global campaigns. The 'Share a Coke' campaign of 2011 was devised by Ogilvy & Mather in Sydney (see Figure 14.1). Responding to the fact that people were increasingly connecting online rather than face to face, the campaign enabled people to connect the brand with their audience in a way that was relevant, fun and personal. By selecting 150 of the most popular Australian names on Coke bottle labels, the campaign hoped to remind Australians of friends or family they had not seen in a while. Its attempt to reach out in a personable and informal way reflected Australia's egalitarian ethos. Commercials aired during major sporting events featured crowd-sourced images of fans drinking a Coke with their own name on it. Interactivity was a central part of the campaign. Over the Labour Day weekend in Sydney, Coke fans could SMS a friend's name, which was then projected onto the famous 'Coca-Cola' sign at King's Cross. The success of the campaign in Australia led Coke to replicate it in New Zealand shortly afterwards. Its success in both markets as well as peer acclamation at the Cannes Lions festival inspired more than 70 countries across the globe to initiate their own variations of the 'Share a Coke' campaign (Moye, 2014). In 2014 Coca-Cola followed up on its successful campaign by harnessing its longstanding 'beach and sunshine' appeal to the irreverent humour shared by Australia and New Zealand, through the use of social media and the careful selection of local comedic stars (Riches, 2015). The '#colouryoursummer' campaign, which ran in Australia and New Zealand across the summer of 2014/15, cost AU$10 million. Running only on social media and limited outdoor sites, the promotion resulted in a 27 per cent uplift in projected sales in Australia (Baker, 2014).

The region's impact can also be felt in the global popularity of digital campaigns. 'Dumb Ways to Die' was created in 2012 for Melbourne's Metro Trains. Within hours of its launch, the catchy song was in the iTunes Top 10 (McCann, 2016). It would go on to become one of the most shared campaigns of all time,

Figure 14.1 Coca-Cola's 'Share a Coke' campaign.

Source: photo credit: Brian Waldron.

Note
Trademarks of the Coca-Cola Company are used with permission; the Coca-Cola Company is not the producer of this guide, nor does it endorse the contents.

and the original advertisement has been viewed over 138 million times on YouTube – more than 30 times the population of Melbourne! Air New Zealand's safety videos have similarly amassed enormous global viewership. Spurning the idea that safety videos should be informative but boring, Air New Zealand sought to insert humour and life into their videos. The airline's initial effort, 'Bare Essentials', was launched in 2009, and featured Air New Zealand staff in body paint. Significantly cheaper than a commercial, the clip was an instant hit (Malkin, 2009). Its 2012 *Hobbit*-themed safety clip was shared over 980,000 times, while the follow-up clip enjoyed more than 510,000 shares (Ward, 2015). This series of clips has attracted over 50 million views alone and generated significant worldwide publicity (Garcia, 2015). Such successes reflect the region's creativity, revealing its continuing contribution to innovation in advertising.

Conclusion

As a region, Australasia has managed to make a significant and continuing con-tribution to global advertising. Although Australia and New Zealand are very much separate markets with distinctive features, the differences between the two countries are often lost on outsiders – much like the Aussie and Kiwi accents. Commercials frequently cross the Tasman Sea with little or no alteration. Despite, or, perhaps, in spite of their size and distance from advertising's tradi-tional global centres, Australia and New Zealand remain important contributors to global networks and their operations. Australasia has not only proven to be receptive to global campaigns and strategies, it has also made meaningful contri-butions to them through creativity, humour and innovation. As these attributes remain integral to advertising and its future, the region will continue to 'punch above its weight' in terms of its contribution to the global advertising business.

References

100% Pure New Zealand (2016) *Official site for Tourism New Zealand.* Available at: www.newzealand.com/au/?cid=p:sem:AU:Google:Always-On:Tourism-New-Zealand-AU-Brand-Phrase:Brand-New-Zealand-Pure-100 (accessed 14 November 2016).

adbrands.net (2015) *Australia's Top-Spending Advertisers in 2014.* Available at: www.adbrands.net/au/top_advertisers_in_australia.html (accessed 14 November 2016).

Australian Bureau of Statistics (2015) *July Key Figures.* Available at: www.abs.gov.au/ausstats/abs@.nsf/mf/6202.0 (accessed 14 November 2016).

Baker, R. (2014) 'Are Coca-Cola's coloured cans the next Share a Coke?' *AdNews*, 28 October. Available at: www.adnews.com.au/news/are-coca-cola-s-coloured-cans-the-next-share-a-coke (accessed 14 November 2016).

Boon, C. (2013) 'Alf Stewart actor Ray Meagher fronts Australian version of Snickers ad'. *Mumbrella.* Available at: https://mumbrella.com.au/ray-meagher-snickers-alf-stewart-ad-153638 (accessed 14 November 2016).

Brailsford, I. (2003) 'US image but NZ Venture: American and fast-food advertising in New Zealand, 1971–1990', *Australasian Journal of American Studies*, 22(2), pp. 10–24.

Burrowes, T. (2009) 'Coca-Cola launches "Open Happiness" campaign' *Mumbrella*. Available at: https://mumbrella.com.au/coca-cola-launches-open-happiness-campaign-13098 (accessed 14 November 2016).

Campaign Brief (2012) *Publicis Mojo Auckland Shuts Shop – Graeme Wills to Start New Agency Joy: ECD Lachie McPherson's Next Move Yet To Be Revealed*. Available at: www.campaignbrief.com/2012/12/publicis-mojo-auckland-shuts-s.html (accessed 14 November 2016).

Christensen, N. (2015) 'OMD claims biggest billings but GroupM still largest holding company in 2015 RECMA table', *Mumbrella*. Available at: https://mumbrella.com.au/omd-claims-biggest-billings-but-groupm-still-largest-holding-company-in-2015-recma-table-306510 (accessed 17 February 2017).

Clemenger BBDO (2016) *Homepage*. Available at: http://clemengerbbdo.com.au/en (accessed 14 November 2016).

Colenso BBDO (2014) *Homepage*. Available at: www.colensobbdo.co.nz/ (accessed 14 November 2016).

Commonwealth Network (2016) *Find Advertising, Marketing and PR Expertise in Papua New Guinea*. Available at: www.commonwealthofnations.org/sectors-papua_new_guinea/business/advertising_marketing_and_pr/ (accessed 14 November 2016).

Communications Council (2015) *Getting Started*. Available at: www.communicationscouncil.org.au/public/content/ViewCategory.aspx?id=525 (accessed 14 November 2016).

Crawford, R. (2008) *But Wait, There's More: A History of Australian Advertising, 1900–2000*. Carlton: Melbourne University Press.

Crawford, R. (2016) 'Opening for business: A comparison of the J. Walter Thompson and McCann Erickson agencies' entries into the Australian Market', *Journal of Historical Research in Marketing*, 8(3), pp. 452–72.

Crawford, R. and Dickenson, J. (2016) *Behind Glass Doors: The World of Australian Advertising Agencies, 1959–1989*. Crawley: UWA Publishing.

Cummins & Partners (2015) *Global Independent Ad Agency Cummins&Partners Today Announced it has Acquired Brooklyn, N.Y Based Creative Agency DC3*. Available at: http://cumminsandpartners.com/news-blog/cumminspartners-acquires-n-y-based-creative-agency-dc3/ (accessed 14 November 2016).

Directory (2015) *The Directory Big Won Rankings 2015*. Available at: www.directnewideas.com/bigwon/ (accessed 14 November 2016).

Dunn, C. (2013) 'Hey, Hey, We're the Monkeys!', *Sydney Morning Herald*, 19 July.

The Economist (2015) 'Technology in New Zealand: Kiwis as guinea pigs'. *The Economist*, 21 May Available at: www.economist.com/news/business/21651858-small-technophile-country-great-place-test-digital-products-kiwis-guinea-pigs (accessed 14 November 2016).

Florida, R., Mellander, C. and King, K. (2015) *Global Creativity Index 2015*. Martin Prosperity Institute. Available at: http://martinprosperity.org/media/Global-Creativity-Index-2015.pdf (accessed 14 November 2016).

Fry, E. (2015) 'Why global business tests its products in Australia', *Fortune*, 26 October. Available at: http://fortune.com/2015/10/26/australia-test-products/ (accessed 14 November 2016).

Garcia, M. (2015) 'Airlines that turn a safety requirement into a content marketing opportunity'. *Skift*, 2 March. Available at: https://skift.com/2015/03/02/airlines-that-turn-a-safety-requirement-into-a-content-marketing-opportunity/ (accessed 14 November 2016).

Grey (2016) Homepage. Available at: http://grey.com/apac/about (accessed 14 November 2016).

Gupta, V. and Hanges, P. J. (2004) 'Regional and climate clustering of societal cultures'. In: House, R. J., Hanges, P. J., Javidan, M., Dorfman, P. W. and Gupta, V. (eds) *Culture, Leadership, and Organizations: The GLOBE Study of 62 Societies*. Thousand Oaks, CA: SAGE, 2004, pp. 183–4.

Hicks, R. (2012) 'Why is advertising so much better in New Zealand than Australia?' *Mumbrella*. Available at: https://mumbrella.com.au/why-is-advertising-so-much-better-in-new-zealand-than-australia-93281 (accessed 14 November 2016).

Hofstede, G. (2016) 'Comparison of Australia and New Zealand'. Available at: https://geert-hofstede.com (accessed 14 November 2016).

IBISWorld (2015) *Advertising Agencies in Australia: Market Research Report (July 2015)*. Available at: www.ibisworld.com.au/industry/default.aspx?indid=2337 (accessed 14 November 2016).

Lawson, V. (2016) 'Goldberg, Frank (1889–1958)' *Australian Dictionary of Biography*, National Centre of Biography, Australian National University, Canberra. Available at: http://adb.anu.edu.au/biography/goldberg-frank-10318/text18261 (accessed 14 November 2016).

McCann (2016) *Dumb Ways to Die*. Available at: http://mccann.com.au/project/dumb-ways-to-die/ (accessed 14 November 2016).

McNickel, D. (2002) '50 years of advertising: The '80s: an overview', *AdMedia*, 17(1) (February), p. 33.

Malkin, B. (2009) 'Airline uses naked crew in safety video'. *Telegraph*, 2 July. Available at: www.telegraph.co.uk/news/newstopics/howaboutthat/5718765/Airline-uses-naked-crew-in-safety-video.html (accessed 14 November 2016).

Medcalf, G. (2006) 'Bye, bye local', *NZ Marketing Magazine*, September 2006, pp. 24–35.

Moye, J. (2014) 'Share a Coke: How the groundbreaking campaign got its start "down under"', *Coca-Cola*. Available at: www.coca-colacompany.com/stories/share-a-coke-how-the-groundbreaking-campaign-got-its-start-down-under (accessed 14 November 2016).

NZONSCREEN (2016a) 'Bugger: Toyota Hilux'. Available at: www.nzonscreen.com/title/bugger-toyota-hilux-commercial-1999 (accessed 14 November 2016).

NZONSCREEN (2016b) 'Hugo and Holly: Kentucky Fried Chicken'. Available at: www.nzonscreen.com/title/kfc-hugo-and-holly/overview (accessed 14 November 2016).

Omnicom Group (2016), *Advertising and Marketing Agencies*. Available at: www.omnicomgroup.com/our-agencies/ (accessed 14 November 2016).

Phillips, H. (2013) *Sell! Tall Tales from the Legends of New Zealand Advertising*. Auckland: Penguin. p. 21.

Riches, N. (2015) 'Coke smashes sales forecast with coloured cans', *AdNews*, 23 March.

Saatchi & Saatchi (2016a) *Australia Homepage*. Available at: https://saatchi.co.au (accessed 14 November 2016).

Saatchi & Saatchi (2016b) *New Zealand Homepage*. Available at: https://saatchi.co.nz (accessed 14 November 2016).

Sinclair, J. (1987) *Images Incorporated: Advertising as Industry and Ideology*. London: Croom Helm.

StopPress (2014) *Last of the Big Spenders: NZ Top 10 a Familiar Story*. Available at: http://stoppress.co.nz/news/last-big-spenders-nz-top-10-familiar-story (accessed 14 November 2016).

Talbot, T. (2012) 'Close-up: Soapbox – What can the UK learn from New Zealand's ad industry?', *Campaign*, 17 August, p. 14.

TBWA (2016) homepage. Available at: www.tbwa.com.au/#/ (accessed 14 November 2016).

Tourism New Zealand (2009a) *Pure As: Celebrating 10 Years of 100% Pure New Zealand*. Available at: www.tourismnewzealand.com/media/1544/pure-as-celebrating-10-years-of-100-pure-new-zealand.pdf (accessed 14 November 2016).

Tourism New Zealand (2009b) 'Ten years young'. Available at: http://10yearsyoung.tourismnewzealand.com/ (accessed 14 November 2016).

Venuto, D. (2014), 'M&C Saatchi pulling out of New Zealand: Local management to take ownership', *StopPress*. Available at: http://stoppress.co.nz/news/flying-solo-local-management-take-ownership-mc-saatchi-nz (accessed 14 November 2016).

Wander, E. (2015) 'How this independent agency is starting its aggressive global expansion plan', *Adweek*, 12 November. Available at: www.adweek.com/news/advertising-branding/how-independent-agency-starting-its-aggressive-global-expansion-plan-168095 (accessed 14 November 2016).

Ward, M. (2015) 'Viral video chart: Australia and NZ's top 10 most shared ads of all time' *Mumbrella*. Available at: https://mumbrella.com.au/viral-video-chart-australia-and-nzs-top-10-most-shared-ads-of-all-time-303408 (accessed 14 November 2016).

WPP (2016) *STW Group and WPP Officially Join to Create WPP AUNZ*. Available at: www.wpp.com/wpp/investor/financialnews/2016/apr/04/stw-group-and-wpp-officially-join-to-create-wpp-aunz/ (accessed 14 November 2016).

Yellow (2016) *Advertising Agencies in New Zealand*. Available at: www.yellow.co.nz/new-zealand/advertising-agencies (accessed 14 November 2016).

Zenith Optimedia (2015) *ZO Review of 2015 Advertising Revenue Forecast*. Available at: http://zenithoptimedia.com.au/industry/zo-review-of-2015-advertising-revenue-forecast/ (accessed 14 November 2016).

15 From global to social

Digital communication and the future of globalisation and advertising

Robert Crawford, Linda Brennan, Dang Nguyen and Lukas Parker

Introduction

Globalisation was supposed to bring about an age of global integration and harmony, as well as enhance efficient business practice throughout the world. A global business culture would smooth the way for partnerships and economic well-being for all would be the result. Globalisation was meant to lead to a greater interdependence of countries, regions and continents, and result in a more efficient flow of ideas, worldviews and aspects of cultures. In sum, global business would lead to world peace and understanding – a borderless world. Advertising has a role to play in the globalisation of ideas and the cross fertilisation of cultures between nations. However, world peace remains unattainable as nationalism is resurging throughout the globe. The borderless world is digital. The digital world is one where people engage and interact beyond their national boundaries, one where ideas flow rapidly and geometrically between people across networks. It is a world in which advertising has become a key player, the player having the financial and technical wherewithal to build aspirational brands and break down metaphorical walls. Increasingly, advertising is using digital tools and relying on social networks for dissemination of the message. As a result, advertising agencies and their partners in the advertising eco-system have opened up offices in many countries throughout the world and, as some of the chapters in this book have shown, have had varying degrees of success in the development of global campaigns.

What is apparent from reviewing the various examples and cases throughout this book is that advertising is regularly taking a regional focus, even if the agency is nationally based. Whereas once advertising would have a city or national focus, it is often now concentrated on regions, whether it be Southeast Asia, the Middle East or Spanish-speaking Latin America. Advertising was expected to take on a more global focus as brands crossed boundaries and transnational communication became efficient and easier. However, time has demonstrated that, while the flow of ideas transcends national borders and digital has become the norm, regional identity and hubs are becoming the standard for agencies and advertisers.

Globalisation of advertising

In Chapter 1 in this collection, John Sinclair notes that globalisation is not a uniform process. This point is underscored by other contributors, whose chapters reveal the multiple ways that globalisation has impacted on advertising practices across different regions and nations. While critics of globalisation have pointed to its capacity to homogenise messages and audiences (Appadurai, 1996, p. 32) more nuanced accounts have revealed a more dynamic interplay between the local and the global as encapsulated in the term 'glocal'. As the chapters in this collection have illustrated, contemporary global advertising practices might be better understood by their hybridity rather than their homogenising influence.

Hybridisation is evident in the changing media landscape. While commentators agree that digital media will become progressively more important as it attracts an increasing share of advertising expenditure, history shows that the emergence of new media platforms results in realignment rather than redundancy. Chapter 14 reveals that digital media in Australasia attracts the largest share of advertising expenditure in the region, but it notes that other media remain integral to advertiser strategies. While Chapters 8 and 9 indicate that digital media use is growing in eastern Europe and sub-Saharan Africa, both regions nevertheless demonstrate that television and radio remain integral to conducting local and global campaigns. For their part, advertisers across the globe are still adjusting to digital platforms and how they might best be integrated into their campaigns. Although there is widespread agreement that a digital presence is essential, advertisers' marketing teams remain more ambivalent about the best way to reach out to a fragmenting audience.

Sinclair's observations about 'deterritorialisation' reveal the complexities of globalisation. While globalisation reflects an increasingly integrated world, nations matter. As some of the chapters in this collection reveal, going beyond the nation remains an ongoing challenge for scholars and practitioners alike – language, culture and geography still present very real barriers to global organisations. To this end, globalisation's relationship with the nation can be paradoxical. For large transnational agencies which have their regional headquarters in one city, their global headquarters in another and their holding company in a third, the geopolitical structure and operations of advertising becomes less important. While Chapters 5 and 6 reveal that New York and London have long been and still remain key advertising centres, they no longer exert the same level of influence. As the case studies in this collection vividly reveal, creativity is increasingly found in branch offices across the globe. Of course, technology has also cultivated closer ties within global networks, facilitating a greater flow of staff and ideas within them. Although global advertisers display similar characteristics, geography may still be an integral part of the brand. McDonald's, Coca-Cola and Nike are all intrinsically viewed as American brands (Johannsson and Carlson, 2015, p. 171).

Further paradoxes can be seen in various campaigns. Tourism campaigns, for example, celebrate national uniqueness but present diverse countries in homogenised ways to global audiences. Advertising was integral to establishing Australia and New Zealand as unique brands while projecting them as viable tourism destinations. These campaigns actively reinforced popular images of both countries and also played a key role in defining them to global as well as local audiences. The chapters on China, India and the United States also remind us that national markets are not necessarily homogeneous, underscoring the need for a further degree of localisation within the glocalisation process.

Digital communication and advertising

As this book shows, global advertising is becoming increasingly digital. In 2015, world social network advertising spending reached US$17.08 billion (eMarketer 2016), and Internet advertising is expected to overtake TV as the largest advertising segment by 2018 (PWC, 2014). According to a white paper by CMO Council (2015), 69 per cent of senior advertisers are currently allocating their budget to website content, development and performance optimisation, while 53 per cent are spending on social media community growth and engagement. The online search market is also booming, with mobile search advertising expected to reach US$12.85 billion in 2015, constituting 50 per cent of the entire search market. However, this book also cogently illustrates that 'becoming digital' entails more than setting up and maintaining a Facebook page or a Twitter profile, responding to customers' feedback on official websites, or increasing online presence through search engine optimisation and buying Google ads. Global brands, agencies and institutions around the world have embraced a new ethos that came with the advent of social media – that of 'being social', or engaging with and creating interest-based communities on social media platforms while utilising advertising services provided by giants such as Google and Facebook. As advertisers work their way through finding optimal ways to catch the attention of some 65 per cent of online adults who are users of social networking sites (Pew, 2015), advertising takes a subtle yet important turn from monologic forms of communication to dialogic forms: from talking at, to conversing with. With the help of digital technology, it now costs less to reach more people, making the globalisation agenda more financially and logistically viable. Nevertheless, perhaps for the first time in history, advertisers find themselves grappling to understand a ubiquitous culture over which they have neither control nor any legitimate claim of authorship in a co-created communication world: the digital culture.

Digital advertising is 'just' advertising but using a rapidly proliferating set of tools. The principles of advertising still apply: be relevant to your target market, offer something of value and be different 'enough' from your competition so that you have an advantage. While the world of digital is more art than science (unless you are actually writing the algorithms), creativity is still critical to engagement. Advertisers can adapt to this by ensuring they have a strong knowledge of technology or that they have technological interpretative capability 'in-house'. Digital advertising is now data-driven. In order to maximise the value of this data, agencies will need to work with different types of brand and different types of product to create innovated advertising. Digital offers promise for efficiency and effectiveness at the same time. The need for agencies to work together in order to optimise the advertising is greater than ever before. Flexible technology platforms will be essential to ensure that digital content reaches the target market and is able to be engaged with at the time and place of choosing of the market. Monetising advertising in a technological environment is about sharing the costs as well as the expertise. Advertisers may pay $1 per click but there may be 20 or 30 service providers that require revenue out of the process; for example, the mobile carrier, the media provider, the publisher, the video producer, and so on. New business models will be necessary to ensure that agencies and their suppliers have sufficient revenue streams to be profitable. As Hook (Chapter 6) illustrates, for global advertisers to have the potential to have teams working concurrently in many countries, all with different cost bases, and therefore to be efficient and cost-effective at the same time, requires a high degree of finesse.

The digital consumer is different to previous conceptions of consumer. Consumers are no longer passive recipients of broadcast messages sitting in front of a screen: they are busy living digital lives and advertising needs to be an adjunct to these lives, not a distraction. Understanding the digital consumer requires expertise and insight on a greater than ever scale. Digital communities form and develop geometrically and new ways of understanding human networks are necessary if advertisers aim to tap into these networks for their own purposes. As Parker, Nguyen and Brennan (Chapter 3) point out 'Far from levelling the playing field for advertisers in a homogenising global market, doing digital marketing with a global outreach means having an increasingly sophisticated understanding of different local markets while recognising and taking advantage of global trends'. The borderless digital world is not geographically bounded despite attempts by some countries to exclude their citizens from interchanges with 'other' (Bender, 2016; Crouch, 2016). As Sreekumar and Varman (Chapter 11) establish, 'other' is a desirable state and will be actively sought by the digital consumer who is seeking alternative realities in which the norm is something (anything) different to their own sometimes mundane lives. Advertising plays a pivotal role in providing access to aspiration in this regard. Elham Arab (2016), an Iranian model, points out that 'All people love beauty and fame, they would like to be seen, but it is important to know what price they will pay to be seen' (Whigham, 2016a). In Iran, the search for fame has led to people having to leave the country and, for example, to Kim Kardashian being proclaimed as a secret agent using Instagram to subvert Islamic values (Whigham, 2016b). Mohammed (Chapter 10) has explanations for how advertising is adapting to Islamic values. In the case of Elham Arab and others, cultures and digital sub-cultures may be changing faster than nation states can keep up with.

The future of advertising

While the world is rapidly globalising, the hegemony of the USA in leading internationalisation is in decline. China and India are becoming more economically empowered and, after the 2016 US Presidential election, the USA may be building walls around its economy that will impact on the future of commerce, and therefore advertising, around the globe. As at November 2016, the Donald Trump presidency threatens to cancel free trade, which has been a formative component of the flow of culture across borders, thereby recreating borders in what has become a threatening borderless world (Reuters, 2016). Whether global industries that benefit from a borderless world permit this to occur remains to be seen. We are indeed living in interesting times and this can be both a blessing and a curse. The growth in the consumer markets demonstrated by the chapters on China (Chapter 13), India (Chapter 11) and Africa (Chapter 9) illustrate a not-so-subtle shift away from the dominant institutional logics currently prevailing. The pressures of globalisation will create new institutions and new models of business over time. Advertising will play a role in this business landscape by adapting to changes and reflecting societal changes in advertising at a national, regional and global level.

One of the most notable aspects of this collection is that, despite the flow of people, trade and culture across borders, the world of commerce is essentially nationally based with multinational advertising agencies making attempts at regionalisation but rarely empowered to work beyond national borders. National consumer identities are on the increase and this means that localisation of advertising is essential if the ad is to connect with the audience. The case studies also show us that a deep understanding of cross-border flows requires a birds-eye view to be able to transcend national agenda. This means that agencies will need to have large teams, and an awareness and understanding of multiple outlooks. Strategic planners and insights generators will have to observe global trends but appreciate local nuances and consumer cultures and indigenous behaviours in order to design apposite advertising campaigns. According to Luca Linder from McCann Worldgroup (Lindner, 2015):

> Global marketers have long faced the challenge of finding the right balance between global brand platforms and evolving local marketing and cultural environments. This important business practice is now entering a new phase again – driven by the combination of the digital technology revolution, the growing marketplace complexity within countries around the world, and the increasing importance of getting local relevance right given the re-energization of local pride movements around the world.

What these chapters also show is that the global consumer may be a mythological creation hopefully constructed by those attempting to save money. Local pride and national identity are growing and advertising creative will need to be localised even if programmatic buying allows for efficiencies on a global scale.

The rise of multinational agencies and media groups, such as those indicated in Chapter 5 by Torras on Latin America and Ling's chapter on Singapore (Chapter 12), is unlikely to abate as agencies need to work together to deliver global services for their multinational clients and brands. Furthermore, materialism and consumerist values are not universal. The slow food movement highlighted in Chapter 7 by Arroyo-Almaraz and Mamic, as well as the examples of advertising provided in Chapter 4 by Grow illustrate a fundamental difference between cultures and advertising practice in different parts of the globe. The narrative that connects green consumers with their brands is one of authenticity. However, being authentic across borders becomes difficult to achieve without a nuanced understanding of the dominant consumer culture. As Jonathan Goodman (2016) asserts: 'Brands can no longer get by with a catchy jingle, instead they search for songs that tell stories, conjure memories and forge genuine connections with people'. Forging connections across national boundaries is problematic in turbulent times.

While there may be no such thing as a global consumer, Torras's work (Chapter 5) highlighted what is possible with shared cultural and language foundations. Her chapter on Latin America has contributed to an understanding of how regionalism is working for advertising in Latin American countries. Advertising in these contexts can be efficient and effective, able to reach related consumers with relevant and targeted campaigns that 'work' because the agencies are deeply embedded within their communities. Conversely, her European counterparts (see Chapters 6, 7 and 8) do not have the same efficiencies evident in their cases, with fragmentation of advertising activities across borders being predominant. However, the chapter on Australasia by Dickenson and Crawford (Chapter 14) illustrates that regionally relevant advertising can be globally exceptional, especially when it comes to winning awards for creativity. These industries are 'standalone' but share a significant proportion of ideas across the region.

The growth of digital is providing capacity for people to avoid advertising like never before. However, the industry's response to digital has been to increase the volume at which they are shouting their messages rather than to provide messages that their consumer wishes to engage with. As cogently argued in the Accenture (2016) report: 'Ad blocking is consumers' response; it's their way to say "enough" … enough of the barrage of unnecessary, unwanted, irrelevant messages'. Consumers are now able to do more than ad blocking: they can create their own relevant messages and find their own credible sources of information, sources they can trust and from people they 'know', however illusory this knowledge might be (e.g. Kim Kardashian's persona has changed often over her media career). What people are searching for is meaning and advertising can provide this. Nevertheless, 'It's time for creative industries to connect with people in a meaningful way, not serve up irrelevant ads' (Goodwin, 2016). Co-creation and user-generated content is only a threat to the advertising industry if they are distanced from their markets and treating them as rogue widgets rather than partners in a system of co-created value. Amy Kean (2016) from

Havas Media makes a good point about the interaction between mainstream advertisers and their online consumers: 'Progress, regardless of how clever, needs human buy-in to happen and become the future'. She cautions that no amount of elaborate technology can overcome the need to be relevant and provide something of value to the consumer.

An important requirement in the future of advertising is the ability to engage with 'big data' where insights into global citizens reside. However, this will require data collaborations between participants in the advertising system on a scale that has not been seen before. Furthermore, a regional or global purview may require multinational agencies that work together for their multinational or global clients (T. Goodman, 2016). As Brennan and Crawford point out in Chapter 2:

> Media convergence and the growth of programmatic advertising make it difficult for a brand to be locally differentiated and remain 'on message' in every market. Keeping the brand story coherent across different cultures, markets, media and platforms can be challenging.

Delivering service value in the borderless digital world may be difficult with national and international restrictions growing stronger. Hook (Chapter 6) highlights some potential considerations for British advertising in a Europe that will no longer include Britain. Nonetheless, at some point, there will need to be business decision-making capacity: regardless of where they are located, someone needs to be in charge, especially of the finances. From this perspective, even though theoretically decision-making could be diffused across the participants in the advertising eco-system, it is likely that increased programmatic buying will see a convergence to Head Office decision making (Still, 2016).

Looking ahead, global advertising shows no sign of abating. While advertising agencies across the globe continue to grapple with the opportunities and the challenges posed by the ever changing digital media space and the new platforms emerging therein, the challenges of operating in a globalised world remain relatively unchanged. Noting that 'the key to successful integrated channel planning is not in innovative use of media and using multiple channels, but in understanding consumers, brand and category', Guy Hearn (2011, p. 31) of Omnicom, underscores the ongoing importance of established advertising principles. Planner Nick Kendall (2016) similarly calls for a return to basics: 'Global branding is complex. As such, global planning requires one intangible skill above all – the skill of simplification'. As the chapters in this collection have mutually shown, understanding contexts in which advertising operates – whether they pertain to regions, nations, media, or culture – is integral to a successful global campaign.

References

Accenture (2016) *The Future of Advertising*. Available at: www.accenture.com/us-en/~/media/Accenture/next-gen/pulse-of-media/pdf/Accenture-Future-Of-Advertising-POV.pdf (accessed 17 November 2016).

Appadurai, A. (1996) *Modernity at Large: Cultural Dimensions of Globalization*. Minneapolis, MN: University of Minnesota Press.

Bender, J. (2016) '6 countries that block social media', *Business Insider*. Available at: www.businessinsider.com.au/the-six-countries-that-block-social-media-2015-4?r=US&IR=T (accessed 17 November 2016).

Crouch, E. (2016) 'Why some social networks still aren't blocked in China', *Tech in Asia*. Available at: www.techinasia.com/social-networks-arent-blocked-china (accessed 17 November 2016).

eMarketer (2016) 'Facebook gets strong majority of world's social ad spending', *Emarketer*. 25 July. Available at: www.emarketer.com/Article/Facebook-Gets-Strong-Majority-of-Worlds-Social-Ad-Spending/1014252 (accessed 15 March 2017).

Goodman, J. (2016) 'Ad Week Europe 2016: Advertising can't afford to stand still', *Guardian*, 27 April. Available at: www.theguardian.com/media-network/2016/apr/27/ad-week-europe-2016-advertising-stand-still (accessed 17 November 2016).

Goodwin, T. (2016) 'Adblocking could be the best thing for the advertising industry', *Guardian*, 21 April. Available at: www.theguardian.com/media-network/2016/apr/21/adblocking-best-thing-advertising-industry (accessed 17 November 2016).

Hearn, G. (2011) 'Asia's integration challenge', *Admap*, June, pp. 30–31.

Johannsson, J. K. and Carlson, K. A. (2015) *Contemporary Brand Management*. Thousand Oaks, CA: Sage Publications.

Kean, A. (2015) 'The future of advertising: What will 2025 look like?', *Guardian*, 16 February. Available at: www.theguardian.com/media-network/2015/feb/16/the-future-of-advertising-what-will-2025-look-like (accessed 17 November 2016).

Kendall, N. (2016) 'How to develop an effective global strategy', Warc Best Practice, October. Available at: www.warc.com/Content/ContentViewer.aspx?MasterContent Ref=744f16bc-934d-45f3-8265-29dc4e78b5c6&CID=A109251&PUB=BESTPRAC (accessed 18 November 2016).

Lindner, L. (2015) 'Why global marketing must move beyond cultural stereotypes and go deep', *Forbes*, 27 October. Available at: www.forbes.com/sites/onmarketing/2015/10/27/why-global-marketing-must-move-beyond-cultural-stereotypes-and-go-deep/#6dd6e1e47f71 (accessed 17 November 2016).

Pew (2015) 'Social Media Usage: 2005-2015'. *Pew Research Center*. Available at www.pewinternet.org/2015/10/08/social-networking-usage-2005-2015/ (accessed: 15 March 2017).

PWC (2014) 'Seizing the initiative: As growth goes digital, advertising spearheads the migration'. *PricewaterhouseCoopers*, 11 June. Available at www.pwc.com/sg/en/pressroom/pressrelease20140611.html. (accessed 15 March 2017).

Reuters (2016) 'Trump's victory is scaring global firms that rely on free trade', *Fortune*, 9 November. Available at: http://fortune.com/2016/11/09/trump-victory-global-firms-free-trade/ (accessed 17 November 2016).

Still, J. (2016) 'What programmatic means for your business: Webchat roundup', *Guardian*, 4 February. Available at: www.theguardian.com/media-network/2016/feb/04/programmatic-means-for-business-webchat-roundup (accessed 17 November 2016).

Whigham, N. (2016a) 'Iran offers ultimatum to social media sites to hand over information or face ban', *News.com.au*. Available at: www.news.com.au/technology/online/social/iran-offers-ultimatum-to-social-media-sites-to-hand-over-information-or-face-ban/news-story/ab9c8f8617b0399dac7f34d01428d12f (accessed 17 November 2016).

Whigham, N. (2016b) 'Iran accuses Kim Kardashian of being a secret agent amid crackdown on social media', *News.com.au*. Available at: www.news.com.au/technology/online/social/iran-accuses-kim-kardashian-of-being-a-secret-agent-amid-crackdown-on-social-media/news-story/018a9a7606fff2d913c6235cccc2db5d (accessed 17 November 2016).

Index